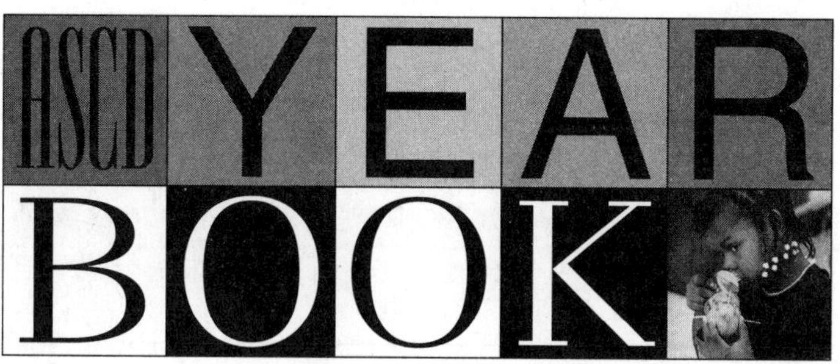

1996

COMMUNICATING STUDENT LEARNING

EDITED BY THOMAS R. GUSKEY

ASSOCIATION FOR SUPERVISION AND CURRICULUM DEVELOPMENT
ALEXANDRIA, VIRGINIA

Association for Supervision and Curriculum Development
1250 N. Pitt Street • Alexandria, VA 22314
Telephone: (703) 549-9110 • Fax: (703) 299-8631

ASCD is a diverse, international community of educators, forging covenants in teaching and learning for the success of all learners.

Printed in the United States of America.

ASCD Stock No. 196000
Price: $21.95
ISSN: 1042-9018

Communicating Student Learning
1996 ASCD Yearbook

Page

Foreword

Do you believe student achievement can improve as educators discover better and more appropriate ways to communicate with parents and students regarding student learning? If your answer is "yes," then I would encourage you to read this 1996 ASCD Yearbook, *Communicating Student Learning*. Most educators would agree that historically we have not achieved heights of greatness in communicating with parents, students, and the community. We have not consistently provided appropriate, relevant, and comprehensible information about student learning. We are still searching for ways to provide accurate, acceptable answers to such questions as "Are students in today's schools performing at acceptable levels of competency?" and "Do student grades accurately reflect student learning?"

We should be grateful that the 1996 Yearbook editor, Tom Guskey, and his fellow authors accepted the challenging task of addressing the issue of communicating student learning. As Guskey notes in the introduction, "Few topics in education are more controversial than grading, reporting, and communicating student learning." Personnel in the school district where I serve have had the opportunity to receive extensive training from Guskey in issues related to this topic, and we have experienced firsthand his passion for finding solutions to the tough questions surrounding assessing, grading, and reporting student learning. Therefore, it came as no surprise when I learned that Tom Guskey would be the editor for this yearbook.

Much discussion and debate in educational circles today concern such issues as assessment, student performance, parent conferences, and related topics. It is appropriate that the 1996 Yearbook address such timely issues. The book provides new information and examples of outstanding reporting systems currently in use in the United States and Canada; and educators from various subject fields and areas of interest will discover chapters related to their specific interests. Contributors to the book have addressed reporting issues in special education, gifted education, students participating in the visual arts, and elementary, middle, and high school students. All educators will find the information contained in the chapter, "Honesty and Fairness: Toward Better Grading and Reporting," by Grant Wiggins, most thought provoking and useful.

In the introduction to the yearbook, Guskey states that he and the other authors "all shared the belief that better thinking, a better knowledge base, and a better understanding of the critical issues involved could bring significant improvements." It was their hope that the yearbook would provide this in-depth understanding. When you complete your review of this publication, I believe you will join me in expressing to Guskey and the other authors our commendation that they accomplished their mission and that their hope has been realized.

CHARLES E. PATTERSON
1995–96 ASCD President

1

Introduction

Thomas R. Guskey

Few topics in education are more controversial than grading, reporting, and communicating student learning. Teachers, students, administrators, parents, and community members all agree that we need better reporting systems. They point out that inadequacies in our present system too often lead to confusion and misinterpretation. But these same groups rarely agree on the form those new systems should take. Researchers point out that much of the current practice in grading and reporting is based more on opinion than it is on evidence. Practitioners counter that the evidence on best practice is blurred.

Many problems related to grading, reporting, and communicating student learning are perennial. These issues have troubled educators for many years and continue to vex those seeking to develop more effective reporting methods and procedures. Given the nature of these problems then, why take on such a difficult and troubled area as the theme for an ASCD Yearbook? Why would we choose to probe this contentious issue at this time?

Actually, four different but interrelated developments led us to this work. First is the growing emphasis in education on student performance and performance-based forms of assessment. Educators today are no longer satisfied with instruction that focuses only on basic skills. Instead they want students to engage in "authentic" problem-solving tasks that require them to think, plan, analyze, integrate, and construct. In developing clear-cut standards to measure how well students can perform these skills, educators discovered that their traditional marking systems were inadequate and obsolete. This, in turn, prompted calls for the development of better and more appropriate reporting systems.

A second development that influenced our work is the growing criticism of education—and a skeptical public that doubts the quality of what is going on in schools and the capabilities of educators. The negative tone of various reports and polls has diminished the public's trust in educators to make decisions that are always in the best interests of students. As a result, parents and community members are demanding more information than ever before about students and instructional programs.

The third development that spurred us in this effort is advances in technology that present many new challenges, but also offer many new opportunities. Today we are able to record and disseminate vast amounts of information with infinite detail. These advances also make it possible for us to do things that were unimaginable in the past. For example, some of the same technology—such as bar coding—that allows supermarkets to itemize every purchase on an individualized charge slip, and permits businesses to provide individualized billings for items bought at locations throughout the world, can be used to produce individualized report cards that show what students are working on, what progress they have made, and what their class is studying and why.

The fourth basis for this book is a growing recognition that grading, reporting, and communicating student learning are one of educators' most important responsibilities. Teachers today engage in some form of reporting nearly every hour they are in the classroom. These reporting activities range from informally checking and correcting students' learning errors, to scoring and recording the results of quizzes, examinations, and performance assessments. Reporting student progress can take the form of checklists, written comments, narrative reports, numerical scores, letter grades, or a formal or informal student conference. Yet despite the importance of these activities, few teachers have any formal training on grading or reporting. Most have scant knowledge of the various reporting forms, the advantages and disadvantages of each, or the effects of different grading policies. As a result, even educators dissatisfied with their present systems lack direction in their efforts to make changes.

My interest in grading and reporting goes back much further. It began many years ago when I first entered education as a middle school teacher. Every nine weeks I was required to reduce to a single symbol all the impressions and information I had gathered on the learning of each of my students. I recorded this symbol on a report card that was carried home by students, signed by one of their parents, and then returned to the school until the end of the next nine-week cycle. When the school year drew to a close, I tallied, summarized, and then recorded yet another symbol that was to represent my students' cumulative accomplishments. This symbol became part of my students' "permanent record" and determined in large part the nature of their academic program the following school year.

Initially I approached the process of grading and reporting rather casually, with little doubt I could be fair and objective. After all, during my 17 years as a student I had experienced a variety of grading practices and policies, and had a good idea of what worked. The first time I sat down to complete report cards, however, I quickly discovered the process to be far more complex than I ever anticipated.

I began at the top of my class list with Angela, who clearly deserved a high mark. She consistently attained the highest score on examinations, and all of her work was well organized and exceptionally neat. But I also knew that none of what we worked on in class required serious effort from Angela, and I had not done a very good job of challenging her capabilities. Still, I recorded the mark and moved on.

Next came Stephen. Although he hadn't done well on examinations, Stephen worked very hard; and his class assignments showed exceptional creativity. I certainly did not want to give him a mark that would discourage the extra effort he was putting forth. Since I would need to consider his case more carefully, I set his report card aside with the intention of coming back to it later.

Then there was Elizabeth. At the beginning of the marking period she really struggled, but in recent weeks had shown remarkable progress. Somehow the mark I gave her needed to reflect her most recent work and show how far she had come. I set her report card aside too.

With each student, the process of grading and reporting became more frustrating and confusing to me. The cases I needed to consider more carefully greatly outnumbered those I could mark with ease. What I imagined to be a simple and straightforward process had turned out to be extremely complex. It seemed impossible to capture all that I wanted to communicate about each student in a single symbol. Further, I began to see the whole process as counter to my role as a teacher. How could I be an advocate for my students and also serve as their evaluator and judge?

Since those early years, the issues of grading and reporting have continued to fascinate and perplex me. Even today in my conversations with teachers, I frequently ask, "What grading and reporting practices do you use and why?" To the first part of my question, elementary teachers generally describe checklists of competencies and narrative reports. Secondary teachers, on the other hand, typically discuss complex mathematical formulae that involve percentages, weighted averages, and various point-tallying options. To the second part of my question, however, the answers come more slowly but are strikingly consistent. Nearly all teachers, elementary and secondary alike, say they really don't like grading and reporting. They then go on to describe the demands of parents and the reporting policies established by their school or district.

When I press a little harder on this issue, it is clear that the majority of teachers have not thought deeply about the process of grading and reporting. Although many find it difficult and troublesome, they still feel compelled to follow policies they had no part in developing. Those with greater latitude in the practices they employ try to replicate what they experienced as students and judged at the time to be fair.

From this context of controversy and confusion, and with a profound sense of the four developments described earlier, we set out to develop the 1996 ASCD Yearbook. The members of the Yearbook Planning Committee and the authors selected to contribute yearbook chapters all recognized the need for better reporting. All were aware of inadequacies in many of our current reporting systems, and all had personal experience with the confusion and misinterpretation resulting from these systems. All were also convinced that muddled thinking in the past had led to these muddled practices in the present. But most important, all shared the belief that better thinking, a better knowledge base, and a better understanding of the critical issues involved could bring significant improvements. That is precisely what we hoped this yearbook would provide.

From the very beginning, our work revolved around three basic premises. These premises guided our exploration of the topics of grading and reporting and shaped our vision of what we hoped the yearbook would be. In addition, they served as the foundation on which we framed the critical issues to be addressed in the yearbook. These premises included the following:

1. The primary goal of grading and reporting is *communication*. Regardless of the format, its purpose is to provide high-quality information to interested persons in a form they can understand and use effectively.

2. Reporting is an integral part of the learning process, much like assessment. It certifies the attainment of learning goals and identifies where additional work is needed.

3. As the goals of schooling become more complex, the need for better-quality and more detailed communication about student learning become increasingly important.

From these premises we framed a set of critical questions about grading, reporting, and communicating student learning. These questions stemmed from the issues considered by the members of the Yearbook Planning Committee to be the most perplexing and most troublesome to educators, policymakers, and parents. With these critical questions clarified, we next set out to identify individuals whose experience, background, and expertise made them uniquely qualified to address these questions. Our hope was to gain the cooperation and involvement of the very best and most knowledgeable people on the topic. As editor, I then contacted these individuals, posed our questions to them, and asked them to develop their answers in a form we could include in the yearbook. To my complete delight, nearly all agreed.

One of the most basic questions we wanted to address was, *"How can we ensure that the goal of effective communication guides the development of reporting systems?"* In the opening chapter, "Bridges Freeze Before Roads," Heidi Watts outlines this process clearly and simply. Arguing that communication is a two-way exchange, and that the key to its success is consideration of the audience, Watts sets the tone for the rest of the book.

"What have we learned about grading and reporting over the years, and how should that inform current practice?" are the questions I address in Chapter 3. I point out that although many of our current reporting dilemmas are not new, lessons from the past and more recent research evidence are frequently ignored in developing modern reporting systems. To develop more effective systems, I contend that educators must first decide what is important to communicate and to whom. Then by following a few basic guidelines, they can make reporting a more meaningful experience for teachers, students, and parents.

Today more and more teachers are using the ideas of cooperative learning in their teaching and are discovering its many valuable benefits for students at all levels. The shift to cooperative learning poses unique challenges to teachers, however, in terms of both assessment and reporting. *"How does the use of cooperative learning affect grading and reporting practices?"* is the focus of Chapter 4 by David and Roger Johnson. In practical and explicit terms, the Johnsons outline the specific steps teachers need to take to ensure that their reporting system communicates clearly what students have learned while remaining aligned with cooperative learning principles.

Current attempts to provide a higher quality of education for *all* students have led to the "detracking" of many schools and the "inclusion" of students with special learning needs in regular classrooms. These changes not only compel educators to make instructional adaptations, but they also require significant adaptations in our reporting systems. *"What changes are needed in reporting systems to accurately communicate the learning of special education students in 'inclusion' programs?"* is the question Russell Gersten, Sharon Vaughn, and Susan Unok Bregelman address in Chapter 5. Gersten and his colleagues argue that by focusing on student progress, educators can develop reporting systems that all students consider fair, equitable, and motivational. In Chapter 6, Kathy Bearden Peckron directs our attention to the problems of students at the other end of the spectrum: the gifted and talented. Addressing the question, *"What adaptations in reporting systems are needed to accurately reflect the special achievements of gifted and talented learners?"* Peckron offers a variety of practical suggestions for meeting the needs of this special population of students.

One school district's ongoing effort to develop more meaningful records of student learning is presented in Chapter 7 by Ken Eastwood. In addressing the question, *"Are there districts that have developed comprehensive information management systems to use in reporting?"* Eastwood describes a technology-based program in his district that systematically tracks students' progress. Teachers, students, and parents then work together to interpret results and design individualized improvement plans.

To come up with clearer standards for performance and accompanying assessment criteria, many educators are turning for guidance to educators in the visual and performing arts. Their areas of study have always demanded the evaluation of student products and performances. In Chapter 8, art educator Bernard Schwartz addresses the question *"How can we accurately and fairly communicate student learning in the visual arts?"* Schwartz describes how art educators approach reporting issues and offers several examples of model reporting forms.

"Are there exemplary models of reporting that educators have developed and find to be working well?" is the question that guided the development of the next two chapters. In Chapter 9, Kathy Lake and Kery Kafka describe a variety of elementary and middle-grade reporting forms and techniques that teachers say are helping them meet the challenge of effective communication. Then in Chapter 10, Jane Bailey and Jay McTighe outline aspects of several innovative reporting systems for secondary-level educators. These include novel approaches to report cards and portfolios of students work, as well as the effective use of student-led conferences.

"What is, or what should be, the relationship of reporting to the assumptions, beliefs, purposes, and culture of the educational organization and community?" is the question Grant Wiggins addresses in Chapter 11. Arguing that honesty and fairness should direct all efforts in this area, Wiggins outlines a set of principles educators should follow to ensure that reporting systems are enhancements, rather than detriments, to student learning.

Advances in technology are changing much of what we do in education, especially the ways we communicate and report student learning. Modern computers allow the storage, retrieval, and aggregation of vast amounts of information that can be used to fashion reports that are much more precise and far more detailed than was ever possible in the past. *"What are the implications of technology for communicating student learning, and what changes might it bring in the near future?"* are the questions Ross Brewer and Bena Kallick address in Chapter 12. Their insightful view of what is possible at the present time and what soon will be possible instills a sense of excitement and wonder.

It should be obvious from this brief description that the chapters in this book are highly diverse. Each was designed to help readers think about grading, reporting, and communicating student learning in fundamental terms. The contributing authors were asked to consider some very basic issues about teaching and learning, and specifically how those processes can be supported and facilitated by better methods of reporting. The prescriptions for better practice offered by these authors are not all the same. In fact, occasionally the perspectives they offer may appear contradictory. But our purpose in developing this yearbook was not to offer "the answer." Rather, our objective was instead to show that improvements in our reporting systems are possible, and that specific and practical ideas are available on how those improvement can be made.

Our hope is that this yearbook will not be just another pretty volume that decorates educators' professional bookshelves. Above all else, we hope it will be used and reused. We hope it becomes one of the most tattered books in schools, with dog-eared pages, paragraphs that are underlined and highlighted, and notes scribbled in the margins. We hope every reader takes an active, thoughtful, reflective, and perhaps even skeptical approach to the ideas presented in each chapter. We hope as a result it simulates further inquiry and action. Most important, we hope it prompts the development of more thoughtful and more critically informed reporting systems that will be considered models of effective communication.

2

Bridges Freeze Before Roads

K. Heidi Watts

The metaphor for this chapter is embedded in the title. I have been collecting titles for some time; and this one, a sign frequently seen on our New England roads warning motorists to be cautious, has long been a favorite. Ice forms faster from rain on bridges over the interstate highway than from rain on the main highway. In the same way, our attempts to communicate from one group, person, or constituency to another often freeze up faster than our attempts to communicate within our own group. Entrance and exit ramps, even driveways, are like bridges: They connect one place to another. In this metaphor, the connection is between one person and another or one constituency and another.

The need for caution in communication is as true for grading and reporting as for anything else, perhaps even more so. Grading and reporting are fraught with overtones of judgment; even when they purport to be objective, they cannot be free of the subjective. Educational jargon, hidden assumptions, and inappropriate reporting make communication all the more perilous.

In 1939, when I was very young, my parents took me to the World's Fair in New York City, and we gazed in amazement at a big model under a glass dome. The model showed what the highways of the future could look like. Big roads crossed over and under other big roads, sometimes becoming networks of three highways, one almost on top of the other. Smaller roads spilled out from the central wheel of crisscrossing highways, like rays from the sun, and these roads ran into even smaller roads that moved across the artist's conception of "The America of the Future" to join larger roads and eventually spin into another great star of intercrossing and overlapping highways. This vision was hard to believe in 1939, but such a picture is commonplace today.

This is the image I have of our communication systems for learning in the future—not a few big highways and a few dusty byways—but a complex system, a map with big thick lines, thin red-and-blue lines, even little dotted lines for the dirt roads that get us to out-of-the-way places. We can draw on the information we get from the big highways, such as grades or standardized tests—generic reporting systems—to the personalized possibilities in a portfolio or parent/teacher/student conference. To stretch the conceit even further, I look forward to a communication system that encompasses both postal patron mail and the UPS truck rattling up to my door with a package just for me.

Traffic Patterns

Communicating student learning implies motion. Something, in this case perceptions about a student's learning, moves from someone or some place to someone else. Who is communicating what? To whom? How? Why? To what effect? Diagraming the possibilities produces a spaghetti bowl as complex as anything on an L.A. freeway. To take one example, how do students know what they are learning, and how is their progress interpreted by other people? Teachers communicate with students about what the students are learning through comments in class and conferences; on papers, grades, and report cards; and in messages to parents, which get relayed back to the students. Schools communicate with students about what they are learning through their teachers; occasionally through a principal; and in a generalized way, through standardized test scores. Students communicate to other students by comments, often as asides, on each other's work; and they communicate again in those rare instances when peer evaluation is officially encouraged. But students also have their own views about what they have learned, and those may be the reports that are least often heard. How often do we ask the students what they have learned?

If we consider how student learning is communicated to parents, we get yet another lengthy list. Avenues of communication run from national policy setters, state education departments, school districts, principals, teachers, other students, and the learners themselves out to parents, community members, school boards, higher and lower echelons in the school, and the students. Then the avenues spiral back. Some are two-way streets; some are not.

Just as I have a choice of at least seven ways of driving to Boston, from the turnpike to a whole lacework of leisurely back roads, I would like to have the same type of choice about reporting information on my students. As a teacher talking to a parent, I'd like to be able to say, "We have many different ways we can show you what your son or daughter is learning in school. What do you want to know? What do you *need* to know? If you can tell me what you really care about, we can figure out which road to take to that destination."

If parents want to know whether their daughter is learning to get along on the playground without conflicts, as a teacher I can invite them to a conference, with or without the child in question, or I can suggest a visit during recess. If parents want to know whether their son is learning to read and write, I can show them a portfolio of his reading and writing work or invite them to an author's meeting where he and other children read their stories. I can send home a list of the books he has read and a copy of the "book" he has published in class. If parents want to know whether their sons and daughters are gaining a sound understanding of U.S. history and government, they can attend an exhibition in which the class acts out the issues surrounding the first constitutional convention. Or parents can read their student's articles in the newspaper the class has written on the outbreak of the Civil War.

Parking: Where, When, and How

Later in this chapter, I address ways we can communicate students' learning, ways that are personalized, specific, and relevant to the receiver's needs as well as to the communicator's. Meanwhile, let me illustrate different needs in knowing by a story a kindergarten teacher told me. Alice teaches in the school that serves the low-income area of her town. She makes a point of visiting all the children in their homes before they come to school, and she tries to keep in close touch with their parents. But the prevalence of single mothers and factory working hours sometimes makes it difficult for parents to come to school conferences. On this occasion, she couldn't seem to find a time when Victoria's mother, coping alone with three young children and a waitress job at a diner, was able to come to school during school hours. Finally Alice said, "Perhaps I could come to you."

They agreed to meet at the diner before it opened at 7:00 a.m. Alice arrived at the appointed time, 6:30 a.m., but Victoria's mother had to open the diner, get her uniform on, start the coffee, and lay out the silverware. Alice sat at the counter and waited. She said that by the time Victoria's mother was ready to talk, it was time to open the diner. The regular clientele, the truck drivers and local folks, shuffled in, perched on the stools, and cast covert glances at the unlikely sight of a schoolmarm in their midst. Victoria's mother was busy pouring out coffee, shouting orders into the back, bantering with the "regulars," and passing out hotcakes and eggs. When a momentary lull occurred, she came over, faced Alice, and said somewhat belligerently, "Well?"

When she told me this story, Alice said, "I realized it wasn't the moment to talk about Victoria's fine motor skills. I looked her straight in the eye and said, 'I just wanted you to know that Victoria is a great kid.'"

She said the woman's whole body relaxed. Her shoulders went down, a spontaneous smile spread across her face, and almost with a sigh she said, "I think so, too."

What Victoria's mother needed to know at that moment was that her daughter was okay. She needed to know that this was not going to be another conference in which she would hear about either her own or her daughter's inadequacies; another conference in which the gulf between herself and the authority of the school would be made plain; or another conference that would make her feel guilty for what she could not do. They did, in fact, get down to talking about what would be useful to develop Victoria's fine motor skills, and about other things, between the orders for hotcakes and coffee, though not in the words educational specialists might have used.

I cite this example not to suggest that teacher-parent conferences should be conducted in diners but to illustrate the importance of figuring out what parents, students, or even school boards really want to know. What Victoria's mother needed to know first was that someone else could see the strengths in her daughter. After that, she could listen to more specific assessments and suggestions.

It is a matter of audience. Writers, speakers, advertisers, and politicians try to assess the interests and expectations of their audiences before they begin to write, speak, act, or plan an approach. Playwrights address themselves to a specific kind of audience. Advertisers will change messages for different publications. Those of us who report on student learning must assess not only what students have learned but also what the audience to whom we are speaking needs to know. The school board needs to know what educational objectives the school field trip to the aquarium will meet. The principal needs to know whether the field trip will contribute to the language program or simply be a day away from it and that the children will treat each other and the people they meet on the trip with respect. One parent wants to know why Michelle is so excited about dolphins these days, and another wants to know what the children can learn about math just from planning the trip. Sometimes these different concerns overlap, and at other times they are idiosyncratic; but all are legitimate.

Highways and Byways

Alternative forms for communicating student learning are linked to alternative forms of assessment and can be divided into four categories:

1. Visible evidence of student growth and achievement through methods such as portfolios, exhibitions, displays of work, presentations, and videos to send home.
2. A ranking or rating of student achievement against clearly stated, predetermined standards such as those found in work sampling, rubrics, and report card checklists.
3. Evidence of learning through student self-assessment or peer evaluation.
4. Opportunities for two-way communication in conferences. What is known is not something one person says to the other, but rather an understanding that is constructed between all parties in the conversation.

Visible Evidence

Using portfolios to communicate student learning is an example of a more holistic approach to reporting, provided a ranking system does not condense the portfolios into yet another superhighway of grades. At the Jonathan Daniels School in Keene, New Hampshire, two 3rd grade teachers, Judy Fink and Tom Julius, have worked out an alternative reporting system in which portfolios that include a selective record of each child's work are coupled with parent/teacher/child conferences, which occur twice a year. In these conferences, children explain to their parents what work is included in the portfolio and why. Parents have the opportunity to see their child's progress in all subjects, from art to zoology, and to hear both the teacher and the child describe what growth has occurred and what new goals should be set (Julius 1993).

The exhibition is another example using visible evidence of achievement, sometimes quite literally a public performance. In *Horace's School,* Sizer (1992) describes creative and highly demanding possibilities for students to demonstrate what they have learned. A science fair, a class play, and a band concert are exhibitions. Similarly, in Antioch New England's Critical Skills program, which is based on learning through real problems, students are given a challenge and a problem to solve. Then they present a report to a panel of people who are knowledgeable or concerned about the issue. For example, a group of middle school science students did an energy audit for their school and presented the findings to a panel composed of the principal, custodian, and school board. The panel questioned the students, and eventually many of their recommendations were incorporated into the building's renovation. These exhibitions combine the features of an oral exam with the possibility of real-world rewards. Something significant happens as the result of one's work.

Rankings and Ratings: Measurement Tools

For any kind of evaluating and reporting, clarity about what is being measured is essential. To say a student is "doing well" establishes a baseline of affirmation but leaves a vacuum crying to be filled by something more specific. Doing well in what? By whose standards? How? As Guskey stresses in Chapter 3, we need clearly stated outcomes, indicators for achieving these outcomes, rubrics to indicate levels of achievement for academic or process tasks, and a comprehensive list of skills to be gained so that specific skills can be seen in context. These are the tools for reporting, which give shape, color, and individuality to "doing well" or to a grade of *A, B,* and *C* or *S* and U. In his chapter, Wiggins offers both rationale and examples of multiple-dimensional modes of reporting for our multidimensional children and society. He describes the difference between "performance scores," such as criterion-referenced, standard-referenced, and exemplar-referenced work, and the traditional letter grade or narrative report and illustrates the description with several examples or rubrics designed for different situations.

Self-Assessment

A colleague, Julie King, says that "self-assessment is gold"; and so it is, for when students are involved in thinking about their learning, learning increases. When we ask students to look conscientiously at what they are learning and to describe for us what they understand, we win on many counts. We learn what they understand about the subject and what they understand about themselves; we tacitly engage them as colleagues in the job of learning rather than as antagonists or inferiors; and we empower them to take responsibility for their own learning. The time spent with students in self-, peer, and group evaluation is time spent on curriculum and instruction, as well as on assessment.

For the three years my daughter was in high school, she barely maintained a 75 percent average, and she failed chemistry. But she passed the advanced placement test in English without taking the course and became a National Merit Scholar.

"If anyone had ever asked me why I was failing chemistry," she said, "if anyone had ever asked why I wanted to finish and get out early, if any teacher had ever asked me anything about what I was learning, I might have been able to figure out why I was failing. I might even know some chemistry now." To be consulted about one's own learning is empowering—not to be consulted is disempowering. Kids without power over their own learning take power in other ways, and some are subverting or resisting what we want to teach them.

Student self-assessment can appear in many forms. It can be a daily or weekly written response to a contract or an informal journal entry. It can be embedded in a learning log, a few minutes of class time devoted to reflecting about one's learning on paper. It can occur in an individual conference with the teacher or in a group debriefing of class work. One teacher asks her students to write individual rubrics for specific learning situations and then evaluate themselves against these rubrics. For one student, "expert" means teaching a math concept to the class; to another, "expert" means the ability to explain it to the teacher. Self-designed rubrics can be a tool for raising standards without sacrificing the need to respond to individual differences. Another valuable form of self-assessment occurs when students make the selections for their portfolios and explain the reasons for their choices in writing, orally to the teacher, or to parents and other audiences.

Conferences

Probably the most valuable and time-consuming form of communication is the teacher/parent, teacher/student conference. Like self-assessment, conferences are an educational experience in themselves if both parties listen to each other. Face-to-face contact enables us to learn the particulars of the audience and shapes our messages to questions we are asked. A constructivist approach indicates that just as knowledge about U.S. history or math facts is constructed by the learner in interaction with other people and the environment, so knowledge about student learning is constructed in the interaction between teachers and learners or parents and learners.

Hawkins (1973) describes the interactive nature of learning as points in a triangle of teacher, student, and content. No two points are sufficient; all three must be in relationships of equality with each other. A similar triangle can be used to describe the interactive nature of communication about student learning. One point is the student's learning, the content of the communication. The other two points are parent and student, or perhaps teacher and student—speaker and listener. In a constructive communication, each speaks and listens, communicating to and learning from the other.

Of course, teachers must be as ready to listen as to tell. The teacher can learn about the nature of the audience in the conference: What is important to these parents? The teacher can also learn about the student from the parents' perspective. Many a parent conference has illuminated some aspect of a child, which helps both sides to work more effectively for the child's good. In addition to the conferences by appointment we hold in schools, many less formal kinds of communication can be just as productive, from a telephone conversation to a few words exchanged in the hallway as Sam looks for his mittens. Communication becomes a two-way street in these formal and informal conversations.

Secondary Roads

Before concluding, I want to acknowledge the hidden messages that schools communicate. In addition to the explicit avenues I have discussed, many implicit ways exist for national bodies, schools, and teachers to communicate students' learning. Like the hidden or implicit curriculum (Jackson 1968, Goodlad 1984), implicit forms of communication are available. In one school, halls and walls attractively display student work for school visitors. Parents can judge for themselves how their children are drawing, writing, and understanding compared to the others whose work is displayed. In another school, all the displays are commercially made or created by teachers. Both schools are communicating something not only about their students but about what they value for students.

In one school, parent conferences are scheduled at 15-minute intervals during the school day, and parents must stand in the hallway outside the teacher's door while waiting their turn. Parent conferences at another school are scheduled for half an hour during the day or in the evening for the convenience of working parents. A welcome sign on the door and comfortable chairs in the hallway add warmth. Coffee is provided, and samples of children's work are on the walls and tables. One schedule invites parents to feel comfortable in the school; the other says take us or leave us. We need to think seriously about how we are communicating what students are learning by the way we treat members of the community and by the environment we create in the school.

Roadblocks

Several potential obstacles and hazards block the way to a more receiver-friendly communication system. Any major change in our reporting systems will require a massive effort in reeducation and time reallocation. Weaning ourselves from reliance on only two measures for communicating student learning—grades and standardized test scores—will not be easy. The United States is hooked on standardized tests, comparative rankings, and sound bite information. I am convinced that parents, teachers, and students themselves want reporting strategies that are more specific, more individualized and, at the same time, more encompassing. But the burden of proof will be on the inventors for awhile. We have become so conditioned to relying on grades and tests, often looking on them as infallible, that developing more individualized and sophisticated systems will require extensive public reeducation.

The difficulty of creating an appreciation for more varied qualitative and unfamiliar quantitative measures is matched only by the difficulty of finding sufficient time and money to do this more sophisticated assessment and reporting. We cannot lay on overburdened teachers and schools the task of creating new forms of reporting without releasing them from other time-consuming tasks. Our present habit of adding new expectations for curricula and instructional changes, without ever taking anything away, is creating such an overload on the classroom teacher that heroic efforts are needed to do anything adequately.

The answer lies in acknowledging the importance of new reporting systems, such as portfolios, exhibitions, and conferences, and agreeing to provide the time *within the school calendar*. We can do this with a clear conscience if we acknowledge and validate the educational values embedded in alternative assessment. Curriculum, instruction, and assessment are all part of the same process. You cannot change one mode without affecting the others. Attention to alternative avenues of communication is in itself part of the curriculum, part of the ways in which we instruct.

Since curriculum, instruction, and assessment are integrally connected, a systems approach to reporting on achievement is essential. I think again of that complex of intersecting and overarching highways I saw at the World's Fair. The problem of how to communicate particular knowledge, different aspects of what students are learning to different audiences, is breathtaking in its complexity but exciting in its possibilities. If we can figure out how to move some communication traffic off the superhighways and onto the secondary roads; if we can build up and improve the blue roads, the roundabouts, and the exit ramps; if we can keep the bridges between school and community, teacher and student, and parent and teacher from freezing up, we will have invented a communication system worthy of the future.

References

Goodlad, J.L. (1984). *A Place Called School*. New York: McGraw Hill.

Hawkins, D. (1973). "I, Thou, It: The Triangular Relationship." In *The Open Classroom Reader*, edited by C. Silberman. New York: Random House.

Jackson, P. (1968). *Life in Classrooms*. New York: Holt, Rinehart and Winston.

Julius, T. (1993). "Creating a Culture of Evaluation." *Democracy in Education* 7, 4.

Sizer, T. (1992). *Horace's School*. New York: Houghton Mifflin.

3

Reporting on Student Learning: Lessons from the Past— Prescriptions for the Future

THOMAS R. GUSKEY

Charged with the task of leading a committee that would revise his school's grading and reporting system, Warren Middleton described the work in this way:

> The Committee On Grading was called upon to study grading procedures. At first, the task of investigating the literature seemed to be a rather hopeless one. What a mass and a mess it all was! Could order be brought out of such chaos? Could points of agreement among American educators concerning the perplexing grading problem actually be discovered? It was with considerable misgiving and trepidation that the work was finally begun (p. 5).

Few educators today would consider the difficulties encountered by Middleton and his colleagues to be particularly surprising. In fact, most probably would sympathize with his lament. What they might find surprising, however, is that this report from the Committee on Grading was published in 1933!

The issues of grading and reporting on student learning have perplexed educators for the better part of this century. Yet despite all the debate and the multitude of studies, coming up with pre-

Special thanks are due Mary Vass of the Education Library at the University of Kentucky, whose help was instrumental in the preparation of historical portion of this chapter.

The resource from which much of this history was drawn is: Kirschenbaum, H., S.B. Simon, and R.W. Napier. (1971). *Wad-ja-get? The grading game in American education*. New York: Hart.

scriptions for best practice seems as challenging today as it was for Middleton and his colleagues more than 60 years ago.

What have we learned about grading and reporting student learning after nearly a century of research on the topic? What do we know works and what doesn't work? Are there guidelines that should be followed to ensure that our grading and reporting practices are fair, equitable, and useful to students, parents, and teachers? These questions form the basis for this chapter.

I begin with a brief description of how grading and reporting practices have evolved in the United States over the past century. Next I consider several consistent findings in the research evidence on grading and reporting. Finally, I outline guidelines for better practice, stemming from this research.

A Brief History

Although student assessment has been a part of teaching and learning for centuries, grading and reporting are relatively recent phenomena. The ancient Greeks used assessments in their teaching, but these were not formal evaluations of student achievement. Instead, their purpose was primarily formative. Examinations provided students the opportunity to demonstrate, usually orally, what they had learned. They also gave teachers a clear indication of what topics required additional work or instruction.

In the United States, grading and reporting were virtually unknown in schools before 1850. Back then, most schools grouped students of all ages and backgrounds together with one teacher. Few students went beyond the elementary education offered in these one-room schoolhouses. As the number of students increased in the late 1800s, however, schools began to group students in grade levels according to their age, and new ideas about curriculum and teaching methods were tried (Edwards and Richey 1947). One of these new ideas was the use of progress evaluations of students' work. In these evaluations, teachers would simply write down the skills each student had mastered and those on which additional work was needed. This was done primarily for the students' benefit, since they were not permitted to move on to the next level until they demonstrated their mastery of the current one.

With the passage of compulsory attendance laws at the elementary level, the number of students entering high schools increased rapidly. Between 1870 and 1910, the number of public high schools in the United States increased from 500 to 10,000 (Gutek 1986). As a result, subject areas in the high schools became increasingly specific; and student populations became more diverse. While elementary teachers continued to use written descriptions to document student learning, high school teachers began to employ percentages and other similar markings to certify students' accomplishments in different subject areas. This was the beginning of the grading and reporting systems we know today (Kirschenbaum, Simon, and Napier 1971).

The shift to percentage grading was gradual, and few American educators questioned it. The practice seemed a natural byproduct of the increased demands on high school teachers, who now faced classrooms with growing numbers of students. But in 1912, a study was published that seriously challenged the reliability of percentage grades as a measure of student achievement.

Starch and Elliott (1912) set out to determine the extent to which the personal values and expectations of teachers influence their grading standards. To do this, they made copies of two English-language examination papers that had been written by two students at the end of their first year in high school. These papers were then sent to 200 high schools, where the teacher who typically taught first-year English was asked to mark the papers according to the practices and standards of the school. A total of 142 schools returned the papers graded.

Both papers were graded on a percentage scale on which scores could range from zero to 100. A score of 75 was considered passing. For one paper, the scores varied from 64 to 98. The other paper received scores ranging from 50 to 97. One of the papers was given a failing mark by 15 percent of the teachers, while 12 percent gave the same paper a grade of more than 90 points. Starch and Elliott found that in addition to their subjective feelings about the papers, many teachers were influenced by neatness, spelling, and punctuation. While some teachers focused on elements of grammar and style, others considered only how well the message was communicated. With more than 30 different scores assigned to a single paper and a range of over 40 points, it is easy to see why this report caused a stir among educators. (It also makes clear that current problems regarding the reliability of portfolio scores is nothing new!)

Starch and Elliott's study was immediately criticized by those who claimed English teachers were naturally prone to be more subjective in their assessments of students' work. Some even argued that good writing is, after all, a highly subjective judgment. To counter this criticism, Starch and Elliott (1913) repeated their study the following year, using geometry papers, and found *even greater variation*. Among the 138 returns, scores on one of the papers ranged from 28 to 95: a 67-point difference! While some teachers deducted points only for a wrong answer, many others took neatness, form, and spelling into consideration.

These demonstrations of wide variation in teachers' grading practices led to a gradual move away from percentage scores to scales that had fewer and larger categories. One was a three-point scale that employed the categories *Excellent*, *Average*, and *Poor*. Another was the familiar five-point scale of *Excellent, Good, Average, Poor*, and *Failing*, or *A, B, C, D*, and *F* (R.H. Johnson, 1918; Rugg 1918). This reduction in the number of score categories served to reduce the variation in grades, but it did not solve the problem of teacher subjectivity.

To ensure a fairer distribution of grades among teachers and to bring into check the subjective nature of scoring, the idea of "grading on the curve" became increasingly popular. By this method, students were simply rank-ordered according to some measure of their performance or proficiency. A top percentage was then assigned a grade of *A*, the next percentage a grade of *B*, and so on (Corey 1930). Some advocates of this method even specified the precise percentages of students that should be assigned each grade. One example was the 6–22–44–22–6 system, in which 6 percent would get *A*'s, 22 percent *B*'s, and so forth (Davis 1930).

Grading on the curve was believed to be appropriate because, at that time, it was well known that the distribution of students' intelligence test scores approximated a normal probability curve. Since innate intelligence and school achievement were thought to be directly related, such a procedure seemed both fair and equitable (Middleton 1933).

In the years that followed, the debate over grading and reporting intensified. A number of schools abolished formal grades altogether, believing they were a distraction in teaching and learning (Chapman and Ashbaugh 1925). Some schools returned to using only verbal descriptions of student achievement. Others advocated pass-fail systems that distinguished only between acceptable and failing work (Good 1937). Still others advocated a "mastery approach," in which the only important factor was whether or not the student had mastered the content or skill. Once the student had demonstrated mastery of a skill, that student would move on to other areas of study (Heck 1938, Hill 1935).

Years later, how student learning is affected by grades and teachers' comments was the focus of an investigation by Page (1958). In this now classic study, 74 secondary school teachers administered a test and scored it in their usual way. A numerical score was assigned to each student's paper and, on the basis of that score, a letter grade of *A, B, C, D,* or *F*. Next, teachers randomly divided students' papers into three groups. Papers in the first group received only the numerical score and letter grade. The second group, in addition to the score and grade, received these standard comments: *A: Excellent! Keep it up. B: Good work. Keep at it. C: Perhaps try to do still better? D: Let's bring this up. F: Let's raise this grade!* For the third group, teachers marked the score, letter grade, and a variety of individualized comments. Page asked the teachers to write anything they wished on these papers, but to be sure their comments corresponded with their personal feelings and instructional practices. Papers were then returned to students in the customary way.

Page evaluated the effects of the comments by considering students' scores on the very next test or assessment given in the class. Results showed that students who received standard comments with their grade achieved *significantly higher* scores than those who received only a score and grade. Those students who received individualized comments did even better. This led Page to conclude that grades can have a beneficial effect on student learning, but only when accompanied by specific or individualized comments from the teacher. Studies conducted in more recent years confirm Page's results (e.g., Stewart and White 1976).

What Do We know?

Today, grading and reporting on student learning remain favorite topics for researchers. In fact, a recent review of the Educational Resources Information Center (ERIC) System found over 4,000 references to journal articles and reports published since 1960 on the topic of grading. But what have we learned from all this research? Is it still the "mass and mess" that Middleton and his colleagues described in 1933, or are there points of agreement in this vast collection of research evidence?

Although the debate over grading and reporting continues, today we know better which practices benefit students and encourage learning. Given the multitude of studies—and their often incongruous results—researchers appear to agree on the following points:

1. *Grading and reporting are not essential to instruction*. Teachers do not need grades or reporting forms to teach well, and students can and do learn without them (Frisbie and Waltman 1992). We must recognize, therefore, that the primary purpose of grading and reporting is other than facilitation of teaching or learning.

Teachers do need to check regularly on students' learning progress, but checking is different from grading. Checking implies finding out how students are doing, what they have learned well, and what problems or difficulties they are experiencing. It is primarily a diagnostic and prescriptive interaction between teachers and students. Grading and reporting, on the other hand, typically involve judgment of the adequacy of students' performance at a particular point in time. As such, it is primarily descriptive and evaluative (Bloom, Madaus, and Hastings 1981).

When teachers do both checking and grading, they must serve dual roles as both advocate and judge for students—roles that are not necessarily compatible (Bishop 1992). Ironically, this incompatibility is generally recognized when administrators are called on to evaluate teachers (Frase and Streshly 1994), but generally ignored when teachers are required to evaluate students. As might be expected, finding a meaningful compromise between these dual roles is discomforting to many teachers, especially those with a child-centered orientation (Barnes 1985).

2. *No one method of grading and reporting serves all purposes well*. Different grading and reporting

methods allow teachers to accomplish the following:

- Communicate the achievement status of students to parents and others.
- Provide information that students can use for self-evaluation.
- Select, identify, or group students for certain educational paths or programs.
- Provide incentives to learn.
- Evaluate the effectiveness of instructional programs (Feldmesser 1971, Frisbie and Waltman 1992, Linn 1983).

Unfortunately, many schools attempt to address all these purposes with a single method and end up achieving none very well (Austin and McCann 1992).

Letter grades, for example, offer parents and other interested parties a brief description of learning progress and some idea of the adequacy of that progress (Payne 1974). Their use, however, requires the abstraction of a great deal of information into a single symbol (Stiggins 1994). In addition, the cut-off between grade categories is always arbitrary and difficult to justify. If the scores for a grade of *B* range from 80 to 89, for example, a student with a score of 89 receives the same grade as the student with a score of 80, even though there is a 9-point difference in their scores. But the student with a score of 79—a 1-point difference—receives a grade of *C* because the cut-off for a *B* grade is 80. Letter grades also lack the richness of other more detailed reporting methods, such as narratives or checklists of learning outcomes.

The more detailed methods are not without their drawbacks, however. Narratives and checklists offer specific information that is useful in documenting progress, but good narratives are extremely time consuming to prepare. In addition, as teachers complete more narratives, their comments tend to become increasingly standardized. That is why many teachers opt to use computer programs in preparing report cards that allow them to select comments from standardized lists.

From parents' standpoint, checklists of learning outcomes often appear so complicated it is difficult to make sense of them. Further, checklists seldom communicate the adequacy of students' progress or whether such progress is in line with expectations for that level (Afflerbach and Sammons 1991). Some schools address this problem by including two marks for each outcome or skill listed. The first indicates the child's status with regard to that outcome (for example, Not Introduced, Beginning, Developing, Mastered, Extending or Advanced). The second mark indicates whether that status is Below, At, or Above expectations for that level. Such a dual marking system gives parents a clearer picture of their child's progress and where assistance may be needed.

Because one method will not adequately serve all purposes, schools must first identify their primary purpose for grading or reporting (Cangelosi 1990). This process often involves the difficult task of seeking consensus among several constituencies. Once the primary purpose is established, the method or combination of methods that best suits that purpose can be selected or developed.

3. *Grading and reporting will always involve some degree of subjectivity.* Regardless of the method used, assigning grades or reporting on student learning is inherently subjective. In addition, the more detailed the reporting method and the more analytic the process, the more likely subjectivity will influence results (Ornstein 1994). This is why, for example, holistic scoring procedures that include only a few score categories tend to have greater reliability than analytic procedures that offer a wide range of scoring options. But subjectivity in this process is not always bad. Because teachers know their students, understand various dimensions of students' work, and have clear notions of the progress made, their subjective percep-

tions may yield very accurate descriptions of what students have learned (Brookhart 1993, O'Donnell and Woolfolk 1991).

When subjectivity translates to bias, however, negative consequences can result. For example, teachers' perceptions of students' behavior can significantly influence their judgments of scholastic performance (Hills 1991). Students with behavior problems often have no chance to receive a high grade, regardless of what they demonstrate, because their infractions overshadow their performance. These effects are especially pronounced in judgments of boys because their conduct typically is perceived as less adequate than that of girls (Bennett, Gottesman, Rock, and Cerullo 1993). Even the neatness of students' handwriting can significantly effect teachers' judgment (Sprouse and Webb 1994, Sweedler-Brown 1992).

Training programs generally help identify and reduce these negative effects, and lead to greater consistency in judgments (Afflerbach and Sammons 1991). Unfortunately, few teachers receive adequate training in grading or reporting as part of their preservice experiences (Boothroyd and McMorris 1992). Also, few school districts provide adequate guidance to ensure consistency in teachers' grading or reporting practices (Austin and McCann 1992).

4. *Grades have some value as rewards, but no value as punishments.* Although educators would undoubtedly prefer that motivation to learn be entirely intrinsic, grades and other reporting methods are important factors in determining how much effort students put forth (Cameron and Pierce 1994, Chastain 1990, Ebel 1979). Most students view high grades as positive recognition of their success, and some work hard to avoid the consequences of low grades (Feldmesser 1971).

At the same time, no studies support the use of low grades or marks as punishments. Instead of prompting greater effort, low grades more often cause students to withdraw from learning. To protect their self-image, many regard the low grade or mark as irrelevant and meaningless. Other students may blame themselves for the low mark, but feel helpless to make any improvement (Selby and Murphy 1992).

Sadly, some teachers consider grades or reporting forms their "weapon of last resort." In their view, students who do not comply with their requests suffer the consequences of the greatest punishment a teacher can bestow: a failing grade. Such practices have no educational value and, in the long run, adversely effect students, teachers, and the relationship they share. Rather than attempting to punish students with a low mark in the hope it will prompt greater effort in the future, teachers can better motivate students by regarding their work as incomplete and requiring additional effort.

5. *Grading and reporting should always be done in reference to learning criteria, never "on the curve."* Using the normal probability curve as a basis for assigning grades typically yields greater consistency in grade distributions from one teacher to the next. The practice, however, is detrimental to both teaching and learning.

Grading on the curve communicates nothing about what students have learned or are able to do. Rather, it tells only students' relative standing among classmates, based on what are often ill-defined criteria. Differences between grades, therefore, are difficult to interpret at best, and meaningless at worst (Bracey 1994).

In addition, grading on the curve makes learning a highly competitive activity in which students compete against one another for the few scarce rewards (high grades) distributed by the teacher. Under these conditions, students readily see that helping others become successful threatens their own chances for success (R.T. Johnson, Johnson, and Tauer 1979; D.W. Johnson, Skon, and Johnson 1980). As a result, learning becomes a game of winners and losers; and because the number of rewards is kept arbitrarily small, most students are forced to be losers (D.W. Johnson and Johnson 1989).

Other unintended, but equally adverse, consequences for students result from grading on the curve. A study by Wood (1994), for example, found the percentage of students receiving *A*'s, *B*'s, *C*'s, and so on, in an urban high school remained virtually the same from the sophomore through senior years. At first glance, teachers throughout the school seemed to be remarkably consistent in their grading. However, each year there were fewer students in the school. Since students who leave are generally those with the lowest grades, this consistency in grade percentages means that as one group of unsuccessful students drops out, it is replaced by a succession of newly created low-grade students who were formerly successful. In other words, additional students are at risk of failing each year. Some students who got *C*'s as sophomores will get *D*'s as juniors, and so on.

Further, other research has shown that the seemingly direct relationship between aptitude or intelligence and school achievement depends on instructional conditions, not a normal probability curve. When the instructional quality is high and well matched to students' learning needs, the magnitude of this relationship diminishes drastically and approaches zero (Bloom 1976). Moreover, the fairness and equity of grading on the curve is a myth.

Learning Criteria

When grading and reporting relate to learning criteria, teachers are able to provide a clearer picture of what students have learned. Students and teachers alike generally prefer this approach because they considered it fairer (Kovas 1993). The types of learning criteria most typically used for grading and reporting purposes fall into in three broad categories. These include *product*, *process*, and *progress* criteria.

- *Product criteria* are favored by advocates of performance-based approaches to teaching and learning. These educators believe the primary purpose of grading and reporting is to communicate a summative evaluation of student achievement (Cangelosi 1990). In other words, they focus on *what* students know and are able to do at that point in time. Teachers who use product criteria often base their grades or reports exclusively on final examination scores, overall assessments, or other culminating demonstrations of learning.
- *Process criteria* are emphasized by educators who believe product criteria do not provide a complete picture of student learning. From their perspective, grading and reporting should reflect not just the final results, but also *how* students got there. Teachers who consider effort or work habits when reporting on student learning are using process criteria. So are teachers who count regular classroom quizzes, homework, class participation, or attendance.
- *Progress criteria* are used by educators who believe it is most important to consider how much students have gained from their learning experiences. Other names for progress criteria include "improvement scoring" and "learning gain." Teachers who use progress criteria look at *how far* students have come, rather than where they are. As a result, scoring criteria may be highly individualized among students.

Teachers who base their grading and reporting procedures on learning criteria typically employ some combination of these three types (Frary, Cross, and Weber 1993; Nava and Loyd 1992; Stiggins, Frisbie, and Griswold 1989). Most also vary the criteria they employ from student to student, taking into account individual circumstances (Natriello, Riehl, and Pallas 1994). Although varying the criteria is usually done in an effort to be fair, it makes interpreting any grade or report very difficult. A grade of *A*, for example, may mean that the student knew what was intended before instruction began (product), did not learn as well as expected but tried very hard (process), or simply made significant improvement (progress).

For this reason, most researchers and measurement specialists recommend the use of product criteria exclusively. They point out that the more process and progress criteria come into play, the more subjective and biased grades are likely to be (Ornstein 1994). How can a teacher know, for example, how difficult a task was for students or how hard they worked to complete it?

Many teachers, on the other hand, point out that if product criteria are used exclusively, some high-ability students receive high grades with little effort while the labor of less talented students is seldom acknowledged. Hence, low-ability students and those who are disadvantaged—students who must work hardest—have the least incentive to do so. These students find the relationship between high effort and low grades unacceptable and, as a result, often express their displeasure with indifference, deception, or disruption (Tomlinson 1992).

A solution to this dilemma is to establish clear indicators of the product, process, and progress criteria to be used, and then to report them separately (Stiggins 1994). That is, marks for effort, work habits, or learning progress should be separated from assessments of achievement. The key to success in doing so, however, rests in the clear specification of those indicators and the criteria to which they relate.

Practical Guidelines

Despite years of research, no evidence exists to indicate that one method of grading and reporting is best under all conditions or in all circumstances. At the same time, evidence does point to three general guidelines educators should follow in developing grading and reporting policies and practices. Although these guidelines may appear simplistic, adhering to them can be difficult because they call into question practices that are widely used in classrooms today. These practices are not the result of careful thought or sound evidence, however. Rather, they are used because teachers experienced these practices as students and, having little training or experience with other options, continue their use.

The following guidelines can help to ensure that grading and reporting practices are fair, equitable, and useful to students, parents, and teachers:

1. *Begin with a clear statement of purpose.* Just as highly effective schools are guided by a clear mission statement, so too an effective grading and reporting system must begin with a clear statement of purpose. The best reporting forms prominently display this statement so it is clear to all who view the form: students, teachers, parents, and administrators. *A statement of purpose should address why grading or reporting is done, for whom the information is intended, and what the desired results are.* Once the purpose of grading and reporting is made clear, all policies and practices should be reviewed in relation to that purpose. Those found to be counter to the purpose—or nonaligned with it—should be revised or abandoned altogether.

2. *Provide accurate and understandable descriptions of student learning.* Regardless of the method or form used, grading and reporting should provide accurate, quality information about what students have learned, what they can do, and whether their learning status is in line with expectations for that level. If process and progress criteria are also used, these must be clearly described as well. But most important, this information must be understood by those for whom it is intended—typically, students and their parents. Grading and reporting should be seen, therefore, more as a chal-

lenge in clear thinking and effective communication than as an exercise in quantifying achievement (Stiggins 1994).

3. *Use grading and reporting methods to enhance, not hinder, teaching and learning.* Although not essential to teaching or learning, grading or reporting can serve as an enhancement to instructional processes. A clear, easily understood reporting form facilitates communication between teachers and parents. When both parties speak the same language, joint efforts to help students are more likely to succeed. Better communication also helps parents ensure that their efforts to assist their children are in concert with those of the teacher.

Developing an equitable and understandable system also will require the elimination of certain long-time practices. Two of the most common of these are the practice of averaging to obtain a student's grade or mark, and assigning a score of zero to work that is late, missed, or neglected.

Averaging falls far short of providing an accurate description of what students have learned. For example, students often say, "I have to get a *B* on the final to pass this course." But does that make sense? If a final examination is truly comprehensive and students' scores accurately reflect what they have learned, should a *B* level of performance translate to a *D* for the course grade? If the purpose of grading and reporting is to provide an accurate description of what students have learned, then averaging must be considered inadequate and inappropriate.

Any single measure of learning can be unreliable. Consequently, most researchers recommend using several indicators in determining students' grades or marks—and most teachers concur (Natriello 1987). Nevertheless, the key question is, "What information provides the most accurate depiction of students' learning at this time?" In nearly all cases, the answer is "The most current information." If students demonstrate that past assessment information no longer accurately reflects their learning, that information must be dropped and replaced by the new information. Continuing to rely on past assessment data miscommunicates students' learning (Stiggins 1994).

Similarly, assigning a score of zero to work that is late, missed, or neglected does not accurately depict students' learning (Raebeck 1993). Is the teacher certain the student has learned absolutely nothing, or is the zero assigned to punish students for not displaying appropriate responsibility (Canady and Hotchkiss 1989, Stiggins and Duke 1991)?

Further, a zero has a profound effect when combined with the practice of averaging. Students who receive a single zero have little chance of success because such an extreme score skews the average. This is why, for example, in scoring Olympic events like gymnastics or ice skating, the highest and lowest scores are always eliminated. If they were not, one judge could control the entire competition simply by giving extreme scores. An alternative is to use the median score rather than the average or arithmetic mean (Wright 1994), but use of the most current information remains the most defensible option.

Meeting the Challenge

The issues of grading and reporting on student learning continue to challenge educators today, just as they challenged Middleton and his colleagues in 1933. But today we know more than ever before about the complexities involved in this process and how certain practices can influence teaching and learning. In addition, we continue to develop new and exciting ways to use grading and reporting to facilitate students' learning progress. Some educators, for example, are having great success with the use of laser disk and video report cards (Campbell 1992, Greenwood 1995).

What do educators need to ensure that grading and reporting practices and policies provide quality information about student learning? We need nothing less than clear thinking, careful planning, excellent communication skills, and an overriding concern for the well being of students. Combining these skills with our current knowledge on effective practice will surely result in more efficient and more effective reporting practices.

References

Afflerbach, P., and R.B. Sammons. (1991). "Report Cards in Literacy Evaluation: Teachers' Training, Practices, and Values." Paper presented at the annual meeting of the National Reading Conference, Palm Springs, Calif.

Austin, S., and R. McCann. (1992). "Here's Another Arbitrary Grade for Your Collection": A Statewide Study of Grading Policies." Paper presented at the annual meeting of the American Educational Research Association, San Francisco.

Barnes, S. (1985). "A Study of Classroom Pupil Evaluation: The Missing Link in Teacher Education." *Journal of Teacher Education* 36, 4: 46–49.

Bennett, R.E., R.L. Gottesman, D.A. Rock, and F. Cerullo. (1993). "Influence of Behavior Perceptions and Gender on Teachers' Judgments of Students' Academic Skill." *Journal of Educational Psychology* 85: 347–356.

Bishop, J.H. (1992). "Why U.S. Students Need Incentives to Learn." *Educational Leadership* 49, 6: 15–18.

Bloom, B.S. (1976). *Human Characteristics and School Learning*. New York: McGraw-Hill.

Bloom, B.S., G.F. Madaus, and J.T. Hastings. (1981). *Evaluation to Improve Learning*. New York: McGraw-Hill.

Boothroyd, R.A., and R.F. McMorris. (1992). "What Do Teachers Know About Testing and How Did They Find Out?" Paper presented at the annual meeting of the National Council on Measurement in Education, San Francisco.

Bracey, G.W. (1994). "Grade Inflation?" *Phi Delta Kappan* 76, 4: 328–329.

Brookhart, S.M. (1993). "Teachers' Grading Practices: Meaning and Values." *Journal of Educational Measurement* 30, 2: 123–142.

Cameron, J., and W.D. Pierce. (1994). "Reinforcement, Reward, and Intrinsic Motivation: A Meta-Analysis." *Review of Educational Research* 64, 3: 363–423.

Campbell, J. (1992). "Laser Disk Portfolios: Total Child Assessment." *Educational Leadership* 49, 8: 69–70.

Canady, R.L., and P.R. Hotchkiss. (1989). "It's a Good Score! Just a Bad Grade." *Phi Delta Kappan* 71: 68–71.

Cangelosi, J.S. (1990). "Grading and Reporting Student Achievement." *Designing Tests for Evaluating Student Achievement* (Chap. 9, pp. 196–213). New York: Longman.

Chapman, H.B., and E.J. Ashbaugh. (October 7, 1925). "Report Cards in American Cities." *Educational Research Bulletin* 4: 289–310.

Chastain, K. (1990). "Characteristics of Graded and Ungraded Compositions." *Modern Language Journal* 74, 1: 10–14.

Corey, S.M. (1930). "Use of the Normal Curve as a Basis for Assigning Grades in Small Classes." *School and Society* 31: 514–516.

Davis, J.D.W. (1930). "Effect of the 6–22–44–22–6 Normal Curve System on Failures and Grade Values." *Journal of Educational Psychology* 22: 636–640.

Ebel, R.L. (1979). *Essentials of Educational Measurement*. 3rd ed. Englewood Cliffs, N.J.: Prentice Hall.

Edwards, N., and H.G. Richey. (1947). *The School in the American Social Order*. Cambridge, Mass.: Houghton Mifflin.

Feldmesser, R.A. (1971). "The Positive Functions of Grades." Paper presented at the annual meeting of the American Educational Research Association, New York.

Frary, R.B., L.H. Cross, and L.J. Weber. (1993). "Testing and Grading Practices and Opinions of Secondary Teachers of Academic Subjects: Implications for Instruction in Measurement." *Educational Measurement: Issues and Practice* 12, 3: 23–30.

Frase, L.E., and W. Streshly. (1994). "Lack of Accuracy, Feedback, and Commitment in Teacher Evaluation." *Journal of Personnel Evaluation in Education* 8, 1: 47–57.

Frisbie, D.A., and K.K. Waltman. (1992). "Developing a Personal Grading Plan." *Educational Measurement: Issues and Practices* 11, 3: 35–42.

Good, W. (1937). "Should Grades Be Abolished?" *Education Digest* 2, 4: 7–9.

Greenwood, T.W. (1995). "Let's Turn on the VCR and Watch Your Report Card." *Principal* 74, 4: 48–49.

Gutek, G.L. (1986). *Education in the United States: An Historical Perspective*. Englewood Cliffs, N.J.: Prentice-Hall.

Heck, A.O. (1938). "Contributions of Research to the Classification, Promotion, Marking and Certification of Pupils." Reported in *The Science Movement in Education (Part II), Thirty-Seventh Yearbook of the National Society for the Study of Education* (pp. 187–199), edited by G.M. Whipple. Bloomington, IL: Public School Publishing Co.

Hill, G.E. (1935). "The Report Card in Present Practice." *Education Methods* 15, 3: 115–131.

Hills, J.R. (1991). "Apathy Concerning Grading and Testing." *Phi Delta Kappan* 72, 7: 540–545.

Johnson, D.W., and R.T. Johnson. (1989). *Cooperation and Competition: Theory and Research*. Endina, Minn.: Interaction.

Johnson, R.T., D.W. Johnson, and M. Tauer. (1979). "The Effects of Cooperative, Competitive, and Individualistic Goal Structures on Students' Attitudes and Achievement." *Journal of Psychology* 102: 191–198.

Johnson, D.W., L. Skon, and R.T. Johnson. (1980). "Effects of Cooperative, Competitive, and Individualistic Conditions on Children's Problem-Solving Performance." *American Educational Research Journal* 17, 1: 83–93.

Johnson, R.H. (1918). "Educational Research and Statistics: The Coefficient Marking System." *School and Society* 7, 181: 714–716.

Kirschenbaum, H., S.B. Simon, and R.W. Napier. (1971). *Wad-ja-get? The Grading Game in American Education*. New York: Hart.

Kovas, M.A. (1993). "Make Your Grading Motivating: Keys to Performance Based Evaluation." *Quill and Scroll* 68, 1: 10–11.

Linn, R.L. (1983). "Testing and Instruction: Links and Distinctions." *Journal of Educational Measurement* 20, 2: 179–189.

Middleton, W. (1933). "Some General Trends in Grading Procedure." *Education* 54, 1: 5–10.

Natriello, G. (1987). "The Impact of Evaluation Processes on Students." *Educational Psychologist* 22: 155–175.

Natriello, G., C.J. Riehl, and A.M. Pallas. (1994). *Between the Rock of Standards and the Hard Place of Accommodation: Evaluation Practices of Teachers in High Schools Serving Disadvantaged Students*. Baltimore: Center for Research on Effective Schooling for Disadvantaged Students, Johns Hopkins University.

Nava, F.J.G., and B.H. Loyd. (1992). "An Investigation of Achievement and Nonachievement Criteria in Elementary and Secondary School Grading." Paper presented at the annual meeting of the American Educational Research Association, San Francisco.

O'Donnell, A., and A.E. Woolfolk.(1991). "Elementary and Secondary Teachers' Beliefs About Testing and Grading." Paper presented at the annual meeting of the American Psychological Association, San Francisco.

Ornstein, A.C. (1994). "Grading Practices and Policies: An Overview and Some Suggestions." *NASSP Bulletin* 78, 561: 55–64.

Page, E.B. (1958). "Teacher Comments and Student Performance: A Seventy-Four Classroom Experiment in School Motivation." *Journal of Educational Psychology* 49: 173–181.

Payne, D.A. (1974). *The Assessment of Learning*. Lexington, Mass.: Heath.

Raebeck, B. (1993). "Exploding Myths, Exploring Truths: Humane, Productive Grading and Grouping in the Quality Middle School." Paper presented at the Annual Conference and Exhibit of the National Middle School Association, Portland, Ore.

Rugg, H.O. (1918). "Teachers' Marks and the Reconstruction of the Marking System." *Elementary School Journal* 18, 9: 701–719.

Selby, D., and S. Murphy. (1992). "Graded or Degraded: Perceptions of Letter-Grading for Mainstreamed Learning-Disabled Students." *British Columbia Journal of Special Education* 16, 1: 92–104.

Sprouse, J.L., and J.E. Webb. (1994). *The Pygmalion Effect and Its Influence on the Grading and Gender Assignment of Spelling and Essay Assessments*. Unpublished Master's thesis, University of Virginia.

Starch, D., and E.C. Elliott. (1912). "Reliability of the Grading of High School Work in English." *School Review* 20: 442–457.

Starch, D., and E.C. Elliott. (1913). "Reliability of the Grading of High School Work in Mathematics." *School Review* 21: 254–259.

Stewart, L.G., and M.A. White. (1976). "Teacher Comments, Letter Grades, and Student Performance." *Journal of Educational Psychology* 68, 4: 488–500.

Stiggins, R.J. (1994). "Communicating with Report Card Grades." *Student-Centered Classroom Assessment* (Chap. 14, pp. 363–396). New York: Macmillan.

Stiggins, R.J., and D.L. Duke. (1991). "District Grading Policies and Their Potential Impact on At-Risk Students." Paper presented at the annual meeting of the American Educational Research Association, Chicago.

Stiggins, R.J., D.A. Frisbie, and P.A. Griswold. (1989). "Inside High School Grading Practices: Building a Research Agenda." *Educational Measurement: Issues and Practice* 8, 2: 5–14.

Sweedler-Brown, C.O. (1992). "The Effect of Training on the Appearance Bias of Holistic Essay Graders." *Journal of Research and Development in Education* 26, 1: 24–29.

Tomlinson, T. (1992). *Hard Work and High Expectations: Motivating Students to Learn*. Washington, D.C.: Office of Educational Research and Improvement, U.S. Department of Education.

Wood, L.A. (1994). "An Unintended Impact of One Grading Practice." *Urban Education* 29, 2: 188–201.

Wright, R.G. (1994). "Success for All: The Median Is the Key." *Phi Delta Kappan* 75, 9: 723–725.

4

The Role of Cooperative Learning in Assessing and Communicating Student Learning

David W. Johnson and Roger T. Johnson

In this changing assessment world, teams have become essential at both the teacher and student level. For teachers, many of the new assessment formats and communication procedures require collegial teaching teams. For students, cooperative learning groups present unique and important opportunities and benefits for instruction, assessment, and reporting results. In this chapter, we discuss the ways that new assessment and communication procedures rely on cooperative learning groups and how such groups can be achieved.

Seven Principles of Assessment and Reporting

In essence, schools need to follow a basic set of seven assessment and reporting principles:

1. Begin your reporting of assessment results with an assessment plan. This plan should include learning and instructional processes, outcomes to be assessed, and the setting in which assessment will take place.

2. Understand and use the many benefits of cooperative learning groups in assessing the impact of instruction and communicating the results to interested audiences.

3. Avoid the use of "pseudo" groups or traditional learning groups in your assessment plan. Such groups are characterized by social loafing, free riding, hostility among members, sabotage of each other's work, and a variety of dysfunctional behavior patterns.

4. Ensure that learning groups are truly cooperative. Cooperative learning groups are characterized by positive interdependence, individual accountability, face-to-face promotive interaction,

the appropriate use of interpersonal and small-group skills, and group processing. It is cooperative learning groups that promote higher achievement, more positive relationships among students, and greater psychological health.

5. Make your assessment practices an integrated whole involving procedures before, during, and after instruction.

6. Involve students, classmates, and parents in reporting assessment results.

7. Use cooperative learning groups to help you individualize the educational goals, learning processes, assessment procedures, and reporting procedures for gifted and disabled students.

Making an Assessment and Reporting Plan

Our first principle is that reporting assessment results begins with an assessment plan for each class. The assessment plan should focus on the following:

1. The processes of learning. Following the advice of W. Edwards Deming and other advocates of total quality management, you focus on assessing and improving the processes of learning as well as assessing outcomes. In the classroom, this is known as total quality learning. The assumption is that if you continuously improve the processes of learning, the quality and quantity of student learning will also continuously improve. To implement total quality, you assign students to teams, and the team members take charge of the quality of work of fellow students. Team members, therefore, must learn how to define and organize work processes, assess the quality of the processes by recording progress indicators, and place the measures on a quality chart for evaluating effectiveness.

2. The outcomes of learning. To assess how much students have actually learned in a class, you directly measure the quality and quantity of their achievement. Achievement is traditionally assessed by paper-and-pencil tests. The new emphasis, however, is on assessing learning outcomes through performance measures. Performance-based assessment requires students to demonstrate what they can do with what they know by performing a procedure or skill. In a performance assessment, the student completes or demonstrates the same behavior that the assessor wants to measure. Students may submit for assessment compositions, exhibitions, demonstrations, video projects, science projects, surveys, and actual job performances. To assess students' performances, you need an appropriate method of sampling the desired performances and a clearly articulated set of criteria to serve as the basis for evaluative judgments.

3. The setting in which assessment takes place. Authentic assessment requires students to demonstrate desired skills or procedures in real-life contexts. Since it is difficult to place students in many real-life situations, you may wish to have students complete simulated real-life tasks or solve simulated real-life problems. To conduct an authentic assessment in science, for example, you may assign students to research teams working on a cure for cancer. They must conduct an experiment, write a lab report summarizing results, write a journal article, and make an oral presentation at a simulated convention. As with performance-based assessment, you need procedures for sampling performances and developing criteria for evaluation. You also need the imagination to find real-life situations or create simulations of them.

Cooperative learning groups are required to implement an assessment plan in an optimal way and to communicate the results to interested audiences. Using cooperative learning groups in instruction and assessment has many important advantages over individual instruction followed by individual assessment. Not every group will do, however. Many types of groups interfere with learning and assessment.

Using Cooperative Learning Groups

Our second principle is to understand and use the many benefits of cooperative learning groups in assessing the impact of instruction and communicating the results to interested audiences. Cooperative learning groups provide the following:

- **Additional sources of labor to conduct assessments and communicate results.** Because new assessment procedures are labor intensive, teachers simply do not have the time to use them without help and assistance. Students are a natural source of help for teachers.
- **More modalities to be used in the assessment and communication process.** Learning in cooperative groups allows for assessment procedures that cannot be used when students work alone, individualistically, or competitively.
- **The possibility for more diverse outcomes.** Cooperative learning groups enable teachers to assess critical thinking and level of reasoning, the performance of taught skills (such as conducting a science experiment), the ability to communicate knowledge, interpersonal and small group skills, self-esteem and self-efficacy, and commitment to producing quality work.
- **Additional sources of information.** Cooperative learning provides self- and peer assessments along with the teacher's. Self-, peer, and teacher assessments can be coordinated and integrated. This allows students, classmates, and teachers to work together in communicating assessment results to interested audiences.
- **The opportunity for the continuous improvement process to become an ongoing part of classroom life.** Cooperative learning groups offer a setting in which instruction, assessment, and continuously increasing achievement can all be part of one process. Total quality in education is based on the premise that all school members are organized into teams working cooperatively to continuously improve the process of learning.
- **A setting in which students may best learn the rubrics used to assess and communicate about their work.** This helps students produce higher-quality work, understand feedback, and assess classmates' work.
- **The possibility for students to learn from the assessment and reporting experiences.** Learning is enhanced when the assessment requires group members to discuss the accuracy, quality, and quantity of their own and each other's work.
- **Less possibility of teacher bias affecting the assessment and evaluation process.** Bias may be introduced into teachers' assessments in numerous ways. Even characteristics such as neatness of handwriting (Sweedler-Brown 1992) and teachers' perceptions of students' behavior (Bennett, Gottesman, Rock, and Cerullo 1993; Hills 1991) can influence judgment of a student's achievement.
- **The support system necessary to implement the improvement plan that results from the communication of the assessment results.** Communication of results must directly point toward what needs to be improved and what the students do next.
- **The opportunity to assess group as well as individual outcomes.** There are times when a group's scientific, dramatic, or creative projects need to be assessed.
- **The means to make assessment procedures congruent with ideal instructional methods.** Instructional and assessment procedures need to be aligned so they work for, not against, each other. Since cooperative learning tends to promote higher achievement and a variety of other important educational outcomes (Johnson and Johnson 1989), it will be used increasingly as the dominant instructional method in most classes. Therefore, we need to identify ways to use the new assessment procedures with cooperative learning.

Knowing What Type of Group Is Being Used

The third principle is to avoid the use of "pseudo" groups or traditional learning groups in your assessment plan. Not all groups are cooperative; seating students in a circle and calling them a cooperative group does not make it so. Study groups, project groups, lab groups, home rooms, and reading groups aren't necessarily cooperative.

Generally, two particular types of classroom learning groups fail to qualify as cooperative groups (Johnson and F. Johnson 1994; Johnson, Johnson, and Holubec 1993). The least effective and most destructive group is a pseudo group. Pseudo groups exist when students are required to work together, but they know they will be evaluated by being ranked from the highest to lowest performer. They see each other as rivals who must be defeated. Thus, they block each other's learning, hide information, mislead, and distrust one another. The result is that the sum of the whole is less than the potential of the individuals. Almost all students would achieve more if they worked alone instead of in a group like this.

The second least effective group is a traditional learning group. These groups exist when students talk to each other while they work individualistically. Students are required to work together, but assignments are structured so that very little joint work is required. Students believe that they will be evaluated and rewarded as individuals, not as members of the group. The result is that the sum of the whole is more than the potential of some of the members, but harder working and more conscientious students would achieve more if they worked alone.

There are ways to tell whether a student group is a pseudo group or a traditional learning group (Johnson and F. Johnson 1994). You know the group is not truly cooperative if members uncritically adopt the first idea suggested, if they loaf and don't try their best, if one member does all the work while others get a free ride, if members lack teamwork skills, or if some members reduce their efforts because they feel exploited.

Understanding the Nature of Cooperative Learning

The fourth principle is to ensure that learning groups are truly cooperative. We use cooperative learning as the primary instructional method in our classes so all students can experience academic success, form positive and supportive relationships with classmates, and make healthy adjustments to school life. Cooperative learning also creates unique opportunities for assessing and reporting students' learning.

Cooperative learning groups exist when students work together to accomplish shared goals. Students perceive that they will reach their learning goals if and only if other students in the group also reach their goals. Thus, students seek beneficial outcomes for all those with whom they are cooperatively linked.

Students are given two responsibilities: to complete the assignment and to ensure that all other group members complete the assignment. Students discuss material with each other, help one another understand it, and encourage each other to work hard. Individual performance is checked regularly to ensure all students are contributing and learning. A criteria-referenced evaluation system is used. As a result, the group is more than a sum of its parts, and all students perform higher academically than they would if they worked alone.

Hundreds of studies conducted over the past 90 years demonstrate that cooperation results in the following benefits when compared with competitive and individualistic learning situations (Johnson and Johnson 1989).

1. Higher achievement. The superiority of cooperative learning has been found to be greater the more conceptual the task, the more problem solving and creativity required, the more higher-level reasoning and critical thinking are desired, and the greater the application to the real world is required.

2. More positive relationships among students and between students and faculty. This was true even with students from different ethnic and cultural backgrounds, social classes, and language groups. It was also true for handicapped and nonhandicapped students. Individuals tend to like others with whom they have worked cooperatively.

3. More positive psychological well-being. Working with classmates cooperatively has been found to promote greater self-esteem, self-efficacy, social competency, coping skills, and general psychological health. Included in this area are students' attitudes toward schooling and subject areas. When they work cooperatively, students tend to develop more positive attitudes toward school, learning, and subject areas. They are more interested in taking advanced courses and continuing their education.

4. A more constructive classroom and school learning environment (Johnson and Johnson 1991a). The more frequently cooperative learning is used, the more students perceive the classroom climate as being both academically and personally supportive and enhancing. The more positive the attitudes toward cooperative learning, the more students report peer and teacher encouragement to exert effort to achieve, the more students perceive themselves to be involved in positive and supportive personal relationships with classmates and teachers, the higher students' academic self-esteem, and the fairer students perceive grading procedures to be.

Making Cooperation Work

To structure instructional units so students in fact work cooperatively with each other, you must understand the basic elements that make cooperation work. Mastering the basic elements of cooperation allows you to:

- Take your existing instructional units, curriculums, and courses and structure them cooperatively.
- Tailor cooperative learning instructional units to your unique instructional needs, circumstances, curriculums, subject areas, and students.
- Diagnose the problems some students may have in working together and intervene to increase the effectiveness of the student learning groups.

For cooperation to work well, you explicitly have to structure five essential elements in each instructional unit (Johnson and Johnson 1989). The five basic elements must be applied rigorously (much like a diet has to be adhered to) to produce the conditions for effective cooperative action. The use of cooperative learning becomes effective through disciplined action.

The first and most important element is positive interdependence. You must give a clear task and a group goal so students believe they sink or swim together. You have successfully structured positive interdependence when group members perceive that they are linked with each other in such a way that one student cannot succeed unless everyone succeeds. Therefore, their work benefits everyone else and everyone else's work benefits them. Positive interdependence may be structured through common goals, joint rewards, being dependent on each other's resources, assigning specific roles to each member, or a division of labor.

The second essential element of cooperative learning is individual (and group) accountability. Each member must be accountable for contributing her share of the work, which ensures that no one can "hitchhike" on the work of others. Individual accountability exists when the results of each student's assessment are given to the group and the individual. The purpose of cooperative learning groups is to make each member a stronger individual in her own right. Students learn together so they can subsequently achieve more as individuals.

The third essential component of cooperative learning is promotive interaction, preferably face-to-face. Students need to do real work together in which they promote each other's success by orally explaining to each other how to solve problems, discussing with each other the nature of the concepts being learned, teaching their knowledge to classmates, and explaining to each other the connections between present and past learning. Cooperative learning groups are both an academic support system (every student has someone who is committed to helping her learn) and a personal support system (every student has someone who is committed to her as a person).

The fourth essential element of cooperative learning is teaching students the required interpersonal and small-group skills. In cooperative learning groups, students are required to learn academic subject matter (taskwork) and also to learn the interpersonal and small group skills required to work together effectively (teamwork). Cooperative learning is inherently more complex than competitive or individualistic learning because students have to engage simultaneously in taskwork and teamwork. Group members must know how to provide effective leadership, decision making, trust building, communication, and conflict-management. Procedures and strategies for teaching students social skills may be found in Johnson (1991, 1993) and Johnson and F. Johnson (1994).

The fifth essential component of cooperative learning is group processing. Group processing occurs when members discuss how well they are achieving their goals and maintaining effective working relationships. Groups need to describe what member actions are helpful and unhelpful and make decisions about what behaviors to continue or change. Continuous improvement of learning processes results from the careful analysis of how members work together and how group effectiveness can be enhanced.

Conducting a Cooperative Lesson

There are three types of cooperative learning groups. Formal cooperative learning groups last from one class period to several weeks. They ensure that students are actively involved in the intellectual work of organizing material, explaining it, summarizing it, and integrating it into existing conceptual structures. They are the heart of using cooperative learning.

Informal cooperative learning groups are ad hoc, lasting from a few minutes to one class period. They are used during direct teaching (lectures, demonstrations, films, videos) to focus student attention on the material, set a mood conducive to learning, help set expectations for what the lesson will cover, ensure that students cognitively process the material being taught, and provide closure to an instructional session.

Cooperative base groups are long-term (lasting at least a year), heterogeneous groups with stable membership whose primary purpose is for members to give each other the support, encouragement, and assistance each needs to progress academically. Base groups provide students with long-term, committed relationships.

In conducting a formal cooperative lesson, you do the following:

1. Make preinstructional decisions. In every lesson you formulate objectives, decide on the size of groups, choose a method for assigning students to groups, decide which roles to assign group members, arrange the room, and arrange the materials students need to complete the assignment.

2. Explain the task and cooperative structure. In every lesson you explain the academic assignment, explain the criteria for success, structure positive interdependence, explain the individual accountability, and explain the behaviors you expect to see during the lesson.

3. Monitor and intervene. While you conduct the lesson, you monitor each learning group and intervene when needed to improve taskwork and teamwork. You also bring closure to the lesson.

4. Evaluate and process. You assess and evaluate the quality and quantity of student achievement, ensure that students carefully process the effectiveness of their learning groups, have students make a plan for improvement, and have students celebrate the hard work of group members.

Understanding the Underlying Structure

The issue of cooperation among students is part of the larger issue of organizational structure of schools (Johnson and Johnson 1994). For decades, schools have functioned as "mass production" organizations that divided work into component parts (1st grade, 2nd grade; English, social studies, science) to be performed by isolated teachers working in their own room, with their own set of students, and with their own set of curriculum materials. Students could be assigned to any teacher because they were considered interchangeable parts in the education machine. W. Edwards Deming, J. Juran, and other founders of the quality movement have stated that more than 85 percent of the behavior of members of an organization can be directly attributed to the organization's structure, not the nature of the individuals involved. Your classroom and school are no exceptions.

By using cooperative learning the majority of the time, you are changing the basic organizational structure of your classroom to a team-based, high-performance one. In other words, cooperation is more than an instructional procedure. It is a basic shift in organizational structure that will affect all aspects of classroom life. Cooperative learning also allows for more sophisticated assessment than competitive and individualistic learning situations.

Focusing on Potential Outcomes

When cooperative learning groups are used, assessment may focus on a wide variety of outcomes (Webb 1994). These need to be identified for each instructional unit. The following are potential categories of outcomes (Johnson and Johnson 1989):

1. Individual effort to achieve. Assessment has traditionally focused on measuring individual subject matter knowledge and expertise, focusing on immediate achievement, retention, transfer of learning, higher-level reasoning, intrinsic motivation to learn, achievement motivation, and other related outcomes. Since the purpose of cooperative learning groups is to increase the individual learning of each member, the pattern to classroom life becomes "learn it in a group, perform it alone." This is known as group-to-individual transfer. Following the social constructivist perspective of Vygotsky (1978), the Connecticut Common Core of Learning Alternative Assessment Program (Baron 1994) has students work individually, then in small groups to complete a complex task or experiment, and again individually to complete similar activities.

2. Group performance. Assessment may focus on the knowledge and skills individuals demonstrate while working with others. For example, a group may be able to solve problems and complete projects that are too complex and difficult for one student to do alone. Examples include science experiments, dramatic productions, field research such as community surveys, engineering projects, and creative projects such as the "Odyssey of the Mind." What students can accomplish in small groups may be especially interesting to potential employers (Hackman 1990, Johnson 1991).

3. Relationships among students. A variety of factors have focused attention on the relationships among students: desegregation of schools; inclusion of students with disabilities; increasing heterogeneity of students' historical backgrounds, languages, and cultures; pressures for equity of educational opportunity; and concern about isolated and alienated at-risk students. The high quality and positive nature of relationships among students is an important instructional outcome.

4. Psychological health. Many at-risk students are attending schools. Their risk factors may include abuse in the family, living in a criminogenic community, poverty, alienation from peers and school, or poor peer relationships. Promoting healthy social, cognitive, and psychological development is an important purpose of schooling. Instructional programs, therefore, have to focus on such outcomes as improving students' social skills, self-esteem, and positive attitudes toward learning and school. Important social skills include coordination of efforts with others, communication, decision making and problem solving, leadership, trust building, and negotiation and other conflict resolution procedures (Johnson 1991, 1993; Johnson and F. Johnson 1994; Salas, Dickinson, Converse, and Tannenbaum 1992). Such social skills must be acquired for workforce readiness (O'Neil, Allred, and Baker 1992).

Implementing the Assessment Procedures

Once cooperative learning groups have been established and the outcomes of interest identified, the assessment and reporting process can move forward. The fifth principle is to make your assessment practices an integrated whole involving procedures before, during, and after instruction.

It is counterproductive to take a fragmented approach to assessment. In every instructional unit, teachers are responsible for ensuring that instruction, assessment, and communication of results take place and are connected. The steps in doing so include specifying instructional objectives, making an assessment plan, and structuring the instructional unit; conducting the instructional unit and monitoring and assessing students' efforts to learn; and assessing student learning and communicating the results following instruction.

Planning Before the Lesson

Communicating the results of an assessment begins with the following activities before a lesson even starts (Johnson, Johnson, and Holubec 1993):

1. Specify objectives. These provide clear guidelines for conducting the instructional unit and assessing and evaluating student progress toward the objectives. Any cooperative lesson specifies objectives for both academic and social skills. The academic objectives need to be specified at the correct level for the students and matched to the appropriate level of instruction according to a conceptual or task analysis. Social skills objectives detail which interpersonal and small group skills will be emphasized during the instructional unit.

2. Design a sequence of instructional tasks aimed at achieving the objectives for the instructional unit.

3. Establish the criteria for success to be used to evaluate student performance (involving students in developing the criteria when it is appropriate).

4. Define the process of learning through which students are to reach the criteria.

5. Establish the plan for collecting the information needed to assess students' learning and the success of the instructional unit.

Conducting the Instructional Unit

Once you have made your plans, you are ready to conduct the instructional unit. During the unit, you will collect much of the assessment information you will eventually communicate to interested audiences. Each lesson may begin with assessing the quality of students' homework. Then, the teacher communicates to students the learning tasks to be completed, the criteria for success, the fact that they are to work together cooperatively, the ways each student will be individually accountable for both learning the assigned material and helping their groupmates, and the behaviors the teacher expects to see while the students work together.

After the students begin working, the teacher systematically monitors each learning group and intervenes when necessary to ensure that students correctly understand the academic content of the assignment. The monitoring and interventions provide opportunities for assessing student learning by observing the students at work in their groups and interviewing the group members. Special attention is given to assessing students' use of the interpersonal and small-group skills required to work together effectively.

Checking Homework. The following procedure can be implemented to check homework quickly at the beginning of each class period (Johnson, Johnson, and Holubec 1993). Students are requested to bring their completed homework to class and demonstrate that they understand how to do it correctly. Students enter the classroom and meet in their cooperative learning groups, which should be heterogeneous in terms of math and reading ability. One member (the runner) goes to the teacher's desk, picks up the group's folder, and distributes materials in the folder to the appropriate members. Members compare answers and quiz each other on the homework assignment.

The cooperative goal is to ensure that all group members bring their completed homework to class and understand how to do it correctly. Two roles are assigned: *explainer* (describes step-by-step how to complete the homework correctly) and *accuracy checker* (verifies that the explanation is accurate, encourages, and provides coaching if needed). The explainer reads the first part of the assignment and describes step-by-step how to complete it correctly. The other group members check for accuracy. The roles are rotated clockwise around the group so that each member does an equal amount of explaining. The group should concentrate on parts of the assignments that members did not understand. Any questions members have about completing the assignment correctly are answered. The runner records how much of the assignment each member completed. At the end of the review time, all the homework is placed in the group's folder and the runner returns it to the teacher's desk.

There is an alternative to this procedure, with students assigned to cooperative learning pairs. The teacher randomly picks questions from the homework assignment. One student explains the correct answer step-by-step. The other student listens, checks for accuracy, and prompts the explainer if she does not know the answer. Roles are switched for each question.

Conducting Observations. While students work together in cooperative learning groups, the teacher systematically gathers observation data about the quality of explanations and intellectual interchange among group members (Johnson, Johnson, and Holubec 1993). Observational procedures are aimed at describing and recording behavior as it occurs. Data may be gathered with formal observation schedules (on which the frequency of behaviors are tallied), checklists, rating scales, or anecdotal impressions.

Teachers assign students to small cooperative groups and give them an assignment. As the groups work, the teacher moves from group to group listening to students interact with each other. From listening to students explain how to complete the assignment, the teacher can assess what students do and do not understand, their level of cognitive reasoning, and their strategies for approaching the assignment. In addition, the teacher can assess how frequently metacognitive strategies are being used. A variety of observation sheets are given in Johnson, Johnson, and Holubec (1993).

Many times students may be able to give the "correct" answer to a question without understanding the principles and theories on which the answer is based. Correct answers on a test and completed homework assignments tell teachers very little about students' reasoning processes and understanding. The only way teachers can be sure that students really understand the subject being studied is by listening to them explain what they know to each other step-by-step. To do so, students must work in cooperative (not competitive or individualistic) learning groups.

Assessing Social Skills. In real job situations, the ability to work with others is often a key component of a work evaluation. The procedure for assessing students' use of social skills is as follows (Johnson, Johnson, and Holubec 1993):

1. Decide which social skill is going to be emphasized and make practicing it one of the objectives of the instructional unit. (Every cooperative instructional unit is a social skills lesson as well as an academic one.)

2. Operationally define the social skill. It is often helpful to have the class generate the list of nonverbal actions and verbal phrases that demonstrate the skill.

3. Teach the social skill to students. The skill may be modeled, explained step-by-step, and practiced by students before the instructional unit begins. Students are informed that use of the social skill during the instructional unit is expected.

4. Prepare the observation form, appoint observers, and explain the observation form to them. There are three possible observers: the teacher, students, and visitors. The teacher is always an observer. Students may be regularly used as observers, either a few who rove and monitor all groups or, preferably, one observer for each group.

5. The observers use the observation form to monitor the interactions among group members while they work on the academic lesson, paying special attention to the targeted social skill. The observations provide objective data about the interaction among group members. Group members' behavior is observed so students may be given feedback about their participation in the group and so inferences can be made about the ways in which the group is functioning. Students assess each other's use of the targeted social skill and provide immediate remediation to help each other master it.

6. All group members may fill out a checklist or questionnaire about their actions in the group in order to assess how often and how well they individually performed the targeted social skill and other small group skills.

7. The observer reports to the group the information gathered, and group members report their impressions of how they behaved. The observer summarizes her observations in a clear and useful manner and describes them to the group as feed-

back. The observer then helps group members make inferences from the observations about how well they group functioned, how frequently and well each member engaged in the targeted skill, and how the interaction among group members should be modified to make it more effective. The observer ensures that all group members receive positive feedback about their actions in the group.

8. The group members reflect on and analyze the effectiveness of their use of social skills. Reflection is needed in order to discover what helped and hindered them in completing the academic assignment and whether specific actions had a positive or negative effect. After small group processing, there is whole class processing in which the teacher shares his feedback to the class as a whole.

9. The group members set goals for improving their competence with the social skills during the next group meeting. Members discuss the goals and publicly commit to achieving them.

Many studies have examined the impact of cooperative learning experiences on the mastery and use of social skills (Lew, Mesch, Johnson, and Johnson 1986a, 1986b; Mesch, Lew, Johnson, and Johnson 1986, 1988; Putnam, Rynders, Johnson, and Johnson 1989). These studies found that socially isolated, withdrawn, and disabled students learned more social skills and engaged in them more frequently in cooperative than in individualistic situations, especially when the group was rewarded for their doing so.

Interviewing Students. In addition to observing students' work, teachers will want to interview students systematically to determine the level of learning, cognitive reasoning, problem solving, and metacognitive thinking (Johnson, Johnson, and Smith 1991). Interviews may take place with the following procedure.

The teacher assigns students to cooperative learning groups that are heterogeneous in terms of math and reading ability. The groups are given a set of questions on Monday and instructed to prepare all group members to respond to the questions. Each class period, the groups are given time to practice their responses to the questions. On Thursday and Friday, the teacher randomly chooses students from each group and gives each one an oral examination.

In conducting the interview, the teacher joins a group and randomly selects one member to explain the answer to a question. The teacher poses a series of questions, listens to student answers, and probes for more information. The teacher tries to activate the student's background knowledge and promote more complex language and expression. When that student finishes responding to the question, other group members can add to the answer. The teacher judges the answer to be adequate or inadequate. The teacher then asks another member a different question. This procedure is repeated until all questions have been answered or until the teacher judges the group to be inadequately prepared. In that case, the group returns to the assignments and practices until members are better prepared. The teacher provides guidance by identifying specific weaknesses and strengths in the answers. All group members are given equal credit for successfully completing the interview.

Assessing and Communicating after the Lesson

Most assessments and reporting procedures are conducted after the instructional unit is completed. Traditional assessment measures are paper-and-pencil achievement tests. In addition, teachers may wish to examine actual student performances. For example, students may offer for assessment compositions, class presentations, or samples of their work in a portfolio. In addition, the academic controversy procedure can be used to assess students' critical thinking. Students can assess themselves and their groupmates with rating scales, and group products can also be used for assessment and reporting.

In communicating the results of assessments, the most important audience may be students themselves and the cooperative learning groups of which they are members. The groups use the assessment information in their group processing and total quality learning processes. Or, students and cooperative learning groups may be involved in conferences with teachers, parents, and other interested audiences in which the assessment results are reported and communicated.

Paper-and-Pencil Achievement Tests. Tests may be given both to assess and increase student learning. There are two advantages of cooperative learning groups in administering traditional tests (Johnson, Johnson, and Holubec 1993; Johnson, Johnson, and Smith 1991). First, allowing students to work together before an assessment can level the playing field. Students can compare understandings and ensure that they all have the same background knowledge to prepare for the assessment. Second, letting students work in groups immediately following the assessment allows each member to discover what she did and did not understand and where the information required to answer the questions is located in the course materials. It also allows the group to provide remediation to members who did not understand the course content covered in the test.

The sequence of using cooperative learning groups in testing is as follows: group review, individual test, then group test (Johnson, Johnson, and Holubec 1993). As before, students are assigned to cooperative learning groups that are heterogeneous in terms of reading and math ability. The groups study together all week. On Thursday, the groups meet to ensure that all group members know and understand the material on which they will be tested. On Friday, an examination is given.

The students take the test individually, making two copies of their answers. They hand one answer sheet to the teacher for scoring. If all members of the group score above a certain criterion on the individual tests (such as 90 percent correct), each member receives a designated number of bonus points (such as 5). These are added to the individual scores to determine a student's individual grade for the test. Students keep the second answer sheet. After all members have finished the test, the group meets to take the test again. Their task is to answer each question correctly. The cooperative goal is for all group members to understand the material covered by the test. For any answer they disagree about or are unsure of, they are required to find the page and paragraph in the text that contains the answer. The teacher randomly observes the groups to check that they are following the procedure.

Peer Editing. In this process, students are assigned to cooperative groups and given the task of writing a composition or report (Johnson, Johnson, and Holubec 1993). Each student writes her own composition. The assignment is structured cooperatively by informing students that all group members must sign a statement verifying that each member's composition meets the criteria set by the teacher. Each group member will receive two scores for the composition. The first is based on the quality of her composition. The second is based on the total number of errors made by the group (the number of errors in their composition plus the number of errors in their groupmates' compositions).

A typical procedure is as follows (Johnson, Johnson, and Holubec 1993). First, the teacher assigns students to cooperative learning pairs with at least one good reader in each pair. The task of writing individual compositions is given. Students are informed that the criterion for success is a well-written composition by each student. Depending on the instructional objectives, the compositions also may be evaluated for grammar, punctuation, organization, content, or other criteria set by the teacher.

Next, Student A describes to Student B what she is planning to write. Student B listens carefully, probes with a set of questions, and outlines Student A's composition. The written outline is given to Student A. This procedure is then reversed, with Student B describing what he is going to write and Student A listening to and completing an outline of Student B's composition, which is then given to Student B.

Third, each student researches the material she needs to write the composition, keeping an eye out for material useful to her partner. If one student does not have the skills required to use reference materials and the library effectively, the partner teaches her how to do so. Then, the two students work together to write the first paragraph of each composition to ensure that they both have a clear start on their compositions. Each student then writes her composition individually. When completed, the students proofread each other's compositions, correcting capitalization, punctuation, spelling, language usage, topic sentence usage, and other aspects of writing specified by the teacher. Suggestions for revision are explained. Each student then revises her composition with the suggested revisions. The two students reread each other's compositions and sign their names, indicating that they personally guarantee that no errors exist in the composition.

While the students work, the teacher monitors the pairs, intervening where appropriate to help students master the needed writing and cooperative skills. When the composition is completed, the students discuss how effectively they worked together, listing the specific actions they engaged in to help each other. They plan what behaviors they will emphasize in the next writing pair, and thank each other for the assistance received.

Class Presentations. When students prepare and conduct a presentation on an assigned topic (Johnson, Johnson, and Smith 1991), the cooperative goal is for all members to learn the material being presented and gain experience in making presentations. First, the teacher assigns students to groups of four, gives each group a topic, and requires them to prepare one presentation that each group member can give in its entirety. The presentation should be given within a certain time frame and should be supported with visuals or active participation by the audience.

Next, the groups are given time to prepare and rehearse so all group members are able to give the presentation. After preparation is complete, the class is divided into four sections (one in each corner of the classroom). One member of each group goes to each section. Each student makes a presentation to her section. The audience rates the performance on a reaction form provided by the teacher. A presentation is evaluated on the basis of the degree to which it was scholarly and informative; interesting, concise, and easy to follow; involving (audience active, not passive); intriguing (audience interest in finding out more on their own); and organized (has introduction, body, conclusion). In addition, the teacher adds criteria uniquely aimed at the purposes of the presentation.

At the end of the presentation, one copy of the rating form is given to the teacher, and one copy is given to the presenter. The teacher systematically observes part of all presentations. Finally, the groups meet to evaluate how effectively each member made the presentation. Remedial help is given to any member who had problems. Any performance given by a student—whether it is a speech, musical performance, science demonstration, dramatic presentation, or videotape project—can be assessed and evaluated by peers as well as a teacher.

Portfolios. Portfolios are used to accumulate student work over time to show how students are progressing (Wiggins 1994, Wolf 1989). This assessment method has been used successfully in art classes for many years. The portfolio allows the student to present her work as a whole. Students collect their work, select representative pieces, and reflect on what the items show about them as learners. The portfolio then allows teachers and other interested audiences to consider multiple sources of data when they examine what students know and can do. A much broader concept of learners' strengths and needs can be formulated.

There are no hard and fast rules as to the contents of a student's portfolio. For example, the portfolio can contain 10 pieces of work that received the best grades, or it may include 10 pieces of work that the student feels best represent her abilities. The portfolio can also contain all or a wide selection of a student's work. Both the teacher and the student need to be satisfied that the portfolio offers a true representation of the student's understanding and abilities.

When students work in cooperative groups, they provide each other with help and support. This raises the question, "Whose work is it?" and it may be unclear what they can do individually. This same question may be asked about a student's work after a teacher has provided academic help or support. Additional complications arise when classwork merges with homework. The amount of help students get from family and friends becomes an additional threat to the validity of interpretations about individual scores.

Portfolio assessments put students who do not receive help from family and peers at a disadvantage. Furthermore, communities in which parents are highly educated professionals may produce student portfolios superior to those produced by students in districts with less educated and wealthy parents. This problem is avoided when portfolios lead to individual performances on demand.

A student, for example, can write a series of compositions during a school year, all of which go through a peer editing process. While the portfolio reflects what the student is capable of doing with feedback from classmates, parents, and teachers, it does not reflect how well the student can write on demand. The teacher, therefore, may wish to give a test in which students are given a certain amount of class time (such as 30 minutes) to write an essay. The extent to which the writing skills learned in constructing the portfolio transfer to new writing demands can then be assessed. Portfolios should show mastery of basic skills and procedures that can be used and applied in new situations.

The cooperative procedure for using portfolios is similar to that used for peer-editing of compositions. The task is for each student to create a portfolio. The criteria for success is a well-constructed portfolio by each student. The cooperative goal is for all group members to verify that each member's portfolio is perfect according to the criteria set by the teacher. Students receive an individual score or evaluation on the quality of their portfolio. The teacher can also give a group score based on the total number of errors in their portfolios. Each student is individually accountable to create her own portfolio. The procedure is as follows (Johnson, Johnson, and Smith 1991):

1. Assign students to groups with at least one good reader and writer in each group.
2. Each item that may be included in the portfolio is created in the context of the cooperative learning groups. Compositions, for example, go through a peer editing process to ensure that they meet the criteria set by the teacher. This peer editing process is key. Although the portfolio is an expression of the quality of work of each student, assessing and giving feedback to groupmates about their portfolios provides skills and experiences that go beyond the feedback received from others.
3. Each member chooses representative items they think should be in their portfolio.

4. Each member explains her portfolio to the other members.

5. The group members provide each student with feedback concerning the quality of their presentation and the wisdom of the choice of the items.

6. If possible, a chart or graph is drawn showing the progress the student has made.

7. A test is given in which students individually create a product similar to those in the portfolio to demonstrate mastery of the skills and competencies reflected in the portfolio.

Portfolios reflect the idiosyncratic work of a single student. Communicating the results of an assessment about the quality of a portfolio can reveal a great deal about the student's talents, competencies, attitudes, and taste. There may be problems with comparing scores, however, if portfolio assessments are used to compare students (Gearhart and Herman 1995). If portfolio scores are used to compare schools or school districts, the problems of comparing scores become less problematic as long as assessment results are aggregated and exclude individual-level data. It may be easier to give a standard test to individual students that measures the competencies reflected in the portfolio than to find ways of making portfolio scores comparable.

Academic Controversy and Critical Thinking. Higher-level reasoning, critical thinking, and the ability to advocate a point of view persuasively are best taught and assessed by two interrelated instructional procedures: cooperative learning and academic controversy. Controversy exists when one student's ideas, information, conclusions, theories, and opinions are incompatible with those of another and the two seek to reach an agreement (Johnson and Johnson 1979, 1992).

In well-structured controversies, a cooperative group is divided into two pairs, which are assigned opposing positions. The pairs thoroughly research their position and develop a persuasive case for its validity, present the best case possible to the other pair, and listen to the opposing position. They then engage in a discussion in which they attempt to refute the other side and rebut the other's attacks on their position, reverse perspectives and present the best case for the opposing position, and then drop all advocacy and seek a synthesis that takes both perspectives and positions into account.

Compared with concurrence-seeking, debate, and individualistic efforts, controversy results in greater mastery and retention of the subject matter, higher-quality problem solving, greater creativity in thinking, greater motivation to learn more about the topic, more productive exchange of expertise among group members, greater task involvement, more positive relationships among group members, more accurate perspective taking, and higher self-esteem (Johnson and Johnson 1979, 1989, 1992). In addition, students enjoy it more; controversy can be fun, enjoyable, and exciting.

The competencies built by engaging in academic controversies are being assessed in an integrated assessment as part of the Connecticut Academic Performance Test (Connecticut State Board of Education 1992/1994), in which students are asked to demonstrate the skills and knowledge they have learned in language arts, mathematics, science, social studies, and other classes. The test assesses the competencies of researching a position, preparing a persuasive argument, and presenting it. The assessment procedure is as follows:

1. Students are assigned a controversial issue.

2. Students are given 10 minutes to discuss the issue with classmates in small groups of 3 or 4 students each. Each small group generates one list of ideas concerning the issue for all members to use in their essay.

3. Each student has 90 minutes to read source materials that present a variety of viewpoints on the issue. The student is given two charts to help her consider the various arguments

for and against the issue and scratch paper to help organize thoughts. The student also must write an individual essay stating her position on the issue and using the information contained in the source materials to support that position. The essay is scored on the basis of whether the student takes a clear stand on the issue, organizes the essay so readers can follow the student's reasoning, supports the position with accurate and relevant information from source materials, and expresses her ideas clearly so that readers understand what the student means.

Self- and Other Ratings. The German writer Thomas Mann once said, "No one remains quite what he was when he recognizes himself." Having students rate themselves and their groupmates is an important addition to most instructional units (Johnson, Johnson, and Holubec 1993). First, students rate the quality and quantity of their learning. Next, students rate the quality and quantity of their groupmates' learning. Third, students discuss and reflect on their learning experiences (under the guidance of an observant teacher), comparing their self-ratings with the ratings they receive from groupmates. Such self- and other ratings allow students to see how the quality of their work has evolved.

Teachers must assess a number of factors besides test scores. Students need to arrive at class on time and be prepared to learn with the essential materials, resources, and attitudes. Students also need to provide academic help and assistance to groupmates and ask groupmates for help when they need it. In using a rating form, students need to understand clearly the purpose of the form and how it will be used, the number of points (if any) the form will count in evaluating students, and the questions on the form. Figure 4.1 shows a sample form.

Group Products. The usual rule for cooperative learning groups is that students learn together and are subsequently assessed as individuals (Johnson, Johnson, and Smith 1991). Though individual assessment is more common than group assessment in school, it is usually just the opposite in real life. In most organizations, the success of the organization as a whole, divisions in the organization, and teams in the division are focused on more frequently than the success of individual employees. Authentic assessment, therefore, most often means group assessment. Thus, there are times when a classroom assignment may be given requiring a group report, exhibit, performance, video, or presentation.

Students need to be clearly briefed when the purpose of assessment is to measure group productivity. For example, students are given the task of completing the assigned project. The cooperative goal is for group members to complete one project in which everyone has contributed a share of the work, can explain its content and how it was conducted, and can present it to the class. The procedure is as follows.

First, students are assigned an initial project and are placed in cooperative learning groups to complete it. The required materials are provided. Second, the group completes the project, ensuring that all members contribute to, agree on, and can explain the results. The teacher systematically observes each group and provides feedback and coaching. Third, the group hands in its report to the teacher, each member presents the results to a section of the class, and a test may be given on the content of the project. Fourth, the assignment can be extended when the teacher presents the relevant algorithm, procedure, concept, or theory required to complete the project. Students are then given a more complex project that requires them to apply what they have just learned.

Group Processing. One audience for assessment results is the cooperative group itself. The results of assessments have to be communicated to students and their groupmates. The group members reflect on the achievement level of each student and how well they are helping and assisting

FIGURE 4.1
STUDENT SELF- AND PEER EVALUATION FORM

This form will be used to assess the members of your learning group. Fill one form out on yourself. Fill one form out on each member of your group. During the group discussion, give each member the form you have filled out on them. Compare the way you rated yourself with the ways your groupmates have rated you. Ask for clarification when your rating differs from the ratings given you by your groupmates. Each member should set a goal for increasing his or her contribution to the academic learning of all group members.

Person Being Rated: ______________________________

Write the number of points earned by the group member:
(4 = Excellent, 3 = Good, 2 = Poor, 1 = Inadequate)

____ On time for class.
____ Arrives prepared for class.
____ Reliably completes all assigned work on time.
____ Work is of high quality.
____ Contributes to groupmates' learning daily.
____ Asks for academic help and assistance when it is needed.
____ Gives careful step-by-step explanations (doesn't just tell answers).
____ Builds on others' reasoning.
____ Relates what is being learned to previous knowledge.
____ Helps draw a visual representation of what is being learned.
____ Voluntarily extends a project.

each other to learn (Johnson, Johnson, and Holubec 1993). Such group processing leads to self-monitoring (Ames and Lau 1982) and self-efficacy, especially when it focuses on positive actions that facilitated the group's work (Sarason and Potter 1983, Turk and Sarason 1983). Group processing of the information about each member's achievement and the interaction among members aimed at promoting learning has been found to increase the achievement of high-, medium-, and low-achieving students (Yager, Johnson, and Johnson 1985). The combination of the teacher leading a whole-class discussion of how successfully students are learning and each cooperative learning group processing the performance of each member increases achievement on problem-solving tasks (Johnson, Johnson, Stanne, and Garibaldi 1990). The combination of group members receiving individual feedback on academic performance and the group as a whole receiving feedback also promotes higher achievement (Archer-Kath, Johnson, and Johnson 1994).

Group processing ends with a group celebration of members' success and progress (Johnson, Johnson, and Holubec 1993). Group celebrations are an important aspect of reward interdependence. Celebrations also unite members through a common identity. Every time a group member makes an effort to learn or to contribute to the learning of others, the effort must be recognized and celebrated. The celebration may be as simple as congratulating each other, or it could be a group cheer, dance, or song.

Total Quality Learning. Traditionally, assessment has focused on the outcomes of instruction. Yet W. Edwards Deming and other advocates of total quality management in business and industry stress that instead of measuring outcomes, we should emphasize improving the process by which instructional and learning take place. Total quality learning is the use of cooperative learning groups to continuously improve students' performances and group effectiveness (Johnson and Johnson 1994). The continuous improvement of instruction and learning encompasses the following seven steps (Johnson and Johnson 1994):

1. Form teams. To promote total quality in a school, both students and teachers must be assigned to teams: cooperative learning groups and collegial teaching teams. The teams are placed in charge of the quality of members' work. Team members, therefore, have to be trained to organize their work, assess its quality daily, and place the results on a quality chart to help evaluate effectiveness.

2. Select a process for improvement. The team needs a specific, definable process to work on. The process needs to be significant, and it must be in the power of the team to change the process.

3. Define the process. The best way to define the process is to draw a picture of it. Two common ways to picture a process are the flow chart and the cause-and-effect diagram.

4. Engage in the process. Team members must engage in the process so they can measure each of its steps.

5. Gather information about the process, display the data, and analyze it. First, the team identifies quantifiable factors, such as time. (If a factor cannot be counted, it cannot be improved.) Next, the team develops a design for gathering the relevant data. This includes specifying what data will be collected, who will collect it, when it will be collected, and how it will be collected. A check sheet or observation form is a common way to gather data. Finally, the team analyzes and portrays the data in ways that help members easily understand it. Common ways to portray data are the Parieto chart, run chart, scatter diagram, and histogram.

6. Create and implement an improvement plan. A plan is created for how the process will be modified to improve its effectiveness. The team then implements the plan. The focus is on making small, incremental improvements in a process day after day after day. The team carefully evaluates the implementation, gathering more data. If the modified process works, the team adopts it. If it does not work, the team redesigns it and tries it out again on a small basis.

7. Institutionalizing changes that work. Team members ensure that there is no reverting to old practices by continuously taking new data samples, analyzing them, revising the plan, and revising the process.

Deming believes that if teachers concentrate on this continuous improvement of learning and instruction, the quality of students' learning will take care of itself.

Conferencing with Students and Parents

Our sixth principle is to involve students, classmates, and even parents in reporting assessment results. Two types of conferences can follow instruction. The first is a student-teacher conference. The teacher presents the instructional goals to students and sets them to work in cooperative learning groups to achieve the goals. The teacher functions as a consultant or coach to improve students' performance and to train students how to facilitate each other's progress. Periodically, an assessment of the student's progress is made by the student, the cooperative learning group, and the teacher. The teacher then meets with each student individually to discuss the student's progress in reaching the goals and helping groupmates reach the goals. Each student gets personal attention and is taught how to present her progress and improvement from the last conference to the present one. The student's, teammates', and teacher's assessment can all be merged into a two-way dialogue about the student's work.

The second type of conference is a student-led, parent-teacher conference. Placing students in charge of the conference makes them individually accountable, encourages them to take pride in their work, and encourages student-parent communication about school performance.

With this type of conference, an assessment of the student's progress is made by the student, the cooperative learning group, and the teacher. The cooperative learning group prepares each member to present her progress in reaching her learning goals and helping groupmates reach their goals. The group helps each member compile evidence for the presentation, prepare effective presentation aids, and practice and refine the conference presentation. Students become well rehearsed in presenting their work and the rubrics used to evaluate it. Students must master the language needed to communicate about their learning goals and academic efforts and learn how to describe their progress. With the teacher serving as a co-leader and coach, each student presents her work to her parents and discusses the next steps to be taken in improving academic accomplishments.

Promoting Heterogeneity in Cooperative Learning Groups

The seventh principle is to use cooperative learning groups to help individualize the educational goals, learning process, assessment procedures, and reporting procedures for gifted and disabled students. When cooperative learning groups are used in assessing and reporting results, two groups are of special interest: students with disabilities and students who are academically gifted. Each has specific assessment and reporting challenges.

Students with Disabilities

When students with disabilities are included in the regular classroom, the most constructive way to manage their instruction is to place them in heterogeneous cooperative learning groups. Low-achieving students often learn more in such groups than in competitive or individualistic learning situations, especially when they receive the help they need and actively participate in the group's work (Azmitia 1988, Johnson and Johnson 1989, Mugny and Doise 1978, Webb 1980). Following is one way to assess and report the learning of disabled students who are included in the regular classroom (Johnson, Johnson, and Holubec 1992):

1. Tailor the learning goals to each student so that the student is academically challenged but can succeed. Students within the same cooperative learning group can have different amounts of work to complete or different levels of work to complete.
2. Tailor the rubrics used to assess and report each student's achievement. Different criteria may be used to evaluate the quality of work of each member.
3. Give the group the responsibility for ensuring that all members succeed in achieving their learning goals.
4. Assess frequently and give the results to the student and her cooperative learning group. Give the group the responsibility for providing remediation when it is needed and ensuring that continuous improvement of learning takes place.

For each member of a cooperative learning group, an individualized learning plan may be applied. Learning goals, instruction, assessment, and reporting results can all be better individualized in cooperative learning groups than in a class of 30 students working individualistically or competitively. No matter what a student's disability, appropriately challenging learning tasks can be assigned, performance can be assessed, and a rubric can be created for evaluating and communicating the results. Members of the group can then implement the next steps in the student's instructional plans.

Academically Gifted Students

High-achieving, gifted students usually perform quite well whether they work with other high-achieving students or with lower-achieving students (Azmitia 1988; Hooper and Hannafin 1988; Johnson and Johnson 1991b; Skon, Johnson, and Johnson 1981). There is even evidence that high achievers learned more in heterogeneous (mixed-ability) than in homogeneously (all high-ability) cooperative learning groups (Webb 1980). High achievers in heterogeneous learning groups benefit from giving more explanations than other group members. In managing the assessment and reporting of gifted students in heterogeneous cooperative learning groups, the same procedures given above may be applied.

The purpose of cooperative learning groups is to increase the learning of each and every member. It is one of the most effective tools schools have to teach low-, medium-, and high-ability students (Johnson and Johnson 1989). Even a small amount of time in a cooperative group influences students' academic learning if cooperative learning is implemented effectively. Wise and Behuniak (1993) revealed that as little as 10 minutes of participating in a cooperative learning group increased the achievement of some students. On some forms of the 90-minute language arts "Response to Literature" assessment, 10th grade students individually read a short story, individually answered two open-ended questions, discussed the story for 10 minutes in three-person groups, and then individually answered five more open-ended questions. The 10-minute discussion was found to improve some students' understanding of the story, leading to new insights about special twists in the story and the characters' motivations. Saner, McCaffrey, Stecher, Klein, and Bell (1994) found similar results in a science assessment developed by the California Learning Assessment System.

The power of cooperative learning is such that the Oregon State Department of Education incorporated group work into several assessment projects (New Standards Project, New Certificate of Initial Mastery) to give students opportunities to learn relevant content that other students may already know (Neuberger 1993). Given the power of cooperative learning, it seems inevitable that more and more teachers will use it more and more of the time.

References

Ames, R., and S. Lau. (1982). "An Attributional Analysis of Student Help-Seeking in Academic Settings." *Journal of Educational Psychology* 74: 414–423.

Archer-Kath, J., D.W. Johnson, and R. Johnson. (1994). "Individual Versus Group Feedback in Cooperative Groups." *Journal of Social Psychology* 134: 681–694.

Azmitia, M. (1988). "Peer Interaction and Problem Solving: When Are Two Heads Better Than One?" *Child Development* 59: 87–96.

Baron, J. (April 1994). "Using Multi-Dimensionality to Capture Verisimilitude: Criterion-Referenced Performance-Based Assessments and the Ooze Factor." Paper presented at the annual meeting of the American Educational Research Association, New Orleans.

Bennett, R., R. Gottesman, D. Rock, and F. Cerullo. (1993). "Influence of Behavior Perceptions and Gender on Teachers' Judgments of Students' Academic Skill." *Journal of Educational Psychology* 85: 347–356.

Connecticut State Board of Education. (1992/1994). *Connecticut Academic Performance Test*. Hartford, Conn.: Author.

Gearhart, M., and J. Herman. (Winter 1995). "Portfolio Assessment: Whose Work Is It?" *Evaluation Comment* 1–16. Los Angeles: UCLA ,Center for the Study of Evaluation.

Hackman, J. (1990). *Groups That Work (And Those That Don't): Creating Conditions for Effective Teamwork.* San Francisco: Jossey-Bass.

Hills, J. (1991). "Apathy Concerning Grading and Testing." *Phi Delta Kappan* 72, 2: 540–545.

Hooper, S., and M. Hannafin. (1988). "Cooperative CBI: The Effects of Heterogeneous Versus Homogeneous Grouping on the Learning of Progressively Complex Concepts." *Journal of Educational Computing Research* 4: 413–424.

Johnson, D.W. (1991). *Human Relations and Your Career.* 3rd ed. Englewood Cliffs, N.J.: Prentice Hall.

Johnson, D.W. (1993). *Reaching Out: Interpersonal Effectiveness and Self-Actualization.* 5th ed. Boston: Allyn and Bacon.

Johnson, D.W., and F. Johnson. (1994). *Joining Together: Group Theory and Group Skills.* 5th ed. Boston: Allyn and Bacon.

Johnson, D.W., and R. Johnson. (1979). "Conflict in the Classroom: Controversy and Learning." *Review of Educational Research* 49: 51–70.

Johnson, D.W., and R. Johnson. (1989). *Cooperation and Competition: Theory and Research.* Edina, Minn.: Interaction Book Company.

Johnson, D.W., and R. Johnson. (1991a). "Cooperative Learning and Classroom and School Climate." In *Educational Environments: Evaluation, Antecedents and Consequences*, edited by B. Fraser and H. Walberg. New York: Pergamon.

Johnson, D.W., and R. Johnson. (1991b). "What Cooperative Learning Has to Offer the Gifted." *Cooperative Learning* 11, 3: 24–27.

Johnson, D.W., and R. Johnson. (1992). *Creative Controversy: Intellectual Challenge in the Classroom.* 2nd ed. Edina, Minn.: Interaction Book Company.

Johnson, D.W., and R. Johnson. (1994). *Leading the Cooperative School.* 2nd ed. Edina, Minn.: Interaction Book Company.

Johnson, D.W., R. Johnson, and E. Holubec. (1992). *Advanced Cooperative Learning.* 2nd ed. Edina, Minn.: Interaction Book Company.

Johnson, D.W., R. Johnson, and E. Holubec. (1993). *Cooperation in the Classroom.* 6th ed. Edina, Minn.: Interaction Book Company.

Johnson, D.W., R. Johnson, and K. Smith. (1991). *Active Learning: Cooperative Learning in the College Classroom.* Edina, Minn.: Interaction Book Company.

Johnson, D.W., R. Johnson, M. Stanne, and A. Garibaldi. (1990). "Impact of Group Processing on Achievement in Cooperative Groups." *Journal of Social Psychology* 130: 507–516.

Lew, M., D. Mesch, D.W. Johnson, and R. Johnson. (1986a). "Positive Interdependence, Academic and Collaborative-Skills Group Contingencies and Isolated Students." *American Educational Research Journal* 23: 476–488.

Lew, M., D. Mesch, D.W. Johnson, and R. Johnson. (1986b). "Components of Cooperative Learning: Effects of Collaborative Skills and Academic Group Contingencies on Achievement and Mainstreaming." *Contemporary Educational Psychology* 11: 229–239.

Mesch, D., M. Lew, D.W. Johnson, and R. Johnson. (1986). "Isolated Teenagers, Cooperative Learning and the Training of Social Skills." *Journal of Psychology* 120: 323–334.

Mesch, D., D.W. Johnson, and R. Johnson. (1988). "Impact of Positive Interdependence and Academic Group Contingencies on Achievement." *Journal of Social Psychology* 128: 345–352.

Mugny, G., and W. Doise. (1978). "Socio-cognitive Conflict and Structure of Individual and Collective Performances." *European Journal of Social Psychology* 8: 181–192.

Neuberger, W. (September 1993). "Making Group Assessments Fair Measures of Students' Abilities." Paper presented at the National Center for Research on Evaluation, Standards, and Student Testing Conference, "Assessment Questions: Equity Answers," University of California, Los Angeles.

O'Neil, H., K. Allred, and E. Baker. (1992). *Measurement of Workforce Readiness: Review of Theoretical Frameworks.* (CSE Tech. Rep. No. 343). Los Angeles: University of California, Center for Research on Evaluation, Standards, and Student Testing (CRESST).

Putnam, J., J. Rynders, R. Johnson, and D.W. Johnson. (1989). "Collaborative Skill Instruction for Promoting Positive Interactions Between Mentally Handicapped and Nonhandicapped Children." *Exceptional Children* 55, 6: 550–557.

Salas, E., T. Dickinson, S. Converse, and S. Tannenbaum. (1992). "Toward an Understanding of Team Performance and Training." In *Teams: Their Training and Performance*, edited by R. Swezey and E. Salas. Norwood, N.J.: Ablex.

Saner, H., D. McCaffrey, B. Stecher, S. Klein, and R. Bell. (1994). "The Effects of Working Pairs in Science Performance Assessments." Manuscript submitted for publication. Santa Monica, Calif.: RAND.

Sarason, I., and E. Potter. (1983). *Self-Monitoring: Cognitive Processes and Performance.* Seattle: University of Washington.

Skon, L., D.W. Johnson, and R. Johnson. (1981). "Cooperative Peer Interaction Versus Individual Competition and Individualistic Efforts: Effects on the Acquisition of Cognitive Reasoning Strategies." *Journal of Educational Psychology* 73: 83–92.

Sweedler-Brown, C. (1992). "The Effect of Training on the Appearance Bias of Holistic Essay Graders." *Journal of Research and Development in Education* 26, 1: 24–29.

Turk, S., and I. Sarason. (1983). *Test Anxiety and Causal Attributions.* Seattle, Wash.: University of Washington.

Vygotsky, L. (1978). *Mind in Society: The Development of Higher Psychological Processes.* (M. Cole, V. John-Steiner, S. Scribner, and E. Souberman, eds. and trans.). Cambridge, Mass.: Harvard University Press.

Webb, N. (1980). "A Process-Outcome Analysis of Learning in Group and Individual Settings." *Educational Psychologist* 15: 69– 83.

Webb, N. (1994). *Group Collaboration in Assessment: Competing Objectives, Processes, and Outcomes.* (CSE Technical Report 386). Los Angeles: University of California, National Center for Research on Evaluation, Standards, and Student Testing (CRESST).

Wiggins, G. (1994). "Toward Better Report Cards." *Educational Leadership* 52, 2: 28–37.

Wise, N., and P. Behuniak. (April 1993). *Collaboration in Student Assessment.* Paper presented at the annual meeting of the American Educational Research Association, Atlanta.

Wolf, D. (April 1989). "Portfolio Assessment: Sampling Student Work." *Educational Leadership* 46, 7: 4–10.

Yager, S., D.W. Johnson, and R. Johnson. (1985). "Oral Discussion, Group-to-Individual Transfer, and Achievement in Cooperative Learning Groups." *Journal of Educational Psychology* 77: 60–66.

5

Grading and Academic Feedback for Special Education Students and Students with Learning Difficulties

Russell Gersten
Sharon Vaughn
Susan Unok Brengelman

How do we provide meaningful feedback on academic performance to special education students and other students with learning problems? Debates about standards, accountability, and other issues have grown more urgent since the early 1980s, with the increased integration of special education students as part of the movement toward providing instruction in general education settings (Carpenter 1985, Michael and Trippi 1987). Current education reform efforts, which advocate reporting how *all* students are doing against high, uniform standards (Wiggins 1994), bring the issue of grading practice for special education and low-achieving students to the forefront once again. The shifting nature of student learning tasks entailed in current educational reform movements is likely to heighten unresolved tensions, as discussed by Guskey in Chapter 3.

There are two, largely polarized, schools of thought regarding grading practices for special education students. The first holds that standards ought to be absolute. Adaptations in test administration may be permissible for special education students (such as giving them more time to finish a test, or reading a test to them when other students must read it themselves), but ultimately an *A* or *B* or *Pass* grade should mean the same things for all students. In other words, teachers may provide special education students with alternative assessment procedures, but the students must acquire and demonstrate the same level of knowledge as others.

This approach, at first glance, appears to be reasonable. As Wiggins notes in Chapter 11, students and parents need to know where they stand in relation to an objectified standard. Yet, Donohoe and Zigmond (1990), investigating the academic careers of 476 learning-disabled students in nine high schools in a large metropolitan district, found that special education students typically received a grade of *D* or lower year after year in mainstream classes such as science, social studies, and health: "79% were earning a *D* or below in social studies; 69% were earning a *D* or below in science; and 63% were earning a *D* or below in health" (p. 26). A similarly bleak picture emerged for the low-achieving students. With the increased focus on high standards for all, this trend will likely intensify.

It is not hard to imagine the debilitating effects of such a system on a special education student who, no matter how hard he works, will only receive a grade of *D*. In fact, McPartland (1992) found this to be one of the major problems in secondary education for low-performing students, and linked the perpetuation of this grading system to students giving up. Similarly, Zigmond and Thornton (1985), studying students with learning disabilities, correlated the long-term consequences of earning poor grades to reduced self-concept as well as to a high risk of dropping out.

Yet, as severe as this may seem to us—and to the special education students—research by Vaughn, Schumm, Niarhos, and Gordon (1993) indicates that the majority of students consider this approach to be fair and that, to some extent, students' perceptions of equity influence their teachers' views as well.

The second school of thought assumes a diametrically opposite position, calling for grading based primarily on individual effort. Although this may seem to be a more humane route, one that special educators often prefer, there are numerous problems with this as well. One difficulty is the fact that effort is virtually impossible to measure; by its very nature, it is subjective. Also, students need feedback that helps guide their future study and learning efforts (Serna, Schumaker, and Sheldon 1992). Grades based on effort are simply too vague to provide much valuable information.

Many teachers base grades for special education students on learning-related behaviors such as handing in assignments, attendance, participating in class, and taking notes. However, there are obvious problems with grades based primarily on these criteria. Students with disabilities effectively learn that all the teacher requires of them is to stay out of trouble, and that no one cares whether or not they learn anything in class.

Calhoun and Beattie (1984) documented this problem over a decade ago through a series of interviews. Special education students told the researchers that "good behavior and good effort (not falling asleep!) . . . (were) the important criteria" (p. 225). One 10th grade English student commented, "For a good grade, sit there and do your work. That's all you have to do. If she asks you a question, answer it. If you can't answer, tell her" (p. 225).

Assessing Students' Growth Rate

In this chapter we review the research on grading and academic feedback for special education students and provide guidelines culled from the literature. Our major focus is on middle and high school, where problems with grading appear most severe. We also share critical issues raised in interviews we conducted with secondary special education teachers.

Although no easy remedies exist for the problem, current information on features of academic feedback and communication systems appears promising; but this research is truly in its beginning stages. The issues of grading and feedback are complex and are often the most difficult problems for special educators.

The wide range of purposes and functions typically associated with grading and performance assessment compound this complexity, as Wiggins notes in Chapter 11. Although considering these multiple purposes is important when teachers assess special education students, the primary focus of this essay is on one aspect of grading—what Wiggins refers to as "growth rate." It should be noted that special education students, as mandated by law, receive regular formal evaluations of their achievement levels, based on standardized measures. Also by law, schools must share these results with parents. Thus parents and students receive feedback on performance relative to national standards.

A recent movement in special education has been to increasingly include special education students in national assessments and, when necessary, to provide adaptations so that students can demonstrate what they know and don't know. For example, some teachers give students more time for the test or read the test to them. This movement seems important because it is likely to shift goals to include concepts and reasoning skills, as well as more basic academic proficiencies. Because this movement is in its infancy, however, our focus will be on *grading based on individual growth rates*.

For special education students and their parents, this type of grading has the most promise for improving communication about learning progress. Rather than trying to assess the elusive concept of effort, it is almost always preferable to assess student academic performance in an *ipsative* fashion—that is, by frequently assessing and giving feedback about how well the student is doing compared to where she was at the beginning of the year. This is not to discount the important contribution of evaluating learning-related behaviors or a student's effort. However, neither of these is sufficient for providing special education students and parents with important information about how well students are learning academic content.

Fairness: Students' Perceptions of Grading and Testing

Researchers have conducted several studies that consider students' perceptions of grading. In two studies (Schumm and Vaughn 1994, Vaughn and Schumm in press) that involved 3,000 elementary, middle, and high school students, representing the full range of achievement groups (high achievers, average achievers, low achievers, and students with disabilities), students turned out to be very good judges of their teachers' behavior. They were sensitive to differential treatment of classmates, even when the teachers believed they were able to conceal how they felt.

For the most part, studies show that students assess grading and testing procedures based on *what they perceive as fair*. In general, they believe that all students should have the same tests, though they feel that modifications in testing procedures are acceptable.

Middle and high school students prefer teachers who make instructional adaptations to meet students' needs over less flexible teachers (Vaughn, Schumm, Niarhos, and Daugherty 1993). However, in issues related to testing, a more complex picture emerges: many of the students surveyed indicated that they thought teachers should treat all students the same. Their rationale was fairness (e.g., "It is not fair to change a test for some students"). Yet during follow-up interviews, most students said it would be all right to give a different test to a student with learning disabilities or to one who spoke English as a second language.

Vaughn, Schumm, Klingner, and Saumell (1995) also found that most students wanted everyone in the class to have the same assignments and homework. Yet middle and high school students with learning disabilities requested adaptations in their assignments. Our recent interviews with students provided some insight into the reasons behind these conflicting opinions (Gersten, Dilliplane, Dimino, and Peterson 1995). While students frequently cited fairness, a second reason was communication. If students have different assignments and homework, they cannot help each other inside or outside of class; other students exclude them from the telephone "loop," leaving them out of the mainstream. According to those interviewed, textbooks, assignments, and homework need to be the same for all students because they provide tangible evidence of class membership and opportunities for social inclusion.

Our interviews conducted with secondary special education students revealed diverse perspectives among the special education students themselves. Some students identified or expressed the need for teachers to modify and grade their instruction and assignments using an adjusted standard. Researchers have begun to identify the importance of engaging these students in self-advocacy training so that they know their rights and understand that they can ask teachers for reasonable adaptations and adjustments.

Another group of students expressed resistance to any communication regarding their school performance. In the words of one teacher, "They perceive their lives as always falling short and themselves as always failing" (at home and at school). These students assumed teacher contact would be negative and would serve only to point out their errors. They appear to require gentle, cautious, nonthreatening opportunities to recognize their accomplishments, less related to grades and more attuned to their own improved performance. Clearly this group would benefit from graphed data that document progress, suggestions for areas of work, or tutoring sessions with a peer or instructional assistant.

A third group of students with disabilities was extremely sensitive about teachers' modifying requirements or standards to meet their needs. These students, in the name of fairness, insisted on the same assignments and instruction without modification, however badly they needed them. Their values and standards were in sync with those in the Vaughn studies cited previously. Their desires to be "the same as other kids" outweighed their ability to recognize the benefit of appropriate accommodations; they refused needed individualization, and thus set themselves up for potential failure. The teachers viewed this group as requiring the most time and energy for communicating feedback on performance and progress, and for developing rapport and trust so that the feedback could be beneficial.

The interviews illustrate that special education students hold differing views of what they consider fair and appropriate in terms of grading standards, test adaptations, and assignments—thus providing teachers with conflicting information.

Teachers' Perceptions and Concerns

Pollard, Rojewski, and Pollard (1993) examined the concerns that secondary education teachers encountered when grading special education students in integrated settings. Results of a survey asking teachers to identify problem areas revealed the following themes: lack of information on student capabilities and individualized educational programs (IEPs); issues related to objectivity and fairness; use of double standards in grading; issues related to maintenance of high standards for high school graduation; lack of training; and the resentment of nonspecial education students toward differential grading of special education students. Rojewski, Pollard and Meers (1990) found that a group of secondary vocational education teachers identified fair and objective grading as their greatest source of frustration when grading special education students in their classrooms.

The quandaries of teachers were well articulated in research by Calhoun and Beattie (1984). Of 26 teachers interviewed, 25 indicated that they had different grading criteria for special education students. Often, report card grades were "bumped upward." A social studies teacher stated, "If they're mainstreamed . . . I grade special education students' papers like the rest of the class. Then I adjust the grade on the report card according to effort. Individually, I tell them I'm proud of their improvement" (p. 222).

In fact, recent research by Putnam (1992) conducted in several states found that many teachers reported making adaptations in test format (52 percent of the teachers) and test procedures (43 percent of the teachers), along with providing some additional types of assistance (87.4 percent of the teachers) for special education students. Although there were wide variations based on subject areas, Putnam noted that the adaptations and modifications generally tended to be fairly minor (e.g., dividing up the test into two sections, reading the instructions aloud, or letting students use class notes).

Many teachers feel that they should hold special education students in general education classrooms accountable to the same standards as the other students in the class (Schumm, Vaughn, and Saumell 1994). This can be a source of friction between general and special education teachers. On the other hand, special education teachers often consider effort and attendance to be important (Calhoun and Beattie 1984). For example, the special education teacher often feels that students who show they can solve a type of problem should receive a satisfactory grade—even if they are able to solve only one third as many as other students on a timed test. Again, the tension between ipsative standards (where the student is compared to her earlier performance) and absolute standards emerges.

Our interviews revealed that many special education teachers attempt to use a combination of effort and performance criteria. All of them noted inherent dilemmas in using some of the grading strategies identified in the literature, such as standardized grading, basing grades on effort or classroom behaviors, or adjusting academic content. These teachers felt it crucial to provide regular, frequent, and specific feedback to students so they know how they are doing and, specifically, where they are improving. The teachers provided feedback both verbally and through progress graphs, special awards, and weekly progress reports. A couple of the teachers disliked the increasingly popular use of computerized "average" grading systems because such systems did not allow students to see the progress they were making.

Teachers also expressed ambivalence about basing grades on learning-related behaviors, noting how merely handing in an assignment seemed inadequate without considering how much of the assignment the student completed, or how accurately. It appears that assessment of learning-related behaviors should not be the sole source for development of a grade. However, this type of assessment can be a useful tool for helping orient students toward behaviors they need for academic success, similar to Wiggins' concept of evaluating students' "habits of mind" described in Chapter 11.

Gustafson (1994) notes that effective evaluation and grading systems should help students improve by providing *specific* grading or evaluation criteria. In other words, the purpose of grading should be to provide the student with specific and comprehensible objectives and to assess progress in these areas.

One teacher we interviewed reported a fairly comprehensive process for establishing grading criteria for special education students that seems to fit criteria noted by Gustafson. Essentially, this grading process (shown in Figure 5.1) involves a contract that spells out the criteria by which a teacher will evaluate a student, using a range of modification strategies to assess several key areas. The student, the general education classroom teacher, and the special education resource room teacher jointly develop the contract.

FIGURE 5.1

SAMPLE OF CRITERIA FOR GRADING A SPECIAL EDUCATION STUDENT

The following procedures could be jointly developed by the school, student, and parent when specifying grading options.

Tests

- Administer test orally, with questions and answers.
- Teacher, other student, or resource teacher reads regular test to student. (Please give resource teacher at least one day's notice.)
- Administer regular test using open book, class notes, or both.
- Modify modality of test, written or oral, such as multiple choice instead of essay questions.
- Redo test if not passed.
- Lower criterion for passing.

In-Class Assignments

- Give regular assignments with lower criteria for passing.
- Shorten the regular assignment (e.g., half the questions).
- Grade assignments as "complete" rather than with a letter grade.
- Modify the set of questions students will answer.
- Pair the student with another student for help.
- Require the student to give oral answers to teacher.
- Redo assignments if incorrect.
- Give credit for appropriate behaviors not normally graded, such as taking notes.

Homework

Same options as "In-Class Assignments."

Class Participation, Behavior, and Effort

- Same expectations as for other class members, but student may need extra encouragement and frequent feedback from teacher.
- Focus on a specific study skill or behavior deficit by giving a Pass/No Pass each day for that behavior. (Examples: coming prepared to class with correct materials, or volunteering answers during class discussions.)

Other Considerations

- Give extra credit for projects that student or teacher suggests.
- Have student aide tape reading assignments or read aloud to student.
- Set expectations for attendance.

Providing Direct Feedback to Students on Their Academic Performance: Curriculum-Based Assessment and Other Formative Systems

As Guskey (1994) noted, "Today we know more than ever before about the complexities involved in grading student performance and how certain practices can influence teaching and learning" (p. 19). Yet, for too many special education students, teachers often employ grading practices without critically examining them for their immediate or long-term effects (whether intended or unintended) on students' learning.

The work on curriculum-based measurement by Fuchs, Fuchs, and Hamlett (1994) is a dramatic exception. These researchers found that sharing academic performance data on a regular (weekly or bimonthly) basis with students improved academic growth in those of average and above-average ability. However, this process did not help special education students or other low-performing students.

Fuchs and her coauthors interpreted their findings as resulting from the inability of students to know what to do with the information. They either need guidance (and perhaps explicit instruction) in how to use the information to focus their studying, or they need to literally walk through the process with a teacher. Currently this group of researchers is exploring the effects of a more elaborate intervention that requires students to use performance feedback to set personal goals and to determine the content of upcoming instructional activities. Other researchers have noticed that, when students in a middle school American history class were given informal, weekly, curriculum-based measures focusing on knowledge of historical concepts (as opposed to historical facts), the students seemed better able to focus their study efforts (Carnine et al. in press). Demonstrating how this type of assessment affects student study habits seems a particularly germane area for future research.

Also encouraging is a wide range of curriculum-based measurement systems teachers are developing and using for special education students in basic academic skill areas (Fuchs and Deno 1994). There are also the beginnings of curriculum-based measurement systems in more complex areas such as expressive writing (Davenroy and Hiebert 1993, Isaacson 1995), and science (Tindal and Hasbrouck 1991).

Although there seems to be some benefit in providing frequent feedback to special education students on their academic performance, it appears that teachers need to guide students in how to use this information to help focus their learning and studying efforts. It is also possible that, as assessments focus more on concepts and their applications and less on facts, students will "get the message" and better orient their studying time. Researchers are currently exploring both topics, including the use of this information to help plan for peer tutoring sessions.

Implications for Practice

Research, however scanty, does suggest guidelines for how to provide academic feedback to special education students and other students deemed at risk for academic failure. It also has helped pinpoint common errors and traps into which teachers unwittingly fall.

Grading is likely to remain a complex and perplexing issue. Teachers must take into account perceptions by many students that adaptations are permissible in almost any area of instruction, but that modifying standards for grades is unfair. Thus grades based on effort or solely on behaviors related to learning (such as percent of assignments handed in) is problematic. Additionally, in contrast to measures of academic progress, effort is extremely difficult to assess. Finally, while behavioral goals are an important part of the assessment picture for many special education students, there should always be an academic or learning assessment component. The teacher interviews we conducted this past year reinforced this notion. Figure 5.2 lists some of the key principles of successful grading practices identified in the literature.

The research of Page (1958), and more recently Serna, Schumaker, and Sheldon (1992), has shown that grading is only a small part of the picture. The crucial piece of ongoing assessment is not *the grade*, whether it is normative or compared to some absolute standard, but rather *the utility of the information conveyed when assessing performance.* For example, the study by Serna et al. indicates that more specific and descriptive feedback, as opposed to general number of points earned, led to improved student performance on writing assignments. Although the research subjects were college students, it is reasonable to extrapolate that specific, descriptive feedback would be equally important for special education students.

We believe ongoing feedback is particularly meaningful if it includes achievable areas where the student needs to direct effort. Further, teachers need to share such information with parents so that they understand not only what students' grades are based on, but also how to encourage and assist their children at home. As Wiggins (1994) noted, "The key to report card change is to make sure that grades, scores, or any other system can be effectively translated by parents" (p. 30).

The work of Goldenberg and Gallimore (1991) in the elementary grades offers some guidelines for establishing communication links with

FIGURE 5.2

PRINCIPLES OF SUCCESSFUL GRADING PRACTICES FOR SPECIAL EDUCATION STUDENTS

Learning-Related Behavior

This often can be part of grades, but grades should never be based solely on appropriate school behaviors. They should always include an academic/cognitive component.

Effort

Grading on effort sounds appealing, but can be fraught with peril. Better to assess student progress.

Graphing

In order to show progress, always graph rather than average scores.

Specificity

Include information on specific areas of strength and relative weaknesses, specific suggestions for what to study, and areas for a peer tutor or instructional assistant to focus sessions on.

Feedback

Remember that students will not necessarily be able to make sense of the graphs unless a teacher helps interpret them.

Communication with Parents

Try to include this type of information in reports to parents as well.

parents that can enhance student learning. In their study, they provided concrete information on what teachers expected of each child in class and identified an array of specific learning activities (involving repeated readings and vocabulary practice) that parents could do with their children.

Secondary special education students and their parents need analogous activities. For example, teachers could outline for parents those key concepts (e.g., in history or science) that students must master to earn a good grade and could offer suggestions on how to review these concepts at home with their children. Teachers could adapt many of the procedures employed in classwide peer tutoring for use by parents and siblings. Giving interested parents specific tools for helping their children learn and succeed, as well as assistance in providing the additional home practice so many students with learning disabilities need, appears to be a potentially powerful direction.

Generally, the best feedback system is an ipsative one, comparing each student's current level of academic performance to past performance. Teacher interviews consistently reveal that graphs documenting progress are far more comprehensible to students than are numerical averages of scores over an entire semester.

Systems such as curriculum-based measurement and other criterion-based assessments seem to provide the most promise. They allow both teacher and student to track the student's progress over time using agreed-on benchmarks. A growing number of curriculum-based measures surpass the earlier "basic skills" emphasis. Educators are developing systems to assess the quality of written products on technical/expository material (Isaacson 1995, Davenroy and Hiebert 1993) and will increasingly broach areas of comprehension, mathematical concepts, and historical concepts (Carnine et al. in press). Because these measures actively orient students toward what they must actually do to succeed, as opposed to simply measuring students' factual knowledge, they will likely increase the quality of student learning.

The work of Fuchs et al. (1994), though troubling, does provide some possible solutions. These researchers found that merely providing students with ipsative information on their progress, without ideas on where to focus their learning efforts, resulted in some minor changes but did not enhance achievement. The research explores current work where teachers take a more active role in helping students use ipsative information for the focus of peer tutoring sessions. Our belief, reinforced by our interviews, is that for many of these students, adults or capable peers will need to spend time in a mediating role. They can "walk the student through" the graphed data and can jointly plan how to interpret the data, pointing out topics that need review or aspects of writing that need work. Together they can develop a plan of action.

Assessing students' individual progress relative to their personal goals rather than to some abstract, possibly unreachable standards, holds great promise. Development of valid measures to do so is still in its infancy. We believe that by using these key principles, educators can achieve sensible assessments that also truly enhance student learning.[1]

References and Resources

Calhoun, M.L., and J. Beattie. (1984). "Assigning Grades in the High School Mainstream: Perceptions of Teachers and Students." *Diagnostique* 9: 218–225.

Carnine, D., D. Crawford, M. Harniss, K. Hollenbeck, and S. Miller. (in press). "Effective Strategies for Teaching Social Studies." In *Strategies for Teaching*

[1] We thank Lynn Fuchs for her assistance in sharing ongoing research findings with us, and Dorothy Dilliplane, Anne Peterson, and Joseph Dimino for their interview material. We also thank Matt Cranor and Carol Munch for their editorial and organizational assistance in putting together this manuscript. This research was supported in part by Grant #H023C20111 from the Division of Innovation and Development, Office of Special Education Programs, U.S. Department of Education.

Students with Diverse Learning Needs, edited by E. Kaméenui and D. Carnine. Columbus, Ohio: Charles E. Merrill.

Carpenter, D. (1985). "Grading Handicapped Pupils: Review and Position Statement." *Remedial and Special Education* 6, 4: 54–59.

Davenroy, K.H., and E.H. Hiebert. (1993). "An Examination of Teachers' Thinking About Assessment of Expository Text." In *Multidimensional Aspects of Literacy Research, Theory, and Practice: Forty-Third Yearbook, National Reading Conference*. Chicago: National Reading Conference.

Donohoe, K., and N. Zigmond. (1990). "Academic Grades of Ninth-Grade Urban Learning-Disabled Students and Low-Achieving Peers. *Exceptionality* 1, 1: 17–27.

Fuchs, L.S., and S.L. Deno. (1991). "Paradigmatic Distinctions Between Instructionally Relevant Measurement Models." *Exceptional Children* 57, 6: 488–500.

Fuchs, L.S., and S.L. Deno. (1994). "Must Instructionally Useful Performance Assessment Be Based in the Curriculum?" *Exceptional Children* 61, 1: 15–24.

Fuchs, L.S., D. Fuchs, and C.L. Hamlett. (1994). "Strengthening the Connection Between Assessment and Instructional Planning with Expert Systems." *Exceptional Children* 61, 2: 138–146.

Gersten, R., D. Dilliplane, J. Dimino, and A. Peterson. (1995). "Interviews with Practicing Special Educators on Issues in Grading." Unpublished manuscript. Eugene Research Institute, Eugene, Ore.

Goldenberg, C., and R. Gallimore. (1991). "Local Knowledge, Research Knowledge, and Educational Change: A Case Study of Early Spanish Reading Improvement." *Educational Researcher* 20, 8: 2–14.

Guskey, T.R. (1984). "The Influence of Change in Instructional Effectiveness Upon the Affective Characteristics of Teachers." *American Educational Research Journal* 21, 2: 245–259.

Guskey, T.R. (1994). "Making the Grade: What Benefits Students." *Educational Leadership* 52, 2: 14–20.

Gustafson, C. (1994). "A Lesson from Stacey." *Educational Leadership* 52, 2: 22–23.

Isaacson, S. (February 1995). *A Comparison of Alternative Procedures for Evaluating Written Expression*. Paper presented at the annual meeting of the Pacific Coast Research Conference, Laguna Beach, Calif.

McPartland, J. (August 1992). *A Conceptual Framework on Learning Environments and Student Motivation for Language Minority and Other Underserved Populations*. Paper presented at the Third National Research Symposium on Limited English Proficient Students, sponsored by the Office of Bilingual Education and Minority Language Affairs, Arlington, Va.

Michael, R.J., and J.A. Trippi. (1987). "Educators' Views of Procedures for Grading Mainstreamed Handicapped Children." *Education* 107, 3: 276–278.

Nolet, V., and G. Tindal. (1994). "Instruction and Learning in Middle School Science Classes: Implications for Students with Disabilities." *Journal of Special Education* 28, 2: 166–187.

Page, E.B. (1958). "Teacher Comments and Student Performance: A Seventy-Four Classroom Experiment in School Motivation." *Journal of Educational Psychology* 49: 173–181.

Pollard, R., J. Rojewski, and C. Pollard. (1993). "An Examination of Problems Associated with Grading Students with Special Needs." *Journal of Instructional Psychology* 20, 2: 154–161.

Putnam, M.L. (1992). "The Testing Practices of Mainstream Secondary Classroom Teachers." *Remedial and Special Education* 13, 5: 11–21.

Rojewski, J.W., R.R. Pollard, and G.D. Meers. (1990). "Grading Mainstreamed Special Needs Students: Determining Practices and Attitudes of Secondary Vocational Educators Using a Qualitative Approach." *Remedial and Special Education* 12, 1: 7–28.

Rojewski, J.W., R.R. Pollard, and G.D. Meers. (1992). "Grading Secondary Vocational Education Students with Disabilities: A National Perspective." *Exceptional Children* 59, 1: 68–76.

Schumm, J.S., and S. Vaughn. (1994). "Students' Thinking About Teachers' Practices." In *Advances in Learning and Behavioral Disabilities*, edited by T.E.

Scruggs and M.A. Mastropieri. Greenwich, Conn.: JAI Press.

Schumm, J.S., S. Vaughn, and L. Saumell. (1994). "Assisting Students with Difficult Textbooks: Teacher Perceptions and Practices." *Reading Research and Instruction* 43: 39–56.

Serna, L.A., J.B. Schumaker, and J.B. Sheldon. (1992). "A Comparison of the Effects of Feedback Procedures on College Student Performance on Written Essay Papers." *Behavior Modification* 16, 1: 64–81.

Tindal, G., and J. Hasbrouck. (1991). "Analyzing Student Writing to Develop Instructional Strategies." *Learning Disabilities Research and Practice* 6, 4: 237–245.

Vaughn, S., and J.S. Schumm. (in press). "Classroom Ecologies: Classroom Interactions and Implications for Inclusion of Students with Learning Disabilities." In *Research on Classroom Ecologies: Implications for Inclusion of Children with Learning Disabilities*, edited by D.S. Speece and B.K. Keogh. Hillsdale, N.J.: Erlbaum.

Vaughn, S., J.S. Schumm, J. Klingner, and L. Saumell. (1995). "Students' Views of Instructional Practices: Implications for Inclusion." *Learning Disability Quarterly* 18, 3: 236–248.

Vaughn, S., J.S. Schumm, F.J. Niarhos, and T. Daugherty. (1993). "What Do Students Think When Teachers Make Adaptations?" *Teaching and Teacher Education* 9: 107–118.

Vaughn, S., J.S. Schumm, F.J. Niarhos, and J. Gordon. (1993). "Students' Perceptions of Two Hypothetical Teachers' Instructional Adaptations for Low Achievers." *Elementary School Journal* 94: 87–102.

Wiggins, G. (1994). "Toward Better Report Cards." *Educational Leadership* 52, 2: 28–37.

Zigmond, N., and H. Thornton. (1985). "Follow-Up of Postsecondary Age LD Graduates and Dropouts." *Learning Disabilities Research* 1: 50–55.

6

Beyond the A: Communicating the Learning Progress of Gifted Students

Kathy Bearden Peckron

How do we adequately and appropriately communicate the learning progress of gifted students when, in many instances, they will go beyond whatever standards we establish? In addressing this challenge, school districts need to analyze their curriculum, assessment procedures, and methods for reporting learning progress to determine if their current practices are meeting the needs of the gifted learners and the expectations of the students' parents.

Critical to understanding the challenge of reporting gifted students' learning progress is the knowledge that standardized test results are not very helpful. Most gifted students experience a "ceiling effect" on standardized achievement tests; that is, their scores cluster at the top of the distribution of test-takers both before and after an educational treatment. As a result, little is known about the effects of the curriculum or the quality of instruction offered to gifted students (Van Tassel-Baska 1992).

Similarly, a grade of *A* may tell gifted students and their parents very little about new knowledge gained. Many gifted students master the learning objectives for a particular grade level one to three years prior to entering that grade. Hence, the *A* may reflect past achievement more than current learning progress.

Virtually no research exists on the issue of adequately and appropriately communicating the learning progress of gifted students. Nevertheless, our experience at the Center for Creative Learning indicates that school districts attempting to meet the challenge of reporting gifted students' learning progress are more likely to be successful if they consider the following guidelines:

I am grateful to the Rockwood School District in Ellisville, Missouri, for providing forms used in this chapter.

1. District administrators should base grading policies on the belief that all learners have the right to an appropriate education, one that recognizes individual differences and unique learning needs. A major step toward illustrating such a belief is a district's strong commitment to, and support of, a formal, multifaceted gifted education program. This means a district must consider implementing K–12 acceleration policies, differentiated assessments, and procedures for giving students credit for prior learning.

2. Administrators should develop comprehensive curriculum documents that allow for and encourage student learning beyond established grade level standards. Such curriculum documents should include activities at the highest levels of the Taxonomy of Educational Objectives (Bloom et al. 1956), as well as a detailed description of creative and critical thinking skills.

3. A monitoring system that tracks and documents students' mastery of objectives and concepts must be in place. This system should allow students who demonstrate mastery of grade-level materials to proceed to materials that go beyond that level. Such materials may extend students' learning by providing opportunities for topics they can explore in greater depth, or they may accelerate students' learning progress. Integral to the monitoring system is the development of appropriate assessments for the objectives and concepts. Staff can computerize or manage the monitoring system via a paper filing system.

4. Working collaboratively, teachers and administrators must develop a multifaceted staff development program that meets the needs of both groups for additional training on alternative forms of assessment (Stiggins 1994), curriculum compacting (Reis and Renzulli 1992), and procedures for recording student learning beyond the standards established for a particular grade level. Staff development should also include information on how best to communicate the learning progress of gifted students to their parents.

5. Teachers need to use multiple assessment measures to illustrate the learning progress of gifted students. Portfolios and other learning products offer an excellent means of documenting learning progress. In addition, teachers must develop point systems, rubrics, and holistic evaluation methods that allow gifted students to go beyond the established standards for that grade. Gifted students may even become engaged in the creation of the scoring rubrics used to evaluate their own work. In fact, it is important that teachers, students, and parents reach agreement among themselves regarding the scoring criteria and how students will meet those criteria (Winnebrenner 1992). Figure 6.1 provides a sample evaluation rubric; Figure 6.2 gives two examples of teachers' written comments based on the rubric.

6. District administrators must clearly establish the relationship between alternative assessment methods and the district's formal reporting system. Several states currently mandate the use of the individualized educational program (IEP) for gifted students. The IEP is a management tool that documents the curricular needs of the student, justifies placement in special programming based on those needs, and ensures special services appropriate to the student's unique learning characteristics. Many IEPs also specify alternative procedures for documenting learning progress (Dettmer 1994). Adminstrators must clarify the linkages between these alternative procedures and the district's formal reporting system, to facilitate effective communication with parents.

7. Policies must support the collaborative efforts of the regular classroom teacher and the teacher of the gifted at all levels. One of the best ways for a school district to provide a better and more accurate picture to parents of their child's learning progress is to allow time prior to parent-teacher conferences for the regular classroom teacher and the teacher of the gifted to collaboratively plan the conference. During this time the teachers can discuss the particular strengths of the

FIGURE 6.1

AN EVALUATION RUBRIC FOR A 5TH GRADE CLASS CONTAINING LEARNING OBJECTIVES THAT RANGE FROM THE 5TH TO 12TH GRADE LEVELS

The Center for Creative Learning
Student Evaluation Form

Dennis L. Peterson. Ph.D.
Superintendent of Schools

Kathy Peckron
Coordinator of Gifted Education

What Every Earthling Should Know About Space
Semester 1, 1994–1995
Grade 5
Mrs. Pam Nazzoli

Technology Used: Linkway, Microsoft Works, Digitizer, CD Rom, SIRS, MAS, Prodigy, Destination: Mars, Planetscapes Laser Disc, The Planets Laser Disc, Space Shuttle Laser Disc, The Living Textbook Laser Discs

Evaluation Rubric

Objective 1: Gathers, records, organizes, and interprets data, and explains the implications of interpretations.

3 Transfers learned concepts to multiple subject areas; assesses and critiques other issues using science ideas.
2 Demonstrates understanding of basic concepts; incorporates concepts into other experiments and products.
1 Exhibits little understanding of science concepts, unable to see relationship of concepts to other learnings.

Objective 2: Uses mathematical skills and applies quantitative reasoning.

3 Chooses appropriate formulas to calculate correct solutions; provides thorough explanation for solution.
2 Calculates correct solutions; applies mathematical formulas to science concepts.
1 Unable to calculate correct solutions; omits significant parts of problem solving process.

Objective 3: Follows research steps to create an informative product.

3 Follows research steps; scrutinizes appropriate data, makes evaluative decisions throughout the process to create a quality product.
2 Follows most research steps; incorporates learned concepts.
1 Research steps are omitted or incomplete; few or no learned concepts are incorporated.

FIGURE 6.1 (*continued*)

Objective 4: Incorporates technology into a multimedia research product and/or scientific investigation.

3 Selects, integrates, and appraises appropriate technology tools needed to create an effective, multimedia presentation.

2 Uses most technology tools independently and with mastery; product reflects learning.

1 Unable to utilize most technology tools independently; lacks experience with most tools.

Objective 5: Employs effective communication skills to convey ideas and information.

3 Demonstrates all effective skills plus incorporates imagery, descriptive language, and humor; utilizes a creative format.

2 Is knowledgeable of topic; demonstrates effective skills such as eye contact, variance in voice rate and inflection, facial expressions, voice volume, clear enunciation.

1 Is not knowledgeable of topic; does not utilize skills effectively; lacks experience with communication skills.

Objective 6: Develops and completes a simulated space product, invention, or experiment.

3 Displays extra effort and commitment toward project; exhibits originality, creativity, and high-level thinking to produce a quality project.

2 Chooses a project, plans steps needed, organizes materials, and completes an effective project which incorporates learned concepts.

1 Omits appropriate steps to complete project; fails to complete project.

student, concepts or skills that the student has already mastered, and areas that need additional attention. Conferences that involve teachers, parents, and sometimes the student as well, can be especially useful.

8. Teachers should develop alternative communication strategies and use them when appropriate. Two alternative strategies for reporting student learning beyond established grade level standards are *independent study agreements* and *learning contracts*. Typically, the teacher and student collaboratively establish study agreements and learning contracts. Also involving parents allows them to be aware of the guidelines for the development of the project and the deadlines for completion. Occasional progress reports might indicate students' work or study habits and comment on the effort needed to complete the project on time. School staff should include copies and photographs of completed projects and learning contracts in the student's permanent school record and in other reporting procedures.

Mentors or specialists from the school district may also be involved in supporting the students' contract work. In this case, they too should give written and verbal feedback to the parents and students regarding the work completed and its relation to grade level standards.

Portfolios offer yet another way to document and communicate learning progress of gifted students. Portfolios typically include examples of the student's best effort as well as work in progress. As such, they can highlight students' critical and creative thinking in real-world tasks and situations (Treffinger and Cross 1995). Examples of portfolio contents include:

- Products or work samples, both completed and in progress;

FIGURE 6.2

EXAMPLES OF TEACHERS' WRITTEN COMMENTS ON AN EVALUATION FORM DESCRIBING STUDENTS' FINAL PROJECTS, WORK, AND STUDY HABITS

Name: JENNIFER
ID Number:
Center Day:
Home School:
Grade: 05

Objective 1:
3 Gathers, records, organizes, and interprets data and explains the implications of interpretations.

Objective 2:
2 Uses mathematical skills and applies quantitative reasoning.

Objective 3:
3 Follows research steps to create an informative product.

Objective 4:
3 Incorporates technology into a multimedia research product and/or scientific investigation.

Objective 5:
3 Employs effective communication skills to convey ideas and information.

Objective 6:
3 Develops and completes a simulated space product, invention, or experiment.

Teacher Comments: Jennifer is an elaborative thinker who eagerly accepts cognitively challenging activities. She thinks in novel ways and approaches problems with clever, unusual solutions. She has the ability to embellish and expand ordinary ideas into unique ones. Her scientific investigation about bone calcification was just one example of her ability to follow proper testing procedures, collect and record data, analyze information, and most of all, draw logical conclusions. Her identification and assessment of variables which may have affected her experiment's results required high-level thinking skills. What a quality project! Jennifer is a positive, effective leader among her peers. She is a goal-setter who determines priorities and meets deadlines. She demonstrated good time management and organizational skills. Jennifer has the courage to take risks, defend her opinions, and dream....

FIGURE 6.2 (*continued*)

Name: JESSICA
ID Number:
Center Day:
Home School:
Grade: 05

Objective 1:
2 Gathers, records, organizes, and interprets data and explains the implications of interpretations.

Objective 2:
2 Uses mathematical skills and applies quantitative reasoning.

Objective 3:
3 Follows research steps to create an informative product.

Objective 4:
2 Incorporates technology into a multimedia research product and/or scientific investigation.

Objective 5:
2 Employs effective communication skills to convey ideas and information.

Objective 6:
3 Develops and completes a simulated space product, invention, or experiment.

Teacher Comments: Jessica has exhibited a great deal of growth since the beginning of this unit. Academically she has become more focused, has developed an understanding of the scientific inquiry method, and has learned to delve into intricate problems or ideas. Her improved work habits have allowed her to be more on-task, productive, and committed. The model and drawings of her innovative space station are just some examples of her efforts. Jessica put a lot of hard work into research and development of this project. She is proficient at written communication. Her Linkway folder indicated true understanding of concepts. I'm very pleased with her progress and hope she will continue to be self-directed and challenged.

- Evaluations of students' work by themselves and others;
- Documentation of participation in activities or specific events;
- Honors, prizes, or awards (e.g., an award won in an "Odyssey of the Mind" competition or a creative thinking skills competition);
- External reviews or evaluations of the works or accomplishments;
- Visual documentation of work completed or in progress (e.g., models, prototypes, videotapes, or photographs); and
- Other items selected by the student for a specific purpose or need.

Teachers can use portfolios to illustrate to parents those areas of student growth or progress typically not shown on the traditional grade card. As students move to more advanced grades, the portfolio can follow, with each successive teacher adding new items and deleting older ones as students and teachers see fit.

9. Teachers should regularly invite parent involvement and feedback on reporting methods for gifted students. The parents of most gifted children are personally involved in their children's education and are more likely to perceive districts that actively seek and implement parents' ideas as meeting their expectations.

In a survey of parents of gifted students, where we asked them to describe the ideal reporting system for sharing information about their child's learning progress, we found that parents

- Want to have more input in the process of reporting student learning;
- Believe that traditional grades do not provide an accurate description of what their child can do;
- Support the use of portfolios and clearly articulated scoring rubrics;
- Value the teachers' written comments about the students' efforts as much as the grades given.
- Want teachers to be able to recognize the special talents and abilities of students even when they do not note them on traditional report cards; and
- Value teachers who allow children to have input in evaluations of their work or products (Peckron, in press).

Many stakeholders are involved in reporting the learning progress of gifted students, including district personnel, teachers, parents, and the students themselves. Flexibility, creativity, collaboration, and constant communication among all these stakeholders are critical if we are to succeed in developing a fair, accurate, and meaningful reporting system for gifted students whose learning is typically far beyond the *A*.

References and Resources

Bloom, B.S., M.D. Engelhard, E.J. Furst, W.H. Hill, and D.R. Krathwohl. (1956). *Taxonomy of Educational Objectives: The Cognitive Domain*. New York: McKay.

Dettmer, P. (1994). "IEPs for Gifted Secondary Students." *Journal of Secondary Gifted Education* 5, 1: 52-59.

Peckron, K. (in press). *Portfolios, Profiles, and Individual Planning for the Gifted*. Minneapolis, Minn: Free Spirit.

Reis, S., and J. Renzulli. (1992). "Using Curriculum Compacting to Challenge the Above Average." *Education Leadership* 51, 2: 51-57.

Stiggins, R.J. (1994). *Student-Centered Classroom Assessment*. New York: Merrill.

Treffinger, D. (1994). "Productive Thinking: Toward Authentic Instruction and Assessment." *Journal of Secondary Gifted Education* 6, 1: 30-37.

Treffinger, D.J., and J.A. Cross. (1995). *Professional Development Module: Authentic Assessment of Productive Thinking*. Sarasota, Fla.: Center for Creative Learning.

Van Tassel-Baska, J. (1992). *Planning Effective Curriculum for Gifted Learners*. Denver, Colo.: Love.

Winnebrenner, S. (1992). *Teaching Gifted Kids in the Regular Classroom*. Minneapolis, Minn.: Free Spirit.

7

Reporting Student Progress: One District's Attempt with Student Literacy

KENNETH W. EASTWOOD

U.S. Secretary of Education Richard W. Riley (1993) has noted that the most important testing for students measures their improvement and compares where students are today with where they were last year and the year before. In the Oswego City School District, teachers and parents share a similar belief about reporting on student performance. Both want a clear picture of what is most important: How much did this child grow academically in the last year?

Four years ago, our teachers and parents expressed concerns about our district's testing policies and practices and how we communicate student performance in reading and literacy development. Teachers were concerned that the results of the standardized tests that were administered did not provide useful information for instruction or remediation. Parents had similar concerns. The information they received told them how their child was doing in relation to other students in the nation, but what did that really mean? Did the child grow during the school year, and was he or she becoming an increasingly literate student?

In essence, parents were looking for a *value-added* accountability system. They wanted information that documented the progress their children were making in school and reports that would help them understand and help their children. Parents were telling us, "If you make the information clear and relevant, we will feel less intimidated and more comfortable in participating in our child's education." Such comments led us to interview teachers, administrators, and parents regarding the standardized tests that were administered and the information provided by the district on student performance.

After carefully considering the feedback provided from these interviews, the Oswego City schools made significant changes in the way student performance in reading and early literacy are assessed and reported. We developed a program that has two main features: (1) It is built around a value-added accountability model, and (2) It informs staff and parents on student growth or progress toward standards of excellence. In addition, we designed a system of reporting that has increased parent involvement in the education of their children.

The program developed by our district has three essential components.

1. We eliminated standardized testing for reading in kindergarten and 1st grade and replaced it with an individual student literacy assessment. We developed this assessment, the Oswego Primary Assessment in Literacy (OPAL), jointly with the Griffin Center for Human Development; and we designed the program to blend with current ongoing instructional practices in our classrooms.

2. We replaced the Stanford Achievement Test in Reading with the Degrees of Reading Power Test for grades 2 through 8. We made this change to obtain a holistic measure of reading comprehension consistent with the International Reading Association (IRA) guidelines. These guidelines call for measures that engage and assess the cognitive processes of reading rather than those that conceptualize reading as being made up of discrete skills (IRA 1989).

3. We developed standards of excellence in reading for each grade. This was done to comply with parent requests as well as calls for change coming from national and state reports.

The next section describes each of these components in greater detail and reviews the documents we use to communicate student performance in reading and early literacy. Embedded in these descriptions are anecdotal comments from staff, parents, and students.

Assessing and Reporting Early Literacy Development: Oswego Primary Assessment in Literacy

OPAL[1, 2] is an instrument for assessing the reading and writing development of children in kindergarten and 1st grade. OPAL asks the teacher to observe, record, and interpret children's behaviors. This procedure stands in marked contrast to the standardized testing setting in which students are asked to respond to and make sense of isolated tasks. Most past assessment tools focused on looking for answers to predetermined questions in a standardized testing setting. OPAL gathers the child's information and understanding in a manner as comfortable and natural for the child as is possible.

OPAL uses several assessment strategies to gather this information. These strategies include observation (kidwatching), book knowledge discussions, read alongs, sound/symbol association checklists, running records, retellings, and writing samples.

Stages of reading and writing development are central to OPAL. These stages include early connections, pre-emergent, emergent, developing, independent, and skilled reader/writer. Teachers using OPAL gather information from all of OPAL's

[1] For further information regarding OPAL, contact the Griffin Center for Human Development, 15 South Fair St., Guilford, CT 06437, phone (203) 453-8563; or Kenneth W. Eastwood, Oswego City School District, Oswego, NY 13126, phone (315) 341-5838.

[2] Much of the anecdotal information in the OPAL section was provided by Terri Cullen-Stacey and Kathleen Bishop-Sharkey, who teach 1st grade in Oswego.

tasks and then study the information to look for clusters of behaviors that describe a particular stage of reading and writing development.

OPAL presents a way to organize the information teachers collect and a way to consider this information in decision making. Specifically, teachers using OPAL gain a thorough understanding of each child's current level of development and are able to use this information to plan appropriate classroom experiences.

In addition, OPAL offers a practical, theoretically sound format by which the results can be presented to parents, other teachers, and administrators. The basic interpretation strategy is to compare the literacy behaviors demonstrated by the child to behaviors consistent with a particular stage of literacy development. This comparison is best made by the child's teacher, who knows the child's literacy progress intimately through daily contact. Thus, OPAL purposefully places the classroom teacher in the position of expert.

OPAL has four specific purposes:

- To define the stage of literacy development in children, using age-appropriate, authentic literacy tasks.
- To aid the teacher in evaluating, modifying, and prescribing appropriate literacy teaching strategies.
- To identify both qualitatively and quantitatively those children who may need increased experiences and more intensive help.
- To provide a portfolio-type document from which to describe a child's literacy development and progress to other teachers, to parents, or to administrators.

The OPAL Literacy Development Profile is a portfolio that represents a child's literacy development over the kindergarten and 1st grade years. The OPAL profile covers nine important literacy areas, reflecting the idea that Wiggins emphasizes in Chapter 11, that "reading" is not one unitary performance but actually many varied performances. These areas include:

- Language Development
- Letter Recognition
- Word Awareness
- Orientation to Print
- Reading Strategies
- Understanding Stories
- Writing Development
- Spelling Development
- Personal Connections with Literacy

This profile also gives clear evidence of literacy development over time, thus aiding teachers in planning appropriate instruction and in determining a child's possible need for extra attention. Figure 7.1 shows the titles and instructions for some of the recording sheets in the OPAL package.

As part of the profile, two pages are dedicated to developing an instructional focus based on the assessment data contained in the profile. These sheets are used to plan or describe effective teaching strategies designed to promote learning and growth. The richness of the information contained in the profiles (e.g., see Figures 7.2 and 7.3) have become invaluable to teachers and parents alike.

The introduction to OPAL was carried out in Oswego in concert with significant staff development. Teachers were brought into school for a three-day summer inservice program during late August. The first day was dedicated to reviewing the philosophy and research on good teaching practices and child and literacy development. During the second and third days, teachers learned about each of the OPAL components and practiced using them.

OPAL was administered twice during the school year, with a debriefing session held after each administration. The purpose of the debriefing

FIGURE 7.1

SAMPLE INSTRUCTIONS FOR OPAL RECORDING SHEETS

Part 1
Language Development

Directions: Using classroom observations and interactions, complete the language checklist. Check all behaviors that you feel the child exhibits. Use appropriate boxes below for additional comments, descriptions, and language samples when necessary.

Part 2
Letter Recognition

Directions: Place the OPAL letter chart (or one of your own) in front of the child. Tell the child to point to each letter and to tell you the name of each letter.

Part 4
Reading Development

Section 2: Reading Strategies
Directions: (1) Have the child read an appropriate book or reading passage to you. Tell the child that he or she will be telling you what the book is about when he or she is done. As the child reads the selection, record the child's words using a running record format (audiotapes may be used). . . .

sessions was to allow for dialogue between teachers on OPAL in general and, more specifically, on how they were able to manage time and use the information to assist instruction.

It is our belief that assessment and instruction go hand in hand. One should not be present without the other. If we do not plan our teaching strategies from the child's abilities, then the child cannot make the greatest possible gains in our classrooms. OPAL provides powerful information and data for parent-teacher conferences.

Two additional sheets were developed at the request of our teachers. First, the Individual Student Profile provides a two-year progress chart for each student and enables teachers and parents to view progress through a single document. As Guskey emphasizes in Chapter 3, this picture of growth over time is an extremely crucial element of assessment. Specific problem areas can then be dealt with more comprehensively through a review of specific components of OPAL. When time is of the essence, for example, in a parent-teacher conference, this is a beneficial and efficient way of explaining a student's literacy development. The second sheet requested and found to be beneficial was the Class Profile, which provides an overview of the entire class. For each student, this profile shows levels of proficiency (i.e., Early Connect, Pre-emergent, Emergent, etc.) for each area (Letter Recognition, Word Awareness, Orientation to Print, etc.), displayed on a grid.

The recording and reporting of emerging literacy through OPAL is proving beneficial for teachers, parents, and students. Teachers talk about how the process helped them become more student-centered and better able to understand each child.

One teacher even remarked, "For the first time, I feel that I am not teaching to the center of the class."

Another said, "OPAL helps me internalize the principles of emergent literacy to the point where I can provide more holistic types of teaching, both on a class and an individual basis."

And another stated: "I am amazed at how much I have learned about my kids."

When students and teachers reflect together on the information collected, evaluation becomes more than just a verification of work done; it becomes an ongoing opportunity for inquiry and enhanced understanding (Lowe and Bintz 1993). When parents are actively engaged in the process as well, it can be even more effective. Teachers changed the way they conducted parent-teacher

FIGURE 7.2

"BOOK KNOWLEDGE" ASSESSMENT SHEET

Part 2
Reading Development

11-16-93 Lindsay

Section 1: Book Knowledge

MATERIALS: A trade book which is unfamiliar to the child. windows, seats wheels, doors, roof, convertible

DIRECTIONS: Say, "Let's pretend I don't know anything about cars. Tell me everything a car has." If no response, say, "A car has wheels, and tires, and doors, etc." Show the child a book and say, "Now let's pretend I don't know anything about books. Tell me everything a book has." Give the book to the child and record responses. IF A CHILD DOES NOT RESPOND, you may use a direct question to elicit a response. Say "What is this part called, etc." If a child still does not respond, you may say, "Show me the front, back, title, etc."

RECORDING: Record child's responses under "Kind Watching" Observations below

- ✓ to represent concepts demonstrated.
- Q✓ to represent concept demonstrated after direct question.
- Q– to represent concept not demonstrated after direct question.
- S✓ to represent concept demonstrated when asked, "show me the…".
- S– to represent concept not demonstrated when asked, "show me the…".

Concepts	Demonstrates?	"Kid Watching" Observations
front and back	✓ sm	"back"
title	sm	went to back of book
author	sm	" " inside of front cover
illustrator	sm	back cover
words/letters	✓	"reading Ⓟ stuff in it"– not sure of the meaning of word
pictures	✓	"balloons in it."
page numbers	sm	a little uncertain about where the page #'s are.
title page	sm	title page (showed the front cover)
punctuation	✓sm	P. mark - question mark on pg. 23
chapters	sm	not sure - pointed to quotation marks
purpose		I.D.K - Ⓟ - because they have + writing in them
story elements		
other		

INSTRUCTIONAL FOCUS:	INSTRUCTIONAL FOCUS:	INSTRUCTIONAL FOCUS:
Lindsay needs further experience in knowledge of books. i.e. (title, title page, author illustrator, chapters, page number – what they mean + location		

FIGURE 7.3

"LETTER RECOGNITION" ASSESSMENT SHEET

upper case did not know U, R, P, N, K, I, G, F, E, D 11/92 10/7 2/94
lower case did not know t, r, q, p, k, j, h, g, f, e, d, b, a down to 7
—13 down to 10

Section 3: Letter Recognition

MATERIALS: Letter Awareness Chart.

DIRECTIONS: Say, "Point to each letter and tell me its name." If child has no response, say "Show me an a, etc."

RECORDING: Circle letters that are omitted, in her name

✓ above each correct response, if incorrect, place child's response above the letter.

S✓ above each correct showing of letter named by teacher when asked to "show me…"

S– above each letter not found when teacher asked, "show me…"

Z Y X W V U T S R Q P O N M L K J I H G F E D C B A

z y x w v u t s r q p o n m l k j i h g f e d c b a

later said that "i" in Lind?

Section 4: Sound/Symbol Association

MATERIALS: Letter Awareness Chart.

DIRECTIONS, TASK ONE: Point to the first picture and say, "This is a picture of a CAT. Cat begins with the letter c." Point to the next picture and say, "This is a picture of a STAR. Can you tell me what letter star begins with?" Accept the child's answer. If the child says no, ask the child to take a guess. Repeat these directions for the remaining pictures. Discontinue if the child fails or does not respond on four consecutive responses.

DIRECTIONS, TASK TWO: If the child is correct on 7 or more consecutive responses, ask the child to name the ending consonants. Use cat as your example. Discontinue if the child fails (or does not respond) on four consecutive items.

RECORDING: Write the child's response next to each picture below. Place a ✓ next to each correct response.

discontinued after 4 consecutive items

	Initial Letter	Final Letter		Initial Letter	Final Letter		Initial Letter	Final Letter
Star	s	h	Frog	knew f sound		Telephone	"phone" +	
Dog	d	b	Pear	peach p	p	Bird	b	
Moon	M moon for	w	Wagon	w sound w then w	?	Apple	c	
Light IDK	I got it ✓	m	House	s, hh – "Heather" then h		Cake	K	

DIRECTIONS, TASK THREE: Say, "What words rhyme with CAT…HOP…RED." If the child is successful, turn over the letter chart and print CAT, HOP, RED at the top of the paper. Say, "Can you write words that rhyme with these words? Show me."

RECORDING: Write the words the child says and writes below.

did not know what rhyming meant until gave example—

	Oral Responses:	Written Responses:
CAT	, rat, bat, sat, mat, nat	
HOP	, nop, sock, nack, sack	
RED	, NED, SED, MED, BED, DED,	

INSTRUCTIONAL FOCUS:	INSTRUCTIONAL FOCUS:	INSTRUCTIONAL FOCUS:
Lindsay had an idea of what rhyming was auditorially—but could not print rhyming words (word families-inst. focus)		

needs reinforcement of upper + lower case names – focus on ending sounds.

conferences to incorporate OPAL results as a focus of reporting students' progress in early literacy.

Teachers appreciate OPAL's comprehensiveness and like seeing examples of children's responses in each of the major areas of literacy development. Teachers were looking for an assessment that would provide genuine information for parents, showing them how well their child was progressing and what the child was capable of doing. In addition, they wanted information that would help them become better teachers. Through OPAL, one teacher remarked:

> I was able to watch, listen, and then understand how the kids were thinking a task or concept through; how they were understanding or not understanding. Previously, I was making assumptions about the kids—assumptions that OPAL helped me understand did not necessarily exist.

For example, one 1st grade teacher assumed that her students understood the concept of rhyming. When she administered the rhyming section of OPAL, some of the kids got creative, while many just didn't understand the concept. This knowledge led her to change her instruction to accommodate those students who needed some help.

Although it took teachers at least two administrations of OPAL to become comfortable and internalize its concepts and processes, once learned, OPAL has become an invaluable tool. One teacher stated:

> OPAL has been a stimulating challenge for me, as opposed to the former mandated obligation that I felt. As a teacher, I believe I have a better understanding of each child's literacy development. I will certainly find even more time to truly listen to and watch my kids.

OPAL has also had large benefits for our staff. Completing the OPAL records and analysis has pulled teachers out of isolation and into more collaborative relationships. This collaboration also helped them develop relationships with teachers from the special areas, especially with reading staff. "The information contained in OPAL is very rich and valuable for me," reported one teacher. "It saves me a considerable amount of time early in the school year from having to assess these same issues."

Second grade teachers, too, have found the OPAL information to be valuable and informative. One teacher wondered "why we didn't provide it long ago. It has helped to better articulate literacy and its associated curriculum across the grades."

Teachers who share OPAL with parents report similarly positive comments. One parent noted:

> For the first time, I came to a parent-teacher conference and understood what they [teachers] were talking about regarding my child. They showed me examples of my child's work and related it to the evaluation comments. I left the conference knowing more about my child and what I could do to help. Seeing OPAL over the year also helped me feel comfortable that my daughter was making progress at school. I could see it.

Another parent talked about how OPAL helped get rid of the educational mumbo-jumbo, laying out the information "in language we could understand. Seeing your child's work alongside the teacher's comments helps make sense of what they are saying. It was nice seeing what your child can do rather than being told only what they are weak in or cannot do."

Parents and teachers alike appreciate the Student Profile Sheet on the back of the OPAL booklet. This sheet provides a two-year synopsis of the child's literacy development. Parents have noted that "you get a complete view of your child in one look," and "it helps in a quick way to see growth and know that the year has been beneficial." Thus,

OPAL has been responsive to our parents' concerns regarding a value-added approach to education.

Students, too, find OPAL to be a positive experience. One child stated:

> I liked working alone with just you and no other kids. It made me feel special. I liked reading for you [the teacher] and talking just me and you. When will we do this again?

Another said, "Now you know how much I'm learning and what you still have to teach me in first grade." And finally, one child said:

> I think we did this so you could see what good readers and writers we all are. Are you going to tell the principal about us?

Teachers use the results from OPAL in explaining to individual children specifics about their growth and strengths.

Responses to OPAL have not all been positive, though. The underlying philosophy and constructs of OPAL were difficult for some teachers to grasp. It took time and considerable inservice work for teachers to relearn, or learn for the first time, the OPAL practices and assessment strategies which require teachers to observe, record, and make sense of children's behaviors, instead of asking children to respond to and make sense of isolated tasks.

The more teachers used kidwatching strategies and then analyzed data, the more they understood. In addition, administering the instrument (taking at least 25 to 35 minutes per student, twice a year) and recording student behaviors only provide the information. The analysis and interpretation of the information requires considerable time. This need for added time has presented frustrating yet rewarding challenges. While the teachers were kidwatching, a variety of programs was used to keep the remaining students on task. Some teachers teamed with reading or other special area teachers during the time that OPAL was being administered. Other buildings reassigned their teacher aides during that period, and some used student teachers to continue instruction during this period.

This point is clear in our district: Truly authentic and developmentally appropriate assessment and reporting to parents, teachers, resource personnel, and administrators takes time and commitment. We took great care to develop an assessment instrument that is theoretically and developmentally sound. We also took steps to provide inservice training and to interact with staff to ensure a high level of interrater reliability.[3] Even given this level of support, the issue of time remained the most difficult hurdle. However, we will continue to develop new ways to implement OPAL and use its results because we have found that the information obtained is too valuable to be without.

Reporting Reading Progress in Grades 2–8

Since continuous growth in reading is important for success in life, measuring a child's growth in reading is part of our district's assessment program. We use a holistic measure of reading called the *Degrees of Reading Power* (DRP 1988) Test.[4] This test measures the process of comprehension rather than specific skills or strategies often associated

[3] Two professors (Pamela Michel and Sharon Kane) from the Curriculum and Instruction Department at the State University College of Oswego acted as neutral facilitators during the OPAL administrations. They visited the buildings and talked with and assisted staff members with OPAL's administration. This served a number of purposes, including the increase of interrater reliability, which is an important requirement of assessment in our district.

[4] For more information regarding the Degrees of Reading Power Test or the District Reading Reports, contact Stephen Ivens at Touchtone Applied Science Associates (TASA) Inc., P.O. Box 382, Brewster, NY 10509, phone (914) 277-4900, or the Oswego City School District, Oswego, NY 13126, phone (315) 341-5838. All TASA documents are used with permission.

with reading. The DRP is constructed so that the child's performance may be interpreted in terms of criterion-referenced as well as norm-referenced test scores. Furthermore, the DRP Test links the difficulty of textual materials to a measure of reading ability. This reporting of student performance on a text-difficulty scale has been recognized as one of the most important technological advances in assessment (Kibby 1981; Klare 1985; Koslin, Zenos, and Koslin 1987).

Although several different levels of comprehension may be reported through the DRP Test, the Oswego City Schools use and report on the Independent and Developing levels. The Independent Level DRP Score indicates the DRP unit rating that a student can read on his or her own; the Developing Level DRP score indicates the DRP unit rating that a student can read with appropriate assistance. Knowing what children can read on their own, as well as knowing what they can read with assistance, is valuable for teachers, as well as for parents who want to take a more active role in the education of their children.

Measuring student improvement and rewarding students or schools that make significant progress are easy concepts to support—at least in theory. In practice, however, the tendency is to focus attention only on end-of-year achievement. Reporting mean or median test scores, national percentiles, percent above the "norm," or some other cut-off score reinforces the common perception that the best students or schools are those with the highest test scores and the worst are those with the lowest. However, the students with the highest scores may have made the least progress; and, conversely, those with the lowest scores, the most. Our parents and teachers alike agreed that evidence of steady progress for all students, rather than simply high test scores, should be the hallmark of success and effectiveness.

Based on the recommendations of parents and teachers, we redesigned the components of the reports we send to parents at the end of the year informing them about their child's performance in reading. The first part of this report is a cover letter that includes a brief overview of the DRP test, what it measures, and how Oswego uses the information (Figure 7.4). This letter is followed by a "Current Performance Chart" (Figure 7.5), which provides an overview of the child's current and past performance in reading. Parents are informed of Oswego's standards of excellence in reading for each grade and are invited to compare their child's performance to those standards. They also are encouraged to call their child's teacher or administrator if they have questions or concerns.

Second, a "Parent Report" (Figure 7.6) designed by Touchstone Applied Science Associates (TASA) is included to provide parents with suggestions for helping with the reading development of their children. We do this in light of the overwhelming evidence that growth in reading is greatest for children who read the most, who are given time to discuss what they read, and who are provided meaningful opportunities to write about what they read. Designed to be responsive to the question, "What can we do to help?" TASA's Parent Reports are tailored to the current interests and reading performance of the child. They list a number of classic and popular titles that the child might read, and suggest activities for engaging the child in meaningful reading and writing activities.

Finally, we send a reading progress chart to parents. This chart displays current DRP test scores, along with those from previous years. The primary purpose of this chart is to help parents focus on student growth and progress toward standards of excellence, in addition to the end-of-year performance of their child. The multifaceted evaluation, as explained by Guskey in Chapter 3 and Wiggins in Chapter 11, is more honest, accurate, and fair than a single score representing only achievement, only in comparison to a normed population, or only individual student growth.

We have received many favorable comments from parents regarding each of the three compo-

FIGURE 7.4

LETTER TO PARENTS ABOUT DEGREES OF READING POWER TEST

CITY SCHOOL DISTRICT of OSWEGO
"Oswego's People Are The Difference"

120 EAST FIRST STREET • OSWEGO, NEW YORK 13126

Lee J. Cravotta
Superintendent of Schools

Kenneth W. Eastwood, Ed. D.
Director of Secondary Education and
Instructional/Administrative Technology
(315) 341-5838
FAX: (315) 341-5877

June, 1994

Dear Mr. and Mrs. Bear:

Each year we administer Degrees of Reading Power (DRP) tests to students in our district. These tests assess how well a student is able to understand the surface meaning of what he or she is reading. This is very important because students who do not adequately comprehend the surface meaning of text find it very difficult to learn from what they read. We use the results of this test to identify students who need extra help in reading, to determine which textbooks and other types of printed material are most suitable for instructional use, and to document the annual growth our students make in reading.

Independent Reader scores indicate the difficulty level of material that students can read on their own. Developing Reader scores indicate the difficulty level of material that students can read with some assistance from teachers or parents. This year, Ted has earned the following DRP scores: Independent Reader 56 DRP Units and Developing Reader 67 DRP Units. In relation to a nationwide sample of students in the same grade at the same time of year, Ted scored as well or better than 87% of the students. You can compare Ted's Independent Reader performance in reading to the following standards that the Oswego City School District has set for students in each grade.

Oswego City School District Reading Standards of Excellence
(for Independent Readers)

Grade	2	3	4	5	6	7	8
Excellence Goal	27	40	46	53	60	64	70
Minimum Standard	17	22	30	37	42	48	54

These reading standards reflect our goal to make sure that all students are prepared for productive employment and further learning when they graduate from high school. Further comparative and longitudinal information on your child's DRP score is contained on the attached performance chart.

Although we are committed to helping all students reach these reading targets, we need your help also. It is well known that the more reading students do, both in and out of school, the better readers they become. Therefore, we have also prepared the enclosed Parent Report to assist you in engaging Ted in meaningful reading and writing activities that are specifically tailored to Ted's current reading abilities.

If you wish additional information about your child's performance on this test or in the classroom, please feel free to contact the school at your convenience.

"Making School a Better Place"

FIGURE 7.5

REPORT OF THE DEGREES OF READING POWER TEST

Oswego City School District • Degrees of Reading Power (DRP) Test

Student: Ted E. Bear **Teacher:** Wonder Full **Grade:** 05

Current Performance		
Developing Reader (D-DRP)	**Independent Reader (I-DRP)**	**Test Information**
This score indicates the most difficult text that a student can comprehend <u>with</u> assistance from teachers or parents.	This score indicates the most difficult text that a student can comprehend <u>without</u> assistance.	Raw Score: 51 Maximum Score: 70 National Percentile: 87 Test Date: 5/01/94
Current Year (D-DRP) Score: 67	Current Year (I-DRP) Score: 56	
District Score of Excellence For Student's Grade: 64	District Score of Excellence For Student's Grade: 53	

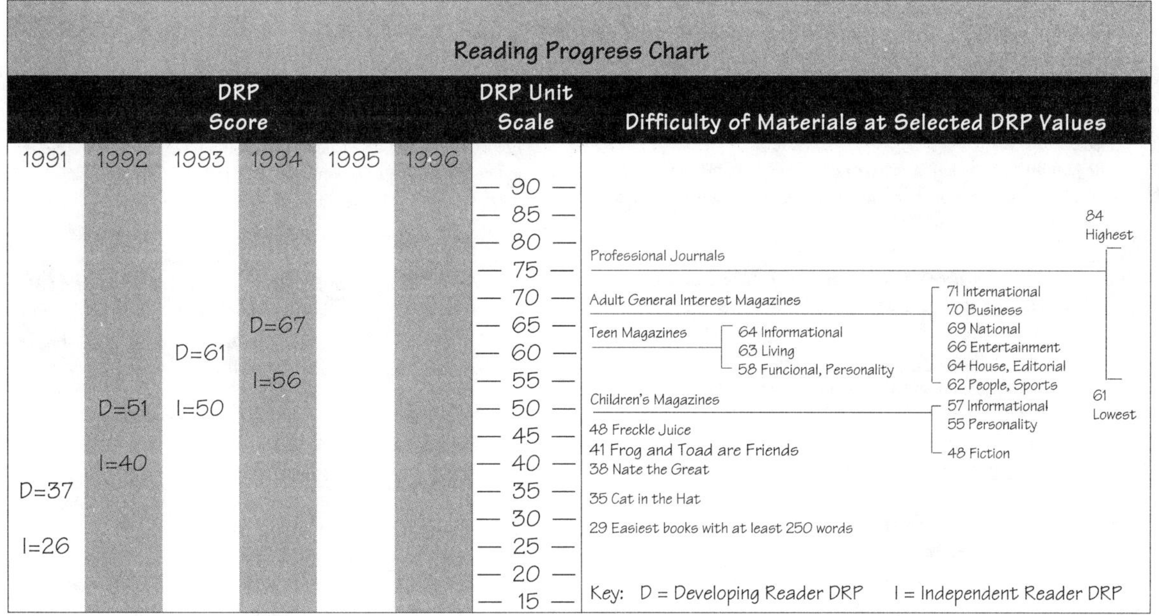

An Alternative to Prime Time Is to Read with Your Children

FIGURE 7.6

DEGREES OF READING POWER PARENT REPORT

Degrees of Reading Power
Touchstone Applied Science Associates

PARENT REPORT

Teacher: Wonder Ful
School: Kingsford Park
District: Osewego C.S.D.

Student: Ted E. Bear

In May of 1994, Ted took a Degrees of Reading Power (DRP) test. This test measures your child' s ability to comprehend the surface meaning of text while it is being read. The Parent Report, which is based on Ted's current performance on the DRP, suggests the kinds of things you can do to assist in your child's literacy development.

Books to Try Now. The following books are among those your child should enjoy reading on his or her own. Most of them are widely available in bookstores, libraries, some grocery stores, and discount stores. Many are published in both hardback and paperback form. It is hoped that one of these books will be so appealing that your child will want to read it again, or read other books by the same author. Your child's teacher or the children's librarian at the school or public library can also help you find books to interest your child.

- Emily of New Moon, Lucy Maud Montgomery.
  When her father dies, Emily Starr is left an orphan. Now the irrepressible Emily must go live with her grim Aunt Elizabeth of New Moon Farm.
- Blood and Guts: A Working Guide to Your Own Insides, Linda Allison
  The human body includes miles of blood vessels, billions of cells. It is a system of levers and pumps, as well as a furnace and a computer.
- The Mystery of Stonehenge, Nancy Lyon.
  Stonehenge is an incredible circle of huge boulders on a plain in England. Almost 5,000 years old, it may have been an ancient observatory.
- Auks, Rocks and the Odd Dinosaur, Peggy Thomson.
  Go behind the scenes at the Museum of Natural History in Washington, D.C. Learn about the Kachina doll and the 5-foot rift worm exhibits.
- Mary McLeod Bethune: Voice of Black Hope, Milton Meltzer.
  Mary McLeod Bethune became a black educator and activist. With $5 and a dream, she started Bethune College.
- Ben and Me, Robert Lawson.
  Unknown to history, Ben Franklin's best friend is a mouse. Amos helps Ben invent the Franklin stove and publish Poor Richard's Almanac.
- Tom's Midnight Garden, Phillippa Pearce.
  During the day, Tom lives in the present. But at night, he sneaks out into a garden of long ago to meet Hatty, a girl of Victorian England.

Books to Try Later. Your child may want to try the following books in the next few months.

- Bagthorpes v. the World, Helen Cresswell
  The eccentric Bagthorpe family has gone bankrupt but Mr. Bagthorpe has the solution: self-sufficiency! They will grow lettuce and get a milk goat.
- The Phantom Tollbooth, North Juster.
  Bored, Milo 'drives through' the toy tollbooth in his room and finds himself in a strange world. He meets King Azaz, and Tock, the dog who ticks.
- Across Five Aprils, Irene Hunt.
  Civil War becomes real to the Creighton family when all the able-bodied men are called. Only young Jethro is left to keep the Illinois farm going.
- Only the Names Remain: The Cherokees and the Trail of Tears, Alex Bealer.
  For 1,000 years, the Cherokee Indians have hunted and fished in the Appalachian Mountains. But in 1837, they are driven away from their homeland.
- What Do You Mean by 'Average'?: Means, Medians, and Modes, Elizabeth James and Carol Barkin.
  Jill Slater is running for Student Council president. Using means, medians, and modes, she sets out to prove that she represents the average student.
- Cowboys of the Wild West, Russell Freedman.
  A century ago in the Old West, cowboys drove herds of longhorn cattle north out of Texas. What were these legendary men really like?
- Earthquakes, Seymour Simon.
  Approximately once every thirty seconds and earthquake occurs somewhere in the world. Learn what causes earth tremors and how to protect yourself during a strong quake.

There are many other things you can do to stimulate your child's interest in reading. Specific activities are recommended on the following page.

050601 PRB

FIGURE 7.6 (*continued*)

Student: Ted E. Bear | Teacher: Wonder Ful

Reading Aloud. Reading aloud is the most frequently recommended at-home activity for encouraging literacy development. It benefits children whether they are the listeners or the readers.

- Ask your child to read aloud to his or her younger brothers and sisters. This will benefit all of the children. It is also a welcome help to busy parents. If there are no younger siblings, try to find another audience for your child: grandparents, an aunt or uncle, younger neighborhood children. Look for someone who will appreciate being read to and will respond positively to your child's efforts.

Reading to Do. Too often, children view reading solely as a school activity. But reading has many purposes. One of the most important and satisfying is reading in order to do something. Encourage your child to experience this type of reading with the following activities.

- Science is an exciting and informative reading-to-do activity. Look for books with science experiments that children can do at home. These books give instructions for projects which use familiar materials to demonstrate simple scientific facts or principles to children. Usually, the projects are easy and fun-to-do. Often, they deal with everyday questions and occurrences, things children and adults may not think of as the subject of "science." For example, and experiment may explain why the damp socks left in the gym bag too long start to smell terrible!
- Cooking is a classic reading-to-do activity and a useful skill as well. Encourage your child to keep developing as a cook. If your child has had some experience making simple dishes from recipes, ask your child to do something in the kitchen that is more challenging. For example, ask your child to make two dishes at the same time. This will require that your child coordinate the instructions on the package of the directions in the recipe. If you haven't started cooking with your child, now would be a good time to start!
- Kits are usually complete, pre-packaged reading-to-do activities. Look for electricity and electronics kits for your child. The range of these kits includes those which demonstrate the basic properties of electricity to those which involve building an operable electric powered widget. Choose a kit which is appropriate for your child's mechanical skill level.

050601 PRA

- Is your child a Scout or a 4-H Club member? Look into the youth organizations available in your community. These groups provide children with many valuable learning experiences. Many of their activities involve reading and writing.

Talking and Reading. Talking to children about what they have read or what they have learned can help them become better readers. Take advantage of everyday situations—riding in the car, waiting in the doctor's office—to talk to your child.

- When you find a magazine or newspaper article that you have enjoyed reading or that you have found interesting or helpful, clip it and share it with your child. Ask your child to read it if you think it will not be too difficult. Then talk about it. Tell your child why you enjoyed it or what you found helpful or interesting. Ask your child for his or her response.
- Ask your child to describe how something works or how something is done. For example, ask your child to explain how to play his or her favorite sport. Ask your child questions about anything you do not understand. Encourage your child to give enough detail so that you rally know how it is done. But don't turn the conversation into a quiz. Be a real listener.

Writing. Writing is sometimes overlooked, but it can be an enjoyable at-home activity. Try combining writing with one of the reading activities listed above.

- Encourage your child to start his or her own recipe collection. Your child can write out his or her favorite recipes, copy others from cookbooks, and clip some from magazines.
- Similarly, encourage your child to start a "lab book" of the science experiments that he or she has done, complete with pictures or drawings and explanations.

Value Reading. You can communicate the value of reading to your child by treating reading as a privileged activity. For example, let your child stay up 15 minutes or so past bedtime, but only if he or she is reading. Give books and other reading materials as gifts. Never use reading as a punishment. Think of other positive ways you can show your child how much you value reading. Try a different one each week.

nents of the district's reading report. One parent commented that this was the first time she felt comfortable with reading about and understanding how her child did during the school year. This mother went on to say that the book list empowered her to take an active role in her child's reading development because she was offered something concrete to do with her daughter. Many parents like the focus on excellence, along with the chart that gives examples of reading materials that are equivalent to their child's DRP test score.

Reporting performance in relation to standards of excellence, however, can raise anxieties. For example, parents whose children have always been "above the norm" ask teachers why their children are below the standards of excellence and what can be done about it. This anxiety can be positive, however, because fruitful discussion often ensues.

Displaying current test scores alongside previous scores enables parents to easily calculate the amount of growth their child made from one year to the next. This has led to inquiries such as, "How much growth is normal or expected?" and "How is it that the test scores for my child this year are the same as, or lower, than those for last year?" As teachers and parents learn from each other, the children ultimately benefit.

The more parents understand, the more they want to know. They will ask questions and, in so doing, take a more active interest in the education of their children. To help teachers and administrators be more responsive to parent inquiries, the district could not overlook the importance of staff development. We held several workshops to help teachers become knowledgeable and feel comfortable talking about what a child's DRP or OPAL results mean. In addition, we found it equally important to have sessions for parents. Many parents attended evening information sessions at which district personnel explained how to interpret and understand the assessment results.

The Oswego City School District's reporting program, along with staff and parent inservice workshops, has created an increased understanding and solid support for our educational assessment and testing programs, leading to a greater sense of trust in and respect for our educational programs. Assessment is now consistent with the philosophy of literacy development in our district, and it directly affects classroom instruction, as well as school-home communication and collaboration.

References

International Reading Association. (1989). "Professional Statements Approved by the IRA Board of Directors." *Journal of Reading* 32, 4: 297.

Lowe, K., and B. Bintz. (1993). *Understanding Literacy Evaluation: Issues and Practicalities.* Portsmouth, N.H.: Heinemann Educational Books.

Kibby, M. W. (1981). "The Degrees of Reading Power." *Journal of Reading* 24: 416–427.

Klare, G. R. (1985). "Matching Reading Materials to Readers: The Role of Readability Estimates in Conjunction with Other Information about Comprehensibility." In *Reading, Thinking and Concept Development* (pp. 233–256), edited by T. L. Harris and E. J. Cooper. New York: The College Board.

Koslin, B. L., S. Zenos, and S. Koslin. (1987). *The DRP: An Effective Measure in Reading.* New York: College Entrance Examination Board.

Riley, R. W. (1993, Summer). "Technos Interview with Richard W. Riley." *Technos* 2, 2: 4–7.

Touchstone Applied Science Associates. (1988). *Degrees of Reading Power Tests.* Brewster, N.Y.: Author.

8

Communicating Student Learning in the Visual Arts

Bernard Schwartz

Artists and arts educators have an innate understanding of assessment and its value for learning. Now they need to reexamine their knowledge so as to use it in promoting the centrality of the arts in education. (*Measuring Up to the Challenge: What Standards and Assessment Can Do for Arts Education.* American Council for the Arts, 1994)

"Parents Pushing to Learn More About Schools" was the headline in a September 3, 1994, article in the *Globe and Mail*, one of Canada's most respected newspapers. As Canadian students begin a new school year, school officials are under increasing—sometimes intense—pressure to report openly on student and school achievement, even to the point of publicly ranking and comparing individual schools. "One way or another," claims J. Lewington, the education reporter, "the writing is on the blackboard: Schools will have to deliver more useful, reliable information than they have ever done in the past" (p. 8A).

Public information on school performance varies greatly across Canada and the United States. The public is showing greater interest in looking for simple reporting on student achievement, as well as finding straight answers about what happens in the classroom and what remedies are in place when things go wrong. At the same time, school districts are attempting to develop more sophisticated forms of evaluation intended to provide a fuller picture of student and school performance. The public's demand for schools to be more accountable is among the most challenging issues for educators today and certainly one of the hottest political topics in education.

The intended audience for this chapter is elementary teachers who teach the entire school curriculum, including art, in their self-contained classrooms, as well as specialist art teachers in elementary and secondary schools, art supervisors, and consultants. Indeed, teachers of all disciplines are likely to find possibilities for the work they do from the experiences of their colleagues in the arts. Administrators, school board members, and parents may also find this chapter to be informative and applicable to their concerns. Arts educators in the visual arts, music, dance, and theater have long sought evidence of learning through student inquiry processes, products, and performances, and the concurrent challenges of grading, reporting, and communicating outcomes to diverse stakeholders. The inherent nature of the arts has predestined its emphasis on product and performance-based assessments (e.g., projects, portfolios, performances, recitals, exhibitions) that are now highly valued features of the growing trend toward alternative assessments in education.

This chapter begins by exploring the current intensity of concern among parents and the public about how well students and schools are doing, then reviews major curriculum developments affecting art education. A presentation of the broad spectrum of assessment techniques employed in art education follows. The chapter concludes with suggested criteria for student assessment and related procedures for reporting achievement.

Standards for the Arts

The education reform movement has generated vigorous activity on many issues, including the complex and critical matter of determining how well schools are evaluating student performance throughout the curriculum. In the United States, music, theater, dance, and visual arts educators have jointly developed and recently published The National Standards for Arts Education (*NAEA News* 1994). These national standards for visual art, in particular, address two different types of standards—content standards and achievement standards—for assessing student accomplishment and progress. They provide a vision for student competencies, as well as for the educational effectiveness of teachers and school art programs. Content standards specify "what students should know and be able to do." Achievement standards specify the understandings and levels of achievement that schools expect students to attain in the various competencies. The authors of these standards claim that

> people unfamiliar with the arts often mistakenly believe that excellence and quality are mere matters of opinion ("I know what I like"), and that one opinion is as good as another. They [the standards] say there is such a thing as achievement, that knowledge and skills matter, and that mere willing participation is not the same thing as education. They [the standards] affirm that discipline and rigor are the road to achievement. And they [the standards] state emphatically that all these things can in some way be measured if not always on a numerical scale, then by informed critical judgment (*NAEA News*, p. 6)

The national standards, which are voluntary for each of the states and local school districts, present content areas for the visual arts, expectations for student experiences, and levels of student achievement. Written into federal law, they are a part of the Goals 2000: Educate America Act, included among the goals for the year 2000 for all students K–12 in the United States. The arts are now to take their place as core subjects, as equals among all subjects in the school curriculum.

In addition, thousands of 4th, 8th, and 12th grade students across the United States will be assessed in forthcoming years in the areas of the arts (visual art, music, theater, and dance) under the National Assessment of Educational Progress (NAEP). This is the first national assessment of this type since the late 1970s. Many educators and researchers are preparing for this important event, which we anticipate will have substantial ramifications for assessment practices, as well as for future directions of the arts in general education.

Discipline-Based Art Education

Visual arts education theory, curriculum development, and teaching practice in schools are undergoing important transformations that began slightly more than a decade ago with the emergence of discipline-based art education, now more commonly known as DBAE, an innovative, comprehensive approach to teaching the arts in general education. What began with a focus on advocacy of the visual arts has grown to include music, theater, and drama. Not only have changes occurred in the schools and in state and provincial curriculum frameworks, but also in preservice education for specialist art teachers and general classroom teachers, inservice education and professional development, and in the increasing publication and availability of a wide array of high-quality instructional resources for use in schools and in college and university teacher education. Furthermore, the research literature, developmental activity, and conference presentations about DBAE point to steadily increasing interest.

The Getty Center for Education in the Arts, a program of the J. P. Getty Trust of Los Angeles, California, has been the catalyst and continues to be the major supporter of discipline-based art education in schools. This comprehensive approach substantially expands the scope of content and teaching strategies used in art education, which traditionally emphasized producing or creating art based on the role model of the professional artist.

Typically, art programs engage students' imaginations, feelings, and emotions mainly through personal expression and creativity with a wide variety of art media and techniques—paint, clay, wood, wire, papers, fibers, and so forth. Now, however, high-quality DBAE art programs from kindergarten to senior high school include the content and methods of inquiry derived from all four of the interrelated visual arts disciplines—art production, art history, art criticism, and aesthetics. Not only are these four disciplines integrated into students' experiences in the art program itself, but they are also integrated into subjects across the entire curriculum. Creating and studying art within each of these disciplines is fundamental to promoting student learning in the philosophy of discipline-based art education.

The major components of quality contemporary art programs in grades K–12 draw from the substantive content of the four interrelated visual art disciplines, each of which has a long history in human activity. Students at each grade level are given the opportunity to become involved with each of these components at their own level of development, as each offers a different set of lenses for experiencing art.

Art production provides students with opportunities to express their ideas and feelings in a variety of two-and-three-dimensional art forms. Emphasis is on the development of technical skills; problem-solving abilities; and creative, expressive, and communicative capacities.

By contrast, art history emphasizes historical and sociocultural understanding. It provides students with knowledge about creative individuals from both past and present civilizations. The study of art history also considers how the visual arts have reflected, communicated, and possibly changed the thoughts, feelings, and beliefs of people.

Art criticism provides students with the methods and content to make works of art more meaningful and satisfying by knowing how to look at art, what to look for, and how to discuss and write about art. Teachers use instructional strategies to involve their students in observing, describing, analyzing, interpreting, and evaluating or judging art. Art criticism promotes sensory awareness, perceptual discrimination, and judgment.

Aesthetics, a branch of philosophy, engages students in philosophical inquiry and reasoning. This involves the study of the nature and significance of art, beauty, and aesthetic experience. Aesthetics helps students understand what motivates people to produce art, and how and why art is used and valued in society. This discipline expects students to gain an understanding and tolerance of alternative viewpoints about the merit of art and encourages them to reflect on a spectrum of criteria and standards of excellence.

Today, educators expect quality art programs to adhere to basic educational principles in their planning, implementation, and evaluation, similar to any other subject included in the school curriculum. This means that art programs at each grade level should be sequential, balanced, and comprehensive in the kinds of experiences and opportunities offered to students.

Today's quality visual art K–12 programs include two interrelated, major dimensions of learning: creating or producing art; and understanding, responding to, and reflecting about art. Thus, art educators design well-rounded programs to attain educational goals with the understanding, attitudes, and skills that will help students to fulfill their personal potential; to become aesthetically, visually literate consumers of products and services of professional artists, designers, and craft-persons; to participate in improving our world for a more humane and community environment; to become active participants (but not necessarily as arts professionals); and to become lifelong supporters of the arts as adult citizens in their own communities.

Assessment and Evaluation Strategies

Along with the other subjects in the curriculum, visual art as a mainstreamed, core subject will require suitable means to evaluate student progress and program effectiveness, and to sensibly report this to its varied constituents: students, parents, principals and other institutional administrators, school board trustees, funding agencies, and the general public. These diverse stakeholders need to be knowledgeable and feel confident in the authenticity and reliability of the assessment techniques and the kinds of criteria and information considered. Requirements for accountability need to be met head-on, yet art educators must not forget the enormous richness, breadth, and complexity of the visual arts, as well as the relationship between the content of our teaching and the standards or criteria we adopt. As the content of art curricula is expanding and changing, it seems reasonable to assume that evaluation strategies will need to shift to accommodate these trends.

In the visual arts the possibilities for assessment and evaluation strategies are many. For example, they may be formal or informal, self or external, quantitative or quantitative, formative or summative, criterion-referenced or norm-referenced. Though the visual arts make a unique contribution to the total school curriculum, they share and can employ many of the same assessment techniques common to other subjects. At the same time, visual art contributes techniques that more appropriately capture and reflect its unique qualities and purposes—as well as its visual, tactile, and other sensory processes and products—thereby presenting a fuller, more accurate representation of student achievement.

In the visual arts, the long-standing tradition of using art and design portfolios, for example, is widely accepted, making a valuable contribution to assessment techniques in virtually every subject. The portfolio technique of assessment in the art classroom exemplifies the authentic, performance-based assessment thrust in education today. It has grown from consisting mainly of finished art products, to include samples of conceptual ideas, art works in progress, written reports and essays, test samples, photographs and videos, audiotapes, and journals and self-critiques, thus presenting a comprehensive picture of a student's progress and achievement. The student's development is therefore depicted sequentially over time, using a range of indicators and perspectives.

A recent newsletter of the Electronic Media Interest Group of the National Art Education Association reported on the latest approach to portfolios: Two teachers in Florida are pilot testing the latest commercial technology, using blank recordable compact discs to produce CD-ROM portfolios of their high school students' artwork. They see this as becoming more feasible and practical as equipment costs drop and districtwide use increases.

Studies in the arts combine affective and cognitive modes of learning, resulting in the development of creative and critical thinking. State and provincial departments of education are developing visual art curriculum frameworks and guides for teachers that mandate goals, objectives, concepts, and content that will engage students in these higher-order processes and behaviors.

Dimensions of Thinking (Marzano et al. 1988), a concise, provocative book published by the Association for Supervision and Curriculum Development, offers an excellent presentation on this subject. Scholars and researchers outline a series of eight "core thinking skills," including the skills of focusing, information-gathering, remembering, organizing, analyzing, generating, integrating, and evaluating. In addition, this subject is highlighted in the visual and performing arts section of the *ASCD Curriculum Handbook*, a comprehensive, multimedia information resource for teachers, administrators, researchers, and curriculum developers (Schwartz et al. 1993).

Application of many of these skills is essential when individuals engage in creating art objects or responding to expression in the arts. The experiences included in comprehensive discipline-based art programs should naturally engage students in using and refining many of these core thinking skills. Further, these skills also serve students' metacognition—that is, their awareness of their own thinking when performing certain tasks—which enables them to control what they are doing (i.e., by "thinking about thinking").

A Repertoire of Techniques

A wide variety of assessment techniques for gathering and analyzing data are available for teachers to use in evaluating student achievement and effort. From this assortment of techniques, teachers can develop a repertoire that serves as a basis for reporting learning to students and others. The following list suggests an array of possibilities:

- *Art products*—the range of two-and-three dimensional art objects created during art class. The teacher can use specific criteria or gestalt/holistic judgments to assess art products on such dimensions as quality of design; expressiveness; originality/imagination/creativity; craftsmanship, skill, and control; and effort or degree of involvement. Included here is the entire continuum of art products, from tentative and exploratory idea sketches to fully developed and polished works.
- *Written work*—research reports, journals, responses to artworks, and exhibition reviews.
- *Tests and examinations*—a variety of structured and open-ended formats (multiple-choice, matching, short answer, essay, etc.) devised to assess the full spectrum of cognitive knowledge and skills.
- *Self- and peer evaluations and critiques*—oral and written critiques and reviews of art processes, products, and experiences of self and others.
- *Checklists, rating scales, and questionnaires*—assessment tools that students and teachers develop and administer.
- *Oral presentations*—based on the student's own studio involvement or research on selected topics.

- *Scrapbooks and sketchbooks*—these are process-oriented, retaining the flow of ideas, interests, concerns, and "problem finding" discoveries of students, in visual and written forms. These informal notations can be extraordinarily self-revealing to the student (and others) of the creative or artistic process as demonstrated in the history of art.
- *Collaborative work*—team and small-group activity that offers opportunities to undertake complex projects while promoting the give-and-take of peer decisionmaking and cooperative learning.
- *Class discussions*—opportunity to promote and assess listening skills, oral communication, critical thinking, and understanding and tolerance of alternative viewpoints.
- *Videotapes, audiotapes, photographs, and slides*—technology that is readily available and accessible in many classrooms to facilitate students' recording and documenting the evolution of their work.
- *Observational and anecdotal documentation*—descriptive data that a teacher records during and after instructional periods, using checklists or narrative notations of student participation, attitudes, concentration, work habits, and cooperation.
- *Student contracts*—these encourage student initiative, planning, choices, follow-through, and responsibility for their own learning.
- *Interviews and conferences*—formal and informal techniques that render opportunities for one-on-one and small-group review, reflection, and determination of what's next.
- *Student exhibitions*—historically, an inextricable part of the visual arts. Students develop skills in selecting, organizing, and presenting their work for public display; reactions from classmates and other viewers are of equal benefit.
- *Portfolios*—may include many of the foregoing techniques as samples; an approach that presents a systematic and informative review, an in-progress snapshot of each student's development in achievement and effort over time.

Portfolios can encompass many of the other assessment tools. Teachers and students will need to take collaborative responsibility for deciding what samples will go into the portfolio (everything, best works, required assignments, or representative selections?). Students, as well as teachers, can prepare a written or oral assessment of their portfolios, in addition to a student-teacher conference on the completed portfolio. The process of creating a portfolio empowers students when they are able to participate in selecting items included, set criteria for these selections, and define criteria for assessing the portfolio itself.

The school will need to resolve both educational and ethical issues. To make the portfolio approach manageable for art teachers and helpful to others while serving the best interests of students, each school will need to establish a policy regarding storing portfolios, deciding which portfolio items to pass on to other teachers, and determining who else will have access to them.

The purpose of this overview of art assessment techniques is to remind teachers of the many possibilities, but more importantly, to encourage them to incorporate a variety of assessment tools into their own assessment repertoire. Teachers can successfully assess their own program goals and lesson and unit objectives, as well as their students' needs, skills, and interests. A balanced assessment plan is imperative: one that employs a variety of techniques for gathering information about what students are learning in today's comprehensive art programs. Determining their students' strengths and weaknesses, their areas of accomplishment and areas for suggested improvement, is fundamental to the practices of all effective teachers.

A teacher can use each of the assessment techniques individually or in combination to obtain meaningful information about what students have learned through a myriad of art experiences. It may be helpful to think of organizing these assessment tools into three broad clusters according to the types of evidence they collect of student outcomes:

- *Observations* (e.g., teacher anecdotal recordings in the context of class lessons, interviews, checklists, or student journal entries);
- *Performance samples* (e.g., art products and media experiments and the associated criterion-referenced rating scales, such as collaborative work and class discussions, oral and written reports, student journals, exhibits, self- and peer evaluations and critiques, video or audio documentation, photographic or slide formats, or portfolios related to a single project or extending throughout the school year); and
- *Tests* (e.g., multiple choice, essay, or matching).

In a unit on painting, for example, with an emphasis on personal color exploration related to how several famous painters use color expressively, a teacher can incorporate all three types of evidence for evaluation and reporting. The teacher may begin with observational approaches during class production lessons by recording anecdotal comments and employing checklists to document students' attention span, their application of basic color mixing skills in a series of directed tasks, and their courage to take risks in open-ended color investigations with tempera paint.

Further observations will include students' application of art vocabulary, interest shown, and insights shared during discussions (integrating the subject matter of art history, art criticism, and aesthetics) of reproductions of artists whose work in using color is exemplary in conveying moods, ideas, and feelings. Performance samples might consist of each student's miniportfolio of color experiments, preliminary sketches, and a mounted and captioned painting; a journal of plans for the color experiments and ideas for the finished painting; a self-evaluation rating scale for the painting; and a brief, illustrated research report (presented orally in small groups) of a painter admired for color usage.

The teacher can test students during the progress of the unit or as one of the culminating activities. A multiple-choice test can determine understanding of basic color mixing theory and procedures, as in the relationships and application of information presented in a color wheel. An essay test can ask students to compare and contrast reproductions of paintings for the ways painters have used various color characteristics and properties and their effects on viewers. Depending upon the importance of such a unit within the program and the grade level, the teacher may choose to report these student outcomes as either formative or summative evaluations, or a combination of both.

Reporting and Communicating Student Learning

Teachers can use several possible scoring systems, in conjunction with their own evaluation criteria and summary comments, to report to students their accomplishments in a unit of instruction, as in the unit example on color discussed above. Communicating student learning to students, parents, school administrators, and others in ways that are valid and reliable, as well as meaningful and useful, requires assessments that consider student achievement and effort in relation to the broad art program goals and the specific lesson/unit learning objectives of the teacher. Many forms of assessment are pertinent to a well-rounded art education program. In fact, using a diverse array of assessment tools is necessary to respond fully to the range of personalities, learning modalities, and cognitive styles of today's students.

What criteria or standards are appropriate for student assessment in art programs and also valid for reporting achievement and effort? For elementary and secondary schools, three broad categories are useful in preparing formative and summative evaluation reports:

- Knowledge, Understanding, or Cognition;
- Attitudes, Values, or Affect; and
- Skills, Craftsmanship, or Psychomotor.

After teachers obtain and analyze a variety of assessment data, these categories and the criteria subsumed within each can provide a structure for evaluation. A comprehensive student evaluation, which assesses both producing art and responding to art, is then reflected in the summary report (Figure 8.1).

The teacher should also record and report the student's achievement, using a scoring system of points or symbols to describe the *level of attainment* for each specified criterion. She can indicate the range of quality by using any one or a combination of the following:

- A 3-, 5-, or 10-point scale representing low-to-high;
- Percentage scores;
- *A, B, C, D, F* (for Excellent to Failing);
- *E, S, N* (for Excellent, Satisfactory, Needs Improvement);
- The symbols + and – (for Presence or Absence);
- *Much, Some, Little;*
- *Credit* and *Noncredit;* and
- *Satisfactory* and *Unsatisfactory.*

When school districts require conventional grades or marks for periodic reporting of student achievement, teachers can also use the suggested criteria and scoring system as the basis for determining an overall grade or mark for each student. Concise, pertinent written statements to complement and illuminate a student's evaluation are highly desirable, especially constructive summary comments. As Wiggins describes in Chapter 11, not only is it more helpful to identify diverse dimensions of performance separately, as subcategories, rather than averaging into composite scores, but the teacher should also summarize the meaning of this data in the form of a brief narrative.

A perennial issue, one of the more perplexing that teachers must deal with in evaluating art, is the *frame of reference* for making judgments about student learning. Educators can use three fundamental frames of reference to determine a student's learning by comparing current performance with (1) his earlier performance, (2) the performance of other students of the same age and grade level, or (3) absolute standards or norms established either by the teacher or by local, regional, or national standards. The first frame of reference focuses on a student's growth or progress, while the second and third present increasingly broader contexts for understanding a student's attainment of expectations. Teachers of art will need to decide under what circumstances they will emphasize each frame of reference (if at all), so that evaluation reports will genuinely serve to inform students, parents, and others.

The sample "Art Summary Report/Report Card" (Figure 8.1) suggests criteria the teacher might include. Because not all criteria will be of equal importance, whenever warranted the teacher can assign different values to certain criteria within the chosen scoring system. Teachers may choose to use this report card or to make changes to satisfy the unique synthesis of their own educational philosophy, characteristics of their students, the grade level, the art program offered, school and district policies, or any other critical factors of their particular setting. A student-teacher conference in conjunction with the completed report card would further enhance its intended benefits. The teacher can also make cer-

FIGURE 8.1

ART SUMMARY REPORT/REPORT CARD

Student Name ______________________ Reporting Period ______________________

Teacher ______________________ Art Grade/Mark (if required) ______________________

A variety of assessments used during this reporting period indicate that the student has demonstrated achievement and effort in the identified goals and objectives of the school art program.

____

(NOTE: Indicate here the desired scoring system and record for each item below, as relevant.)

Knowledge/Understanding/Cognition

- Gives evidence of conscious awareness, knowledge, and use of design elements and principles in art production. ______
- Knows and applies art processes and procedures. ______
- Exhibits sensory awareness of details, shapes, colors, how things feel, and other features. ______
- Shows awareness of design in art, in the built-environment, and in nature. and is able to discuss design using a variety of criteria. ______
- Knows, uses, and applies art vocabulary in oral and written experience.
- Can discuss ideas about art objects using description, analysis, interpretation, analogy comparison/contrast, etc.; supports judgments. ______
- Tries to understand the art of other students, as well as professional artists, designers, and craftpersons. ______
- Demonstrates originality, inventiveness, and curiosity (creativity) in generating ideas for artworks; thinks through, experiments, and explores with materials and ideas in diverse solutions to art problems; goes beyond the superficial or most obvious. ______
- Grasps processes and concepts associated with the study of art history and aesthetics. ______
- Able to organize workspace, plan use of time, and plan stages of projects or assignments. ______

Attitudes/Values/Affect

- Artworks reflect expressive content from personal experiences, interests, point of view, and involvement. ______
- Shows interest in and works with a range of tools, media, art forms, themes, and subjects. ______
- Has the courage to take risks and chances; confident and eager to express self in several modes—art production, oral, written. ______

(Continued on next page)

FIGURE 8.1 (*continued*)

- Is an active participant in class discussions through willingness to share own perceptions, ideas, experiences, and evaluations of art. ______
- Maintains respect for, tolerance, empathy, and acceptance of the ideas, work, and efforts of others. ______
- Respects public and private property during art experiences. ______
- Accepts constructive criticism of strengths and weaknesses of own performances and is able to incorporate these into future experiences as a result of self- and external evaluations. ______
- Responds positively and flexibly to a variety of new art experiences and situations. ______
- Contributes to classroom maintenance; helps with distribution and clean up, displays, etc. ______

Skills/Craftsmanship/Psychomotor

- Evidence of increasing attention span and concentration. ______
- Is diligent and persevering; completes work; does not give up easily. ______
- Demonstrates control over and suitable care of media, tools, and equipment. ______
- Performs skills in handling a variety of art processes and techniques from simple to complex. ______
- Elaborates and refines work ("polishes") commensurate with intent. ______
- As appropriate, generates quantity of ideas and products, as well as quality. ______

Summary Comments: ____

____

____

____

tain items on the report card either more specific, more broad, or can relate items to a particular art experience. Students and teachers always have the choice of collaboratively generating other criteria or standards.

The "Art Summary Report/Report Card" is structured around the three categories of (1) knowledge/understanding/cognition, (2) attitudes/values/affect, and (3) skills/craftsmanship/psychomotor. Many state and provincial education systems develop curriculum frameworks and subject matter guides based on this conception, considering it an appropriate organizing structure for the content of instruction. Many commercial producers of teacher education publications and instructional resources for schools also employ this structure. Teachers and other education personnel are generally familiar and comfortable with this approach, which is widely used in other curriculum subjects. This reporting instrument includes various criteria, highly valued in the visual arts, that point out student work-related habits, attitudes, and dispositions—similar to the "habits of mind" that Wiggins discusses in Chapter 11. Recipients of this report will want to know this information about each learner. Informed professional consensus is the basis for using this rubric as the overarching umbrella for organizing the particular criteria included within each category.

The *Report/Report Card* will work well at all grade levels. It is comprehensive in specifying criteria relevant to the nature of experience and learning in the visual arts. Educators can adapt it easily to assess and report student art-making encounters with any art form, as well as activities in appreciating art. Furthermore, the instrument also accounts for the four interrelated components of discipline-based art education, the curriculum philosophy and content that is steadily growing in popularity and implementation. Teachers can use parts of this instrument with any of the enumerated scoring systems when preparing formative evaluations related to the suggested criteria. Alternately, they can use the entire instrument as summative evaluation for quarterly or end-of-year reporting periods.

The teacher's frame of reference is critical throughout the procedures involved in evaluating and communicating student learning outcomes. As Guskey emphasizes in Chapter 3, learning criteria should be the basis for grading and reporting since these tend to provide greater understanding about what students have learned. Guskey describes the three broad categories of learning criteria that teachers use most often: product criteria, process criteria, and progress criteria.

Overall, the student's welfare will benefit most when schools give precedence to the element of *change in learning behavior*—that is, when evidence of growth or progress in achievement is accorded highest value. A teacher should compare a student's performance with her earlier performance to determine the degree of movement toward specified criterion-referenced objectives. The teacher then reports on how well (i.e., the quality/quantity of student learning) the student has achieved the desired objective by indicating the level of attainment using the particular scoring system employed. A synthesis of cumulative outcomes can be especially informative when reported in the form of a written summary statement.

The visual arts will continue to make a unique contribution to the benefit and welfare of all students within the total curriculum. Accordingly, it seems reasonable and responsible that art educators remain persistent in the challenging task of assessing the impact of their efforts on student learning and in effectively reporting and communicating outcomes to the diverse stakeholders of the educational enterprise. Such efforts will serve students well and place the visual arts more securely within the curriculum, where they deserve to be.

References and Resources

Lewington, J. (September 3, 1994). "Parents Pushing to Learn More About Schools." *The Globe and Mail*, A8.

Marzano, R.J., R.S. Brandt, C.S. Hughes, B.F. Jones, B.Z. Presseisen, S.C. Rankin, and C. Suhor. (1988). *Dimensions of Thinking: A Framework for Curriculum and Instruction.* Alexandria, Va.: Association for Supervision and Curriculum Development.

Mitchell, R., ed. (1994). *Measuring Up to the Challenge: What Standards and Assessment Can Do for Arts Education.* A report with excerpts from papers presented at an American Council for the Arts Symposium, New York.

"The National Visual Arts Standards." (June 1994). *NAEA News* 36, 3: 6.

Schwartz, B., K. Seidel, L. Kahlich, P. Bennett, L. Davidson, D. Davis, G. Graves, D. Selwyn, B. Moore, B.C. O'Brien, and M. Palmer. (1993). "Visual and Performing Arts." In *ASCD Curriculum Handbook*, edited by F. Betts and J.A. Walter. Alexandria, Va.: Association for Supervision and Curriculum Development.

9

Reporting Methods in Grades K–8

Kathy Lake and Kery Kafka

Since the early 1900s, reporting systems or report cards have been as much a part of American schools as chalk and pencils. Early report cards were largely narrative descriptions of students' learning and progress toward specified goals. With increasing numbers of students came a greater reliance on quantitative methods of reporting student achievement.

Modifying reporting systems to more effectively communicate what students are learning and how well they are learning it is an important part of many school reform efforts in the United States today. The specific content, purpose, and format of reporting systems vary greatly, based in part on the intended audience; the developmental level of students; people's beliefs about teaching, learning, and assessment; the nature of the learning being reported; and the goals and standards set by national groups, districts, schools, and individual teachers. In all cases, however, the effectiveness of a reporting system as a communication tool hinges on the clarity of both the learning objectives and the description of the student's performance in meeting those objectives.

In this chapter, we describe some common reporting methods and present examples of reporting systems used in schools across the United States. The example we chose all meet the following baseline test: The recording of information about a student's progress and achievements should serve a useful purpose and, in particular, should benefit the student. Each example illustrates specific points, and each represents different beliefs about teaching, learning, and the role of student self-assessment and goal setting. Some schools, we discovered, have more than one reporting system—perhaps one for kindergarten, one for primary grades, and one for intermediate grades. When possible, we have included exam-

Authors' Note: We extend our thanks to all those who sent us samples of their reporting systems. We regret that space considerations prohibit us from including more of those examples here.

ples from different levels to illustrate the need for attention to the developmental appropriateness of reporting systems. We have also tried to represent a variety of effective reporting systems. Finally, to illustrate how the process of revising a reporting system can vary, we've included descriptions of the revision processes of an elementary school and a middle school, showing how educators in each school followed a different path as they move toward a reporting system that matches their beliefs about learning.

A Focus on Developmentally Appropriate Practice

At what age should children be exposed to a reporting system? This question has no hard-and-fast answer because different kinds of reporting systems may or may not be appropriate for a specific age group. Many schools wait until 1st grade to begin reporting on students' progress, while others start in kindergarten but keep the reporting systems less formal for the youngest children. Some schools have multiple versions of reporting systems for different age groups.

Many districts hold off on letter grades until the 3rd grade or even the 6th grade, believing that letter grades do not reflect the nature of the developmental progress of young children. Instead of using letter grades, these schools tend to favor checklists or narratives. Checklists are further differentiated by the type of items in the checklist. Some simply list isolated skills while others have a more global perspective. For example, a simple progress report may list skills such as these: listens and responds to questions, directions, statements; stays with topic of conversation; reads well orally; computes accurately; or knows number facts. A report with a more global perspective may include items such as these: demonstrates critical thinking, applies reading strategies, explores new and unfamiliar learning situations, or uses multiple strategies to solve problems.

"Developmentally appropriate practice" is a phrase frequently used in discussions about early childhood education. It refers to both age appropriateness and individual appropriateness (Bredekamp 1987). The importance of being developmentally appropriate, however, transcends any one age group of students, as the schools in this section confirm.

North Bay, Ontario, School System

Reporting systems used in kindergarten typically include those aspects of physical, mental, and emotional development considered important for young children. The reports are generally written in a way that indicates support for the development of the whole child. For example, the kindergarten reporting system in the North Bay, Ontario, school system has a space on the cover for a photo of the child involved in a kindergarten activity. Inside the report are the words of the child, responding to the teacher's questions: "My friends at school are . . . My favorite things to do in Junior Kindergarten are . . . " The child draws a picture, the teacher provide narrative information, based on observations, and the parent comments about the child's growth and development, attitude toward school, and the parent's feelings about the program.

Starms Early Childhood Center

Developmentally appropriate practice permeates the reporting system at Starms Early Childhood Center in Milwaukee, Wisconsin. The school program and the report card reinforce each other. Figure 9.1 shows a small part of the parent observation component—the rubric and examples for oral communication and part of the reading assessment checklist. Parents may complete the observation form at home or during a conference.

FIGURE 9.1

EXCERPTS FROM THE REPORTING SYSTEM OF THE STARMS EARLY CHILDHOOD CENTER

Milwaukee Public Schools
Starms Early Childhood Center

SAMPLE

PARENT OBSERVATION CHECKLIST (POC)

Child's Name________________________ Date ________________________

Parent's Name(s)________________________ ________________________

N = Not Yet Seen **S** = Sometimes Seen **O** = Often

Circle one letter

SOCIAL/EMOTIONAL	
Plays next to other children	N S O
Imitates adult action during play	N S O
Attempts to solve problems with other children	N S O

SELF HELP	
Uses spoon and cup to feed self	N S O
Removes coat by self	N S O
Brushes teeth by self	N S O

MOTOR SKILLS	
Scribbles	N S O
Kicks a ball	N S O
Catches a ball	N S O

COMMUNICATION	
Follows simple 1 step directions	N S O
Enjoys being read to	N S O
Is curious and asks many questions	N S O

Comments/Concerns: ________________________

MacDowell Montessori School

MacDowell Montessori School has three reporting systems, one for ages 3 to 6, one for ages 6 to 9, and one for ages 9 to 11. The stated purpose of the reporting systems is "to evaluate the individual child's progress without comparison to the other children. Our intent is to describe the child's progress." Each reporting system includes items appropriate for the specific age group. The older children have the opportunity to complete a checklist with items related to their work in school. Items include: "I can make appropriate choices," "I care for the environment/property," and "I can accept change and disappointment." The student notes whether this is a consistent ability, a developing ability, or an area that needs improvement.

Lakeland School District

Starting with the question "What do we want our kindergarten student to look like and be able to do as he/she exits kindergarten?" Kindergarten teachers and support staff of the Lakeland School District in Shrub Oak, New York, developed a Kindergarten Instruction Assessment Model on which teachers note and document progress in 11 categories. At the end of the year, the model is forwarded to the 1st grade teacher. By listing identified behaviors in categories such as "Learning-to-Learn Skills" and "Collaborative Skills," the teachers are able to give clear indications of the child's development in areas of importance and relevance for this age group.

Bellingham Public Schools

In the reporting system of the Bellingham Public Schools in Bellingham, Washington, students' performance in each subject falls in one of the following categories: Emergent, Beginning, Developing, Capable, Strong, or Exceptional. An explanation of each of these levels for reading, writing, listening, speaking, mathematics, social studies, and art is included on the reporting system.

The focus of this reporting system is a complete view of the student in multiple areas of development. The descriptions give a developmental picture of each area and serve as a guide for teaching and student progress. To illustrate, here is an example of a description from the intermediate reporting system:

Social Studies

Strong: Shows interest and enthusiasm; demonstrates understanding of concepts; participates very well independently and in a group; high quality work on assignments; sometimes extends self beyond requirements; sometimes uses additional resources.

Thus, to make an evaluation about social studies, teachers have to make sure that students have had an opportunity to work independently and in groups. Here is another example from the primary reporting system:

Mathematics

Capable: Solves problems independently; applies previously learned math concepts; shows accuracy on math tasks; recalls and uses math facts.

We can see, then, that a teacher of primary mathematics area needs to make sure students have the opportunity to work independently and apply math concepts. Both these examples show reporting systems that are consistent with teachers' beliefs about teaching and learning.

By reviewing the descriptors for every grade, parents and students can see the big picture and know what level of development is expected next. Figure 9.2 shows the math descriptors for several grade levels.

The staff at Bellingham Schools also share their beliefs about the purpose of reporting systems with parents by making the following statement on their reporting system:

Teachers and parents can never know all that a child knows. A report card is merely a snap-

FIGURE 9.2

BELLINGHAM PUBLIC SCHOOLS MATH DESCRIPTORS

Descriptors for Grades K–2

EXPLORATION: Becoming aware of math concepts; interacts with materials.

EMERGENT: Benefits from monitoring and help in problem solving; is beginning to understand math concepts; needs assistance to produce work.

BEGINNING: Solves problems with assistance; needs assistance learning math concepts; needs support to complete math tasks successfully; beginning to learn and use math facts.

DEVELOPING: Solves problems with occasional assistance; understands math concepts; usually completes math tasks accurately; can recall and use some math facts.

CAPABLE: Solves problems independently; applies previously learned math concepts; shows accuracy on math tasks; recalls and uses math facts.

EXPERIENCED: Uses a variety of strategies to solve problems independently; independently applies previously learned math concepts; demonstrates high accuracy on math tasks; confidently recalls and uses all math facts.

Descriptors for Grades 3–5

EMERGENT: Descriptors supplied by the teacher.

BEGINNING: Can solve problems and complete assignments with support; some understanding of math concepts; requires support to produce accurate work, is learning to use math facts.

DEVELOPING: Completes required assignments; solves problems with assistance; needs assistance learning math concepts; needs support to produce accurate assignments; beginning to use math facts.

CAPABLE: Completes required assignments; solves problems with occasional assistance; understands math concepts; usually accurate on assignments; recalls and uses math facts.

STRONG: Does some enrichment/extra credit math work; solves problems independently; applies previously learned math concepts; shows accuracy on assignments; confidently recalls and uses math facts.

EXCEPTIONAL: Extends self with math enrichment/extra credit work; uses thinking strategies to solve problems independently; independently applies previously learned math concepts; demonstrates high accuracy on assignments; confidently recalls and uses all math facts.

shot—a tiny slice of a child's learning over a given period of time. It is through talking with a child, looking at what a child creates, and watching the child in action that we gain a clearer, more comprehensive understanding of a child's progress.

A Focus on Parent Involvement

Using Parent/Teacher Conferences

Mountainview Elementary School

At Mountainview Elementary School in Morgantown, West Virginia, 1st grade teachers developed a plan for educating parents about a new reporting system that moves away from letter grades and includes a thorough assessment of the student.

The focus of this plan was communication between parents and teachers. Parent/teacher conferences provided an opportunity to fully explain a student's strengths and weaknesses and to take remedial steps where necessary (for instance, a child whose difficulties are detected early may be referred to Chapter One).

Thanks to successful implementation of this plan, parents now accept and understand the new reporting system. In fact, some parents have gone out of their way to make sure that parents who didn't attend the parent briefing session would understand and support the new reporting system. The teachers also made sure there were many opportunities for questions to be answered.

The Mountainview Elementary School plan included the following steps:

August	1st Grade Open House: Present draft of new reporting system and get feedback from parents
September	All-School Open House: New reporting system introduced again
October	Parents Academy: In-depth explanation and response to questions from parents
October	Local School Improvement Council: Present reporting system and answer questions
November	Send home first progress report
November	Conferences
January	Send home progress report Conferences as requested
May	Send home questionnaire about progress report

The teachers report that this process was very successful. It gave parents ample opportunity to ask questions and become familiar with the new reporting system before the first progress reports were sent home. By asking for parent feedback at the end of the school year, the teachers got information to use the next year as they continued to revise the reporting system.

Surveying Parents and Students

Washington Elementary School

When Washington Elementary School in Independence, Kansas, began to design a new reporting system, the staff surveyed parents and students as they worked through various revisions. The following is an excerpt from the survey distributed to parents. We have selected representative questions that deal with a range of issues related to the reporting system.

Washington School Report Card Survey

In keeping with quality performance accreditation, the teachers at Washington School have been working since August on a new student reporting system. The purpose of this report is to provide more information to parents about the progress of their child. This report is being used on a trial basis and we would like to hear your opinion.

Please select the one response from the choices below that best represents your view.

1 = Strongly Agree
2 = Agree
3 = Tend to Agree
4 = Disagree
5 = Strongly Disagree

____ The most important items on a report card deal with student work habits.

____ I believe the new report card requires the student and the teacher to be more responsible for what is learned.

____ The new report card gives me more usable information than the old one.

A simplified version of this survey was given to students. Seventy-four percent of the students and parents returned the surveys, and the results showed that parents and students both were pleased with the new system. The survey confirmed the wisdom of the changes the teachers had made and answered questions about choices in format and focus.

Inviting Parents into the Classroom

The Nipissing Schools

Educators generally agree that communication between parents and teachers is a key element of successful education. The Nipissing Schools in North Bay, Ontario, Canada, are opening up new lines of communication by inviting parents into the classroom. Figure 9.3 shows the invitation that teachers send to parents. Parents first observe the class and then conference with the teacher; in this way, parents' observations become part of the reporting system. During the conference, teachers also ask parents about their child's attitude toward school and discuss the child's growth and development in the school program. This emphasis on eliciting information from parents gives added dimension to the reporting system.

Using a "Reverse Report Card"

McDowell High School

A teacher at McDowell High School in Erie, Pennsylvania, has created a "Reverse Report Card" to evaluate whether students are applying their classroom learning to their own family situations. She looks particularly at interpersonal skills and communication. The two-sided report includes a rubric for communication and interpersonal skills on one side, with descriptions of "exemplary, "competent," and "in progress" behaviors. For example, the area of effective interpersonal skills is described in this way:

- Consistently and actively helps promote effective family interaction in ways that are sensitive to all family members (Exemplary).
- Consistently participates in family interaction, readily expresses self and is sensitive to family members (Competent).
- Rarely participates in family interaction without arguing or demonstrating sensitivity to other family members (In progress).

The report card works in reverse of the usual report card because the teacher asks parents to rate their child, make comments about each subject area, and return the card to the teacher. The report is completed at the beginning and end of the marking period.

Distributing a School Handbook to Parents

Highland Park Elementary School

At Highland Park Elementary School in Grove City, Ohio, parents receive a handbook that

FIGURE 9.3

PARENT CONFERENCE INFORMATION LETTER

Dear Parents,

I should like to invite you to visit the JK/K class on_____________________________at_______________________.

In this class your child continues the learning started with you at home. There are opportunities to find out about the world and all the other people in it. You are welcome to come and join in with the children's activities, to observe what your child does in the program that day and to discuss progress with me. I shall be free to talk to you for a few minutes at the end of the class. Naturally, while the children are there, I shall be working with them.

You may find the attached booklet* useful in thinking about your child at school, or you may have specific ideas you wish to discuss.

Please let me know whether you will be able to attend.

Yours sincerely,

Teacher

- -

(Cut and Return)

____ I shall be able to visit the class on ____.

____ Phone me to make an alternative appointment.

Signed:____

Parent

---

*The booklet referred to includes information about the mission and curriculum of the school.

describes the school schedule and procedures, the curriculum content and objectives, and the assessment and reporting system used in the school. Here is an excerpt from that handbook:

AUTHENTIC ASSESSMENT

Authentic assessment encourages teachers, students, and parents to take a more active role in forming decisions about teaching and learning. One component of authentic assessment is the portfolio; however, at Highland Park, we use a variety of ways to evaluate children's progress including:

- daily work
- effort
- observational notes
- district course of study expectations
- student self-evaluation
- teacher-made tests
- journals
- competency tests
- student records
- standardized tests
- reading logs
- pre-tests and post-tests
- student/teacher conferences

Authentic assessment also includes frequent parent contacts (conferences, phone calls, notes); weekly newsletters focusing on curriculum objectives; collections of student work; progress reports to parents; "open room" nights where parents can visit the classroom in the evening and participate in various activities with their child; and teacher portfolios.

PORTFOLIOS

Portfolios are a systematic, meaningful, and purposeful collection of children's work. They are used to showcase the students' progress, efforts, and achievements over a period of time. Portfolios may be organized in many ways: however, there are some common elements that most portfolios will include:

- lists of books read
- responses to literature through art, reading, and writing
- writing of different types and in different stages of completion
- books the child has authored
- tape-recorded readings from favorite books
- spelling words
- pre-tests and post-tests from unit work
- student self-assessments
- work that shows current learning
- recently mastered work

Portfolios will have work selected by the children, but may also have pieces chosen by the teacher, parents, or the class as a whole.

DISTRIBUTING A DISTRICTWIDE STATEMENT TO PARENTS

■ WETHERSFIELD PUBLIC SCHOOLS

The Wethersfield Public Schools, in Wethersfield, Connecticut, provide a districtwide statement to parents that is similar to the handbook distributed by Highland Park Elementary School. Here is an excerpt:

THOUGHTS ON STUDENT ASSESSMENT AND EVALUATION

The assessment and evaluation of student work by teachers is a critical form of communication. The process provides an opportunity to communicate to students specific and meaningful feedback in as positive and constructive a manner as possible. It also provides the student with a clear understanding of areas mastered or in need of practice, and encouragement and motivation for undertaking new learning challenges.

Student performance is evaluated using a variety of techniques, including numerically rated tests and quizzes; daily individual and group work; participation; and teacher observation.

Ongoing student assessment is accomplished in a variety of ways in order to gain a more comprehensive picture of each student's performance. Ongoing assessment may include narrative descriptions, checklists, logs, rating forms, running records, portfolios, drawings, paper/pencil tests, oral presentations, end-of-unit assessments, or districtwide testing. It is important to note, however, that teachers determine the appropriateness of different assessment strategies by considering the subject area, the material being taught, the level of difficulty, student profiles, and the number and types of student assessments previously completed for specific skills.

It should not be expected that each individual unit or activity will be assessed by all of the strategies mentioned above. The teachers' goal is to collect samples of student work in as many different forms as possible in order to evaluate each student's performance over time and report such observations through the progress report and other communication to parents.

Quakertown Community School District

Quakertown Community School District in Quakertown, Pennsylvania, provides information on learning goals, how children learn, and assessment in a booklet that begins with a message from the child. The purpose of the booklet is to explain the district's elementary education program, which is based on a state framework for language arts. Both the curriculum and progress report are based on this state framework.

Each section of the booklet is written in clear language, for example: "Our goal is to provide the experiences and instruction that will help students to listen and think critically." The booklet addresses each area of the language arts curriculum: reading, writing, extending reading and writing, investigating language, and learning to learn. In each area, curriculum examples are provided, such as "Students will learn the writing process (prewriting, drafting, revising, editing, and publishing)" or "Students will learn to reflect and express themselves as a response to reading." The booklet also describes the elements of the language arts portfolio and how adults can facilitate learning.

Using Three-Way Communication

Beacon Heights Elementary School

At Beacon Heights Elementary School in Edmonton, Canada, parents, students, and teachers use the reporting form shown in Figure 9.4 to avoid misunderstandings and to support the team approach to education, a focus of this reporting system.

A Focus on Narrative Feedback

Using Narrative Feedback Combined with Letter Grades

Potomac High School

At Potomac High School in McLean, Virginia, students receive extensive narrative comments on their progress from their teachers. Teachers never give a letter grade on a progress report without accompanying narrative feedback. The format of letter grade and narrative feedback,

FIGURE 9.4

BEACON HEIGHTS ELEMENTARY SCHOOL REPORTING FORM

FIRST REPORTING PERIOD	SECOND REPORTING PERIOD
Student Comments or Goals ____________________ Student Signature	Student Comments or Goals ____________________ Student Signature
Parent Comments or Goals ____________________ Parent Signature Additional Conference Requested ____Yes ____No	Parent Comments or Goals ____________________ Parent Signature Additional Conference Requested ____Yes ____No
Conference Summary ____________________ Teacher Signature Date	Conference Summary ____________________ Teacher Signature Date

with a focus on individualized comments, is helpful for students who are assessing their own learning and for parents who are looking for insights into their child's developmental progress. Here is an excerpt of narrative feedback for a student in a biology course:

> It is important to [student's name] that he truly understand the concepts we discuss. He is not satisfied by simply being able to give a correct answer. He searches for the relation between data and the theories they support. During laboratory session, he looks for the applications to an experiment. He prefers, I believe, to think about ideas which are new to him for a while before commenting or asking questions. Ultimately, this gives him a deeper understanding of the material.

Pius XI High School

At the Pius XI High School in Milwaukee, Wisconsin, learners and their parents have accepted a narrative report, coupled with grades. Both parents and students are asked to sign and comment on the progress report, which has a separate page for each subject. The focus is on student self-assessment and the development of the individual. Teachers seek input on conceptual understanding, performance, effort, participation, behavior, and attitude. At the end of the year, copies of the reports from each marking period are put together to create a running record for each student.

Teams of teachers at Pius XI High School are working together to design and implement performance assessments that will enhance learning and provide important information relating to student progress for parents, students, and teachers. Performance assessments that include an emphasis on conceptual understanding, effort, and group and indivudual participation are consistent with the goals of the current progress report.

A Focus on Lifelong Learning Skills

A partial focus of a reporting system may be the skills or attitudes that a student is developing. For instance, a progress report drawn from the work of Marzano, Pickering, and McTighe (1993) includes descriptors such as "Is aware of own thinking," "Is sensitive to feedback," "Restrains impulsivity," and "Pushes the limits of own knowledge and ability." Descriptions like these provide added dimensions to our view of the student as a learner. We received several reporting systems that contain similar descriptors.

Building on Student Progress

Garfield Elementary School

At Garfield Elementary School in Milwaukee, Wisconsin, the reporting system changes to build on what students and teachers have learned in the previous year. The assessment model focuses on six abilities. In addition to a coded reporting system for each ability, the student receives detailed narrative feedback related to each content area, as shown in Figure 9.5.

A Focus on Identified Goals, Standards, and Beliefs

In many school districts, it is difficult to get a sense of a district's or school's beliefs by looking only at the reporting system. Most reporting systems are composed of isolated lists of observable behaviors, without detail or an explanation of how these skills fit into the overall learning picture. We have tried to include here some examples of schools that have taken that next step and are trying to report progress based on the goals, stand-

FIGURE 9.5

GARFIELD AVENUE MATH/SCIENCE SCHOOL PROGRESS REPORT

Milwaukee Public Schools
Garfield Avenue School

SAMPLE

REPORT OF STUDENT PROGRESS

Student's Name: ____________________ School Year: ____________________

Teacher: ____________________ Grade: ____________________

Days Absent ____1 ____2 ____3 ____4 Times Tardy ____1 ____2 ____3 ____4

____________________ is reading at the __________ grade level.

Excellent Progress **G**ood Progress **S**ome Progress **N**ot Yet Progressing

Student First Name:	In class				In fine arts		In phys ed	
COGNITIVE ABILITIES	1	2	3	4	2	4	2	4
Sets goals								
Persists in reaching goals								
Makes appropriate choices								
Uses alternatives in problem solving								
Follows the scientific method								
Formulates questions								
Identifies problems								
Exhibits research skills								
Collects and organizes information								
Draws conclusions								
Understands math concepts								
COMMUNICATION SKILLS								
Communicates ideas clearly when speaking								
Expresses ideas clearly in writing								
Listens well								
Reads with fluency								
Reads with understanding								
Uses technology								

ards, and beliefs to which the district has committed itself. As more districts adopt standards, outcomes, or goals for all learners, reporting systems may look very different. Parents, students, and teachers will be confronted with the question of how to report progress on standards that describe what students will know and be able to do across the curriculum and outside the classroom. The purpose of the reporting system will then be to clearly report students' level of learning relative to the identified standards.

The schools in this section have identified standards, outcomes, or goals that inform their reporting systems.

Incorporating the Goals of the Curriculum

Lincoln School

When teachers at Lincoln School in Madison, Wisconsin, began to use the teaching strategies described in *Cognitively Guided Instruction* (CGI) (Peterson, Fennema, and Carpenter 1989), their reporting system reflected the change to parents by including the problem-solving strategies that students were learning to use. According to staff, CGI is more of a philosophy than a recipe. To implement CGI, teachers learn how the knowledge about children's mathematical thinking can help them learn about their own students. They decide how to use that knowledge to make instructional decisions. They recently revised their report system again to better reflect their CGI work (see Figure 9.6). Note that the mathematics section of the report card is more developed than that of other content areas, and the rubric used in the mathematics section reflects developmental rather than judgmental ranking of skills.

Thus, the focus of the reporting system became the goals that were part of the established curriculum. For instance, for the math strategies listed, teachers note whether a strategy has been introduced and whether students are applying the strategy or developing the strategy.

Incorporating Core Objectives, Standards, and Scales of Progress

Washington Elementary School

Washington Elementary School in Independence, Kansas, uses core objectives, standards, and scales of progress as a focus of the system. These elements guide both teaching and the reporting of progress. Here are some examples of objectives in various subjects:

- *Math.* Student solves multistep problems using multiplication and division.
- *Communication.* Student demonstrates an understanding of how language changes and uses a variety of resources to provide information to enhance writing by preparing oral and written summaries.
- *Science.* The student will use these process skills as tools for problem solving: Inferring—making observations and gathering data in order to make an informed tentative explanation for their experimentation.

Teachers rate students on a scale from 1 ("unacceptable") to 5 ("excels"). Detailed lists describe the curriculum and the goals for the students. The rating scale format is easy to read and accessible to both parents and students.

Using a Performance Profile

Caledonia Community School District

In Caledonia, Michigan, teachers use a Performance Profile to describe a student's performance as a Communicator, Scientist, Historian, Writer, Reader, and Mathematician. The content and processes of each area are part of the reporting system. For example, under the category of Historian is listed the following:

- Applies historical events to bridge the gap between the past and present.

FIGURE 9.6

LINCOLN ELEMENTARY SCHOOL
GRADE 5

Student____________________ Teacher ____________________ Principal Muriel Simms Quarter 2 3 4

E= Excellent S = Satisfactory P = Making Progress N = Needs improvement

READING PROGRAM

Materials Used:______________

___ Reads with understanding
___ Is able to write about what is read
___ Completes reading group work accurately and on time
___ Shows interest in reading

Reading Skills

___ Decodes new words
___ Understands new words

Independent Reading Level:

Below At Grade Level Above

LANGUAGE ARTS

___ Uses oral language effectively
___ Listens carefully
___ Masters weekly spelling

Writing skills

___ Understands writing as process
___ Creates a rough draft
___ Makes meaningful revisions
___ Creates edited, legible final draft

Editing skills

___ Capitalizes
___ Punctuates
___ Uses complete sentences
___ Uses paragraphs
___ Demonstrates dictionary skills

Writing skill level:

Below At Grade Level Above

MATHEMATICS

Problem Solving

____Solves teacher-generated problems
____Solves Self/Student-generated problems
____Can create story problems

Interpreting Problems

____Uses appropriate strategies
____Can use more than one strategy
____Can explain strategies in written form
____Can explain strategies orally

Math Concepts

Understands Base Ten

Beginning Developing Sophisticated

Multiplication, Basic facts

Beginning Developing Sophisticated

2 digit Multiplication

Beginning Developing Sophisticated

Division

Beginning Developing Sophisticated

Geometry

Beginning Developing Sophisticated

Overall Math Skill Level:

Beginning Developing Sophisticated

Attitude/Work Skills

____Welcomes a challenge
____Persistence
____Takes advantage of learning from others
____Listens to others
____Participates in discussion

It Figures

Is working on: ______________

Goal: ______________

Is working on achieving goal:________

SOCIAL STUDIES

____Understands subject matter
____Shows curiosity and enthusiasm
____Contributes to class discussions
____Uses map skills
____Demonstrates control of reading skills by interpreting text

Topics covered: individual cultures, Columbus- first English colonies

SCIENCE

____Shows curiosity about scientific subject matter
____Asks good scientific questions
____Shows knowledge of scientific method
____Uses knowledge of scientific method to help set up and run experiment(s)
____Makes good scientific observations
____Has researched scientific topic(s)

Topic(s) ______________

I Wonder

Is currently working on ____________

WORKING SKILLS

____Listens carefully
____Follows directions
____Works neatly and carefully
____Checks work
____Completes work on time
____Uses time wisely
____Works well independently
____Works well in a group
____Takes risks in learning
____Welcomes a challenge

HOMEWORK

____Self-selects homework
____Completes work accurately
____Completes work on time

PRESENTATIONS/PROJECTS

____

HUMAN RELATIONS

____Shows courtesy
____Respects rights of others
____Shows self-control
____Interacts well with peers
____Shows a cooperative and positive attitude in class
____Shows a cooperative attitude when asked to work with other students
____Is willing to help other students
____Works well with other adults (subs, student teacher, parents, etc.)

Attendance

	1st	2nd	3rd	4th
Present				
Absent				
Tardy				

Placement for next year: __________

- Uses and creates graphics, written materials, and other media to communicate information.
- Understands the significance of current events.
- Has an awareness of the geographical relationship of the United States and the world.

A Scientist is one who does the following:

- Demonstrates a working understanding of the scientific processes and sees the relationship in the physical, earth, and life sciences.
- Utilizes hands-on opportunities and predicts outcomes based on prior knowledge to complete quality activities.
- Implements scientific terminology and content.
- Keeps accurate records.

Teachers also report on the student's progress in what has been defined as "life skills." Life skills include areas such as confidence, motivation, caring, teamwork, decision making and problem solving, and personal management. Instead of using traditional letter grades, teachers use the following descriptors: behavior shown consistently, student is working in this area, personal goal, see goals/comments section, or indicates mastery.

The reporting system also includes the school district's mission statement and outcomes. The focus is on the development of lifelong abilities within and across content areas. Taken as a whole, the progress report gives a clear picture of the student as an individual in areas identified as important by the district.

A Focus on Student Self-Assessment and Goal Setting

Effective reporting systems help students assess their own progress and make plans for future learning. While many schools involve students in some level of goal setting as part of the self-assessment process, we have included examples of reporting systems that include a formal goal-setting component. These examples show the purpose of using report cards as a mechanism for student self-assessment.

Clearly, the complexity of goal setting depends on the developmental level of the student. Students may independently set goals, or they may set them with guidance from parents and teachers. An element of self-assessment is found in some reporting systems. The focus on self-assessment may be in addition to goal setting or may be a stand-alone part of a reporting system.

Helping students develop the ability to set their own goals and assess their own performance is an important part of education. The lifelong learner, the student who goes beyond the classroom to explore learning in a variety of settings, needs to be able to set goals and assess his or her own performance. The initial steps toward this goal are taken as early as kindergarten, when children assess their own work and set goals for future learning (Bredekamp and Rosegrant 1992). The process continues through high school, with students becoming increasingly more able to set realistic learning and behavioral goals that will lead to career choices.

Incorporating Simple Forms of Self-Assessment

Self-assessment and goal setting are part of a process that must be reinforced. Some teachers give students specific feedback on the goals set by students, others ask students to copy the goals onto 3 X 5 cards and tape them to their desks or tables and refer to them throughout the next marking period. As students become more aware of their role in the learning process, they are more able to accept responsibility for learning.

Ben Franklin Elementary School

At Ben Franklin Elementary School in Madison, Wisconsin, the teacher structures students' self-assessment. For instance, kindergarten students fill a shape that corresponds with "I'm doing well," "I'm working on this," or "I don't do this yet." As illustrated in Figure 9.7, the items being assessed are those important for kindergarten success, such as "I can make a plan and follow it." Students also set learning goals, as in the section stating, "The thing I most want to learn about is . . . ."

GARFIELD ELEMENTARY SCHOOL

Educators at Garfield Elementary School in Milwaukee, Wisconsin, decided to use the reporting system envelope to record goals set by students. Each marking period, every student is asked to identify at least one goal, state how the goal will be achieved, who can help the student achieve the goal, and how the child will feel when the goal is met. The envelope containing this information is then signed by the parents and student and returned to the school.

PRINCETON SCHOOL

A less structured example of student self-assessment is illustrated by the Princeton School Student Reporting system from Edmonton, Canada. The focus is still on student goal setting. The reporting system includes space for parent comments and student goals for each marking period. Both parents and students sign the reporting system. Students are encouraged to set goals for achievement and performance. The goals are set in discussion with teachers and parents.

WHEELER ELEMENTARY SCHOOL

Reporting systems may contain areas for student comments if teachers encourage self-assessment and goal setting. For instance, Wheeler Elementary School's reporting system provides space for students to comment on their progress and on the teacher's evaluation of their performance. Figure 9.8 shows part of Wheeler's evaluation form.

A FOCUS ON PORTFOLIOS

REINFORCING STUDENT SELF-ASSESSMENT AND GOAL SETTING

Many teachers realize the value of student self-reflection and include students' own review comments in portfolio collections of student work. These formats can be a source of evidence for judgments made on reporting systems or a complement to a reporting system. Along with teacher feedback, student reviews may even serve as the entire reporting system. Volumes have been written in the past several years about portfolios and portfolio review processes (see, e.g., Grace and Shores 1992; Martin 1994; Tierney, Carter, and Desai 1991). We do not wish to review that information in this chapter, but we do want to acknowledge that portfolios are a rich source of evidence of students' developing abilities and increasing understanding of content.

The translation of the portfolio review to a progress report is often hampered by a lack of clear information about the goals of the portfolio pieces and the learning experiences described in the portfolio. Those schools that clearly identify learning goals in ways that are understandable to students and parents are better able to move between a summary of a portfolio and a reporting system. A brief explanation of this process at one elementary school may serve as an illustration.

GARFIELD ELEMENTARY SCHOOL

At Garfield Elementary School in Milwaukee, Wisconsin, teachers have designed learning and assessment experiences that both teach and assess for the identified goals of the curriculum. These goals include communication, citizenship, and cognition. As teachers prepare a learning experience or assessment, they write a paragraph describing the experience and stating which of the goals are taught and reinforced though this experi-

Figure 9.7

FRANKLIN ELEMENTARY SCHOOL KINDERGARTEN SELF-ASSESSMENT

Mark the shape that tells about you:

□ **I'm doing well.** △ **I'm working on this.** ○ **I don't do this yet.**

I can get dressed to go outdoors.	□ △ ○
I stay with my group.	□ △ ○
I follow the bus rules.	□ △ ○
I can cut with scissors.	□ △ ○
I follow directions. "Please walk."	□ △ ○
I help clean up our room.	□ △ ○
Something I do really well is...	
My name is	

I use words to tell how I feel. "I'm mad!"	□ △ ○
I can count to 123	□ △ ○
I listen while others talk.	□ △ ○
I follow our safety rules at school.	□ △ ○
I try to help other children.	□ △ ○
I can make a plan and follow it.	□ △ ○
The thing I most want to learn about is...	
Today is	

Figure 9.8

JEFFERSON COUNTY PUBLIC SCHOOLS
WHEELER ELEMENTARY SCHOOL
PILOT INTERMEDIATE STUDENT EVALUATION

Student:______________________________ School Year: 19____–_____

Principal:______________________________ Homeroom Teacher/Team:____________________

Quarter Report (Circled): 1 2 3 4 Attendance: Present____ Absent____ Tardy____

A narrative summary of your child's development:

Linguistic Development Teacher:____

Oral Communication • Writing • Reading • Research Skills • Participation

Areas of Strength:____

____

Areas of Needed Concentration: ____

____

Interpersonal Development Teacher:____

Recognizes Patterns and Connections with People and Places • Cooperation • Goal Setting • Meets Responsibilities • Participation

Areas of Strength:____

____

Areas of Needed Concentration: ____

____

Parent and Student Comments:

FIGURE 9.8 (*continued*)

Logical-Mathematical Development Teacher:____________________

Problem Solving • Reasoning • Mathematical Communication • Connections of Core Concepts • Participation

Areas of Strength:____________________

Areas of Needed Concentration: ____________________

Scientific-Investigative Development Teacher:____________________

Problem Solving • Reasoning • Scientific Inquiry • Collects Accurate Data • Draws Conclusions • Participation

Areas of Strength:____________________

Areas of Needed Concentration: ____________________

Cultural and Physical Development

Cooperation • Involvement • Meets Responsibilities + = Is actively involved ✓ = More effort needed

Area	Teacher	Evaluation
Computer/Writing Development		
Strategies		
Music		
Physical Education		
Information Skills		
Instrumental Music		

Areas of Strength:____________________

Areas of Needed Concentration: ____________________

JEFFERSON COUNY PUBLIC SCHOOLS

Equal Opportunity/Affirmative Action Employer Offering Equal Educational Opportunities ence. A copy of this information is distributed to each student. As students participate in the experience, the teacher records feedback on this one-page description. These sheets are then put in each student's portfolio. Later, when teachers are preparing progress reports, they refer to the portfolios for evidence about student progress in each area of development. Figure 9.9 contains an example of one of these situations and some of the criteria.

Using Guided Reflection

Guided reflection questions help students focus on particular aspects of work. For example, at Franklin School in Madison, Wisconsin, the kindergarten and 1st grade students are asked to find samples of work that fit the following categories: "How your writing has changed," "Work that was challenging," "Work that you are proud of," "How your drawing has changed" and "Work that you want to do more of." These samples complement other elements of the reporting system where the teacher makes judgments about progress. Another supplement teachers use at this same school asks students to describe something interesting they did in science, to write a math story problem, to make a pattern, to draw a picture of friends and write their names, and to write a story or draw a picture and write some words about it. Doing this each marking period gives teacher, parent, and student a basis for comparison with the previous ability level. It also gives a clear picture of the student's ability in math, science, and writing and supports decisions made by the teacher.

Although including examples of student work in reporting systems may be cumbersome, it is very helpful as parents strive to know what their children are doing in school. Educators who want to educate parents about the richness of the curriculum can include student work to improve that understanding. Conferences with parents are a good time to review portfolio samples because the student or teacher can explain the process used to create the work and discuss the meaning of the sample. Clear criteria for each assignment allow students to be specific in their self-assessment and to identify areas of strength and areas that need further development. Conferences focusing on portfolio items can give teachers, students, and parents a clearer understanding of learning goals and the kinds of work needed to meet those goals.

Seeking Change Through Portfolios

Mount Laurel School District

The Mount Laurel School District in Mount Laurel, New Jersey, is in the process of revising its assessment program and its reporting system. As is so often the case in the change process, the staff at Mount Laurel are finding that their work will never be done: Assessments and reporting systems are fluid entities that grow and change as the adults who manage them grow and change.

The current reporting system is a traditional grade-based system coupled with student portfolios that include items from four categories: products, processes, scores, and tests. Figure 9.10 shows the list of suggested portfolio items that is provided on the back of the portfolio checklist.

A list of important objectives for students is being continually developed to augment the more general reporting system. This list is available to students and parents and contains such items as "Uses prewriting strategies," "Participates in familiar and new situations," and "Identifies characteristics of specific cultures." These objectives are grouped in the larger categories of Communications, Numeracy, Personal and Social Growth, Work Skill, and Cultures and Environments. For each objective, the teacher notes if evidence of this area has been observed or assessed and is avail-

FIGURE 9.9

GARFIELD ELEMENTARY SCHOOL—MILWAUKEE, WISCONSIN ABILITIES-BASED ASSESSMENT

Brief description of the activity

The students were asked: "My neighbor has a peculiar orchard. He has five apple trees, five pear trees, five peach trees, five apricot trees, and five plum trees. The trees are planted in a square. There are five rows with five trees in each row. Each row has one tree of each kind of fruit tree and so do the center diagonals. How are the trees planted?" Each child was given a bag of manipulatives (gram cubes, colored blocks, Unifix cubes, or snap cubes), work space, and told that they could use their pencil or crayons. They were given the definition of a diagonal and reminded to keep in mind the problem-solving strategies they have used to solve the problems (Beyer 1993).

Abilities measured and criteria identified

The criteria and anecdotal identified below are associated with the following abilities listed on the report card: Cognitive Abilities (Makes appropriate choices, Uses alternatives, Draws conclusions, Understands math concepts), Communication Abilities (Communicates ideas clearly in writing, Expresses ideas clearly when speaking)

Not Understanding	Developing	Understanding/Applying
Cannot explain answer or explanation makes no sense	Recognizes that answer is incorrect or unreasonable but doesn't know how to correct it	Is able to use more than one strategy
Does not name strategy used	Can name strategy but poor explanation	Explains strategy and answers logically and coherently

Anecdotal (written by teacher): ______________________________

____

____

____

____

FIGURE 9.10

SUGGESTED PORTFOLIO ITEMS

Products	**Processes**
Self-Portrait Name Sample Writing Samples Reading Log Student Interview Special Projects Journal Sample Interest Inventory Audio/Video Tapes	Student Self-Evaluations Anecdotal Records Parent Conference Notes Student Conference Notes Parent Surveys
Scores	**Tests**
Read-Retell Scores Holistically Scored Writing Samples Analytically Scored Writing Samples Selected Worksheets Class Assignments Homework Assignments	Standardized Test Results Chapter Tests Unit Tests Pre- and Post-Tests

Source: Mount Laurel School District, Mount Laurel, New Jersey. Adapted by permission.

able. An area for notes or comments allows the teacher to expand on any specific area.

WHEN AND HOW TO USE REPORTING SYSTEMS

Traditionally, reporting systems are sent home with students or mailed to parents. The timing often coincides with parent-teacher-student conferences. Some schools have found it more useful to distribute reporting systems at conferences, thus giving all concerned an opportunity to discuss the strengths and areas that need further attention. Conference distribution, of course, assumes that students will be active participants in conferences, describing their experiences as learners and providing evidence for comments or grades.

Reporting systems should be considered a means of communication rather than a hidden weapon to be held over students as a threat. Thus, it is important that the reports be distributed in a way that encourages students to participate in conversations about their performance and to be involved in goal setting (remember that young children need goals that will allow them to quickly see progress during a specific marking period).

Quarterly distribution of progress reports seems to be the norm, with districtwide dates determined on the basis of the school calendar. When teachers and students are involved in ongoing review of progress, the timing of the distribution of a progress report is not as critical. Portfolio review, for example, is an ongoing process through which students and teachers make judgments about progress, even without a formal progress report.

Current practices generally link parent-teacher-student conferences with at least one progress report. If the progress report serves as a vehicle for communication, with the portfolio as evidence of progress, it is very logical to combine the two. Similarly, if the student is involved in self-assessment, it is helpful for the student to actively participate in the conference, perhaps even leading the discussion as he or she gives examples of learning from the previous marking period. There may be some instances in which conferences should include only the parent and the teacher, such as when a sensitive decision will be made about a young child and there is a need to discuss the issue privately before involving the child.

Teachers involved in narrative reporting systems offer some suggestions for the time crunch that often prohibits the use of this type of reporting system. Examples from Edmonton, Canada, illustrate the effective use of technology in streamlining narrative reporting. Another suggestion from teachers is simply to not send all reporting systems on the same day, but instead to distribute them over a period of three to four weeks. Teachers then have time to carefully give meaningful feedback. Since the goal of the reporting system is individual development, it isn't important that all reports be sent home before an arbitrary cut-off date.

Although some reporting systems may refer to videotaped samples of students' work, we didn't receive any examples of reporting systems that were dictated on either audiotape or videotape; such systems would be an exciting development, especially for parents who are not literate. Nor did we receive any reporting systems contained solely on computer discs, although many teachers do write their narrative comments on the computer and then send home the printout.

Transitions Between Old and New Systems

In the samples we received, the consistency between stated goals and what appeared on the progress report varied. Many schools include aspects of development and education in goal statements without reporting on student progress in those same areas. We found no examples of reporting systems that explicitly referred to current national standards, such as those developed by the National Council of Teachers of Mathematics. We did find examples of schools that have matched their reporting systems to either their own standards and benchmarks or to district standards and benchmarks. We also noted reporting systems that displayed great consistency between the reporting system and the stated goals for students. For instance, Grand Avenue Middle School in Milwaukee, Wisconsin, which draws its teaching philosophy from Howard Gardner's work in multiple intelligences, has built its reporting system on the same beliefs that guide the teaching and learning experiences (Gardner 1993a, 1993b). Thus, the reporting system includes statements describing how students are performing in each intelligence.

Two Examples of Processes for Revising a Reporting System

Grand Avenue Middle School

The Grand Avenue Middle School in Milwaukee, Wisconsin, provided us samples of several versions of their reporting system, illustrating the changes made after feedback from students, parents, and teachers. A public school established in 1991, Grand Avenue had the opportunity to start fresh and design a reporting system that fit their beliefs about learning and reporting student progress.

A group of teachers met throughout the summer before the opening of the school to design the new reporting system. The school was already committed to basing its curriculum on Howard Gardner's theories of multiple intelligences, and the teachers wanted the reporting system to reflect this philosophy. They were consistent in their belief that assessment drives both curriculum and reporting systems. The first reporting system, eight pages in length, included four pages of lists describing each of the multiple intelligences. Students were rated as "developing" or "strong" in each area. The remaining pages had space for narrative comments about art, music, and physical education; community involvement; extracurricular activities; student comments; parent comments; and advisor comments. To illustrate, the reporting system described Gardner's concept of logical/mathematical intelligence as follows:

This is the ability to understand logical or numerical patterns and to make decisions and problem solve.

- Uses numbers with understanding
  - The relationship between numbers
  - The process signs
- Performs arithmetic operations
  - In written form
  - Mentally
- Understands the principals of measurement
  - Reads graphs and tables
- Is able to problem solve
  - Is proficient with calculators
- Is computer literate
  - Is able to gather data accurately
- Develops a hypothesis
  - Experiments with multiple strategies
- Draws conclusions
  - Demonstrates the connections between global and local issues

Each of these areas was marked "developing" or "strong." The reporting system had a great deal of information, but the teachers quickly agreed that they had tried to include too much in one document. Parents and teachers were both dissatisfied. The assessment committee, which had been in place from the opening of the school, reviewed the reporting system and began the process of developing rubrics for each content area.

By the beginning of the school's second year, the teachers had learned how to complete the reporting systems on the computer, saving much time. The focus shifted from creating a reporting system to creating an assessment system. The system that evolved was one to which every teacher could add information at a different time, eliminating the need for all the teachers who worked with a student to meet together to complete the reporting system. A six-stage rubric was developed for each content area, and a descriptor for the stage that best described the student's performance was also included in the report. For example, a student may have met the criteria for a level 4 in Science Concepts and a level 3 in Science Problem Solving. In addition to the numbers that represent the rubric score, the reporting system would include the descriptors from the rubrics at the identified level. For example, the progress report of a student identified as performing at level 4 of Problem Solving would include a description of problem solving at that level. The reporting system also included a brief statement describing the major topics of study for that marking period. Here, for example, is a topic statement for Language Arts: "Stereotypes in television, fairy tales and novels, racism and sexism in film, African novels, fables, and proverbs."

This second version of the reporting system was more manageable, but it lost the element of student self-assessment and the focus on multiple intelligences.

Year three saw a change to trimester reporting systems, half of which focused on personal skills such as effort, output, and quality and half of which focused on learning and understanding concepts. Self-assessment was reinstituted and suggestions for improvement were added.

Although the third reporting system was much more streamlined, teachers and parents were concerned about the elimination of the focus on multiple intelligences. The reporting system used in the fourth year included a report on the intelligences that were areas of strength for a student, a summary of the major areas of study in a given trimester, and an evaluation in content areas based on the rewritten rubrics. The assessment committee met during the summer to rewrite the rubrics, making the focus positive—that is, rewriting statements such as "Does not predict events" to "Needs help to draw conclusions."

The committee members also designed rubrics for an area they called Foundational Skills and Competencies. Foundational skills, based upon qualities identified by the Secretary's Commission on Achieving Necessary Skills (SCANS 1991) as required skills for effective workers, are a combination of subject skills, thinking skills, and problem-solving skills. Competencies, also drawn from the SCANS report, represent the student's ability to effectively use resources, organize information, work with others, understand work systems, and use technology to get work done.

Self-assessment took the form of a letter to students' parents or guardians. The letter included academic and personal goals.

The assessment committee continues to play a critical role in the review of the reporting system. They periodically update the rest of the staff and use feedback from parents, students, and teachers to keep the reporting system valid and relevant. The commitment to a philosophy has proven to be a guide for all of the changes the reporting system has seen. The lack of letter or number grades has not been an issue. At first, teachers offered to convert the progress information to a grade-point average for 8th graders who were thought to need "grades" for high school. Teachers haven't received even one request,despite the fact that the students go to a variety of high schools when they leave Grand Avenue Middle School.

Garfield Math/Science Elementary School

The staff at Garfield Math/Science Elementary School in Milwaukee, Wisconsin, recognized the need for a new report card. They had been learning and practicing the instruction of reading through whole language and the instruction of science through a process of "search, solve, create, and share." They had also been focusing on integrating the curriculum and making it more multicultural. Yet the reporting system still used letter grades applied to discrete content areas to describe students' performance.

Over the summer of 1991, they decided to meet informally in small groups and design a new reporting system. By the middle of the first meeting, they realized that they needed to design a new assessment system, from which would come a new progress report.

To accomplish this task, they knew they needed a broader knowledge base and so formed an action research team. They also visited schools that had been identified as knowing how to work with authentic assessment, and they consulted with Alverno College, nationally recognized as an expert in abilities-based assessment. From these experienced sources, the school staff learned that their efforts would be successful only if the entire school community reached agreement on their beliefs about assessment. For example, they decided they believed that all learners have multiple abilities that are demonstrated in multiple ways and need to be assessed in multiple ways. That decision results in an assessment and reporting system quite different from one built on the belief that children should demonstrate knowledge in only one way.

This design process was hard work. People talked about their heads hurting from thinking so hard. But no one wanted to stop and return to the much easier method of grading. As adult learners, staff members were having fun learning how to do something better. They now acknowledge that they didn't know all the tasks that needed to be done ahead of time. Rather, they defined the essential tasks as the work progressed. Each teacher had a different understanding of ability-based assessment, and each attached different personal meaning to the process and terms being used. Although some teachers were afraid they would not understand the system well enough to be able to explain it to parents, and others were nervous about learning the computer skills needed to make the system work efficiently, collegiality and trust carried everyone through.

During the following year, Garfield put an abilities-based assessment model into practice. The staff paid close attention to educating parents and students about the recommended model and to discussing their concerns. They appreciated the magnitude of the paradigm shift and the need to remain flexible in incorporating recommendations from many stakeholders. Two 5th grade students, who had produced a video depicting the new reporting system, which eliminated letter grades, told their teachers, "I want you to check off what is right or wrong. I don't want you to tell me about my progress. I want an *A* so I can stop working. How will my mother pay me for *A*'s, when there won't be any?" This is an example of the many difficulties that had to be worked through in the process of adopting the new system. The first of many modified reporting systems was used during the first marking period.

The reaction from parents and students was positive. Everyone was allowed thinking space to talk about and understand the changes they were going through. By the third marking period, teachers were saying that they would never go back to the old way of doing things. Parents were saying that they had never received such a comprehensive picture of their children, and they, too, did not want to return to letter grades.

The staff at Garfield continue to educate parents and to learn more themselves. They also continue to modify their reporting system based on their latest thinking.

Concluding Thoughts

We have learned a great deal from reviewing the many progress reports sent to us. What stands out most clearly is that the process of developing an effective reporting system is never complete. The better you get at reporting, the better the assessments you use, the better your instruction becomes, the more you need to update your reporting system to reflect the changes in instruction, and on and on. The impetus to change a reporting system occurs primarily when the discrepancy between what is being reported and what is being taught becomes so great that the tension causes people to redesign their reporting system. Constructive changes in reporting systems signal that the school truly is a learning organization.

REFERENCES

Beyer, A., ed. (1993). *Alternative Assessment.* Ann Arbor, Mich.: Dale Seymour Publications.

Bredekamp, S., ed. (1987). *Developmentally Appropriate Practice in Early Childhood Programs Serving Children from Birth Through Age 8.* Washington, D.C. : National Association for the Education of Young Children.

Bredekamp, S., and T. Rosegrant, eds. (1992). *Reaching Potentials: Appropriate Curriculum and Assessment for Young Children.* Washington, D.C.: National Association for the Education of Young Children.

Gardner, H. (1993a). *Frames of Mind: The Theory of Multiple Intelligences.* 2nd ed. New York: Basic Books.

Gardner, H. (1993b). *Multiple Intelligences: The Theory in Practice.* New York: Basic Books.

Grace, C., and E. Shores. (1992). *The Portfolio and Its Uses: Developmentally Appropriate Assessment of Young Children.* Little Rock, Ark.: Southern Association of Children Under Six.

Martin, S. (1994). *Take a Look: Observation and Portfolio Assessment in Early Childhood.* Don Mills, Ontario: Addison-Wesley.

Marzano, R. , D. Pickering, and J. McTighe. (1993). *Assessing Student Outcomes: Performance Assessment Using the Dimensions of Learning Model.* Alexandria, Va.: ASCD.

Peterson, P., E. Fennema, and T. Carpenter. (January 1989). "Using Knowledge of How Students Think About Mathematics." *Educational Leadership* 46, 4: 42–46.

Tierney, R., M. Carter, and L. Desai. (1991). *Portfolio Assessment in the Reading-Writing Classroom.* Norwood, Mass.: Christopher-Gordon.

ADDRESSES OF SCHOOLS CITED

Beacon Heights Elementary School
Edmonton Public School Board, District #7
Center of Education
1 Kingsway Avenue
Edmonton, Alberta, Canada T5H4G9
Bellingham Public Schools
Bellingham School District
P.O. Box 878
Bellingham, WA 98227

Ben Franklin Elementary School
Madison Metropolitan School District
545 West Dayton Street
Madison, WI 53703

Caledonia Community School District
203 Main Street
Caledonia, MI 49316

Garfield Math/Science Elementary School
2215 North Fourth Street
Milwaukee, WI 53212-3199

Grand Avenue Middle School
2430 West Wisconsin Avenue
Milwaukee, WI 53233-1828

Highland Park Elementary School
Southwestern City School District
2975 Kingston Avenue
Grove City, OH 43123

Lakeland School District
1086 Main Street
Shrub Oak, NY 10588

Lincoln School
Madison Metropolitan School District
545 West Dayton Street
Madison, WI 53703

MacDowell Montessori School
Milwaukee Public Schools
P.O. Box 2181
Milwaukee, WI 53201-2181

McDowell High School
Millcreek Township School District
P.O. Box E
Mill Creek, PA 17060

Mount Laurel School District
330 Morristown-Mt. Laurel Road
Mount Laurel, NJ 08054

Mountainview Elementary School

Monongalia County School District
13 South High Street
Morgantown, WV 26505-7546

The Nipissing Schools
Nipissing Board of Education
P.O. Box 3110
North Bay, Ontario, Canada P1B8H1

Pius XI High School
Milwaukee County School District
P.O. Box 2181
Milwaukee, WI 53201-2181

Potomac High School
Prince William County School District
16706 Jefferson Davis Highway
Dumfries, VA 22026

Princeton School
Edmonton Public School Board
District #7, Center of Education
1 Kingsway Avenue
Edmonton, Alberta, Canada T5H4G9

Quakertown Community School District
600 Park Avenue
Quakertown, PA 18951-1588

Starms Early Childhood Center
Milwaukee Public Schools
P.O. Box 2181
Milwaukee, WI 53201-2181

Washington Elementary School
Independence School District
300 East Myrtle
Independence, KA 67301-3796

Wethersfield Public Schools
Wethersfield School District
51 Willow Street
Wethersfield, CT 06109-2798

Wheeler Elementary School
Jefferson County School District
5410 Cynthia Drive
Fern Creek, KY 40291

10

Reporting Achievement at the Secondary Level: What and How

JANE BAILEY AND JAY MCTIGHE

In his 1993 book *Renewing America's Schools*, Carl Glickman devotes a chapter to "Dealing with Tough Questions of Practice." In this chapter, he says, "There are profound questions about current educational practices that need to be openly debated" (p. 94). One of the "tough questions" raised by Glickman concerns prevalent grading practices. He says, "Grades come from a tradition of weighing and ranking students according to supposedly objective psychometric scales." He goes on to say that grading is just one of the conventions in schools that has become a "sacred cow. . . . A school that is considering how best to develop an educational environment consistent with its principles of learning needs to probe and scrutinize its current practices." Then, Glickman asks, "Do grades really reflect what students have learned and should be learning and what will be most helpful?" (p 95).

With this question in mind, we began to look at this sacred cow: grading and reporting practices in today's secondary schools. Other authors have discussed the history of grading and press us to think about why we need better grading and reporting systems (Guskey 1994) or *why* we need grades at all (Kohn 1994). It is not our intent here to answer why. Rather, we address the question of *how* grading and reporting systems in secondary schools are changing to more accurately reflect student achievement. We also examine different types of grading and reporting systems designed to communicate to various audiences. In this chapter, we present examples collected from secondary schools across North America that illustrate how some schools are attempting to improve their grad-

We are grateful to many schools and districts for sharing their systems of reporting student achievement. These schools, located in Alaska, Florida, Michigan, and Canada, are listed in the section "Participating Schools and Districts."

ing and reporting systems to better communicate student learning.

Grading and Reporting: What and How

Any communication system consists of four components: *content (what* is being communicated), *process* or method *(how* it is being communicated), *purpose (why* it is being communicated), and *audience (for whom* it is being communicated). Educators have used grades and reports for many purposes (e.g., to provide performance incentives for students, to identify students for special programs and academic honors, and to evaluate teachers and educational programs). In this chapter, however, we focus on the primary purpose of secondary level grades and reports—to communicate student achievement to students, parents, school administrators, postsecondary institutions, and employers.

Before looking at the examples, let's consider the options for a grading and reporting system. Figure 10.1 shows a framework for examining these grading and reporting options.

Secondary schools have typically graded and reported student achievement in terms of content knowledge in subject areas. Content achievement may be reported as a single grade for a course (e.g., Algebra 1, World History) or in terms of more specific content standards (e.g., understanding mathematical concepts, problems-solving strategies).

Figure 10.1

REPORTING STUDENT LEARNING: A FRAMEWORK OF OPTIONS

What?	For Whom?	How?
❍ content knowledge ❍ life/workplace skills	❍ students ❍ parents	❑ letter grades ❑ numerical scores/percentages
❑ achievement ❑ progress ❑ other factors (e.g., effort)	❍ teachers ❍ policy makers/boards of education ❍ post secondary institutions	❑ checklists ❑ rating scales ❑ written narrative reports
❍ norm-referenced ❍ standards/criterion referenced	❍ employers ❍ general public ❍ other:________	❑ work samples/portfolios ❑ oral reports/conferences ☆ teacher led ☆ student led

In addition to grading and reporting on content knowledge, some schools and districts are including a broader set of "workplace" or "life" skills. Such inclusion reflects attention to the recommendations of national reports, such as the SCANS (1991) report, *What Work Requires of Schools,* and attempts to strengthen the "school-to-work" transition by emphasizing more generalized competencies (e.g., communication, teamwork) and habits of mind (persistence, attention to quality) that transcend particular subject areas (see Marzano, Pickering, and McTighe 1993). For example, Academy High School in Fort Myers, Florida, has developed a "Work Ethic Checklist" for use in conjunction with a senior portfolio as part of an internship program (see Figure 10.2). The checklist assesses workplace skills deemed important in both school and the workplace.

Regardless of whether they concentrate on content knowledge or include workplace or life skills, teachers and schools need to consider exactly what their grades and reports intend to communicate.

Other authors in this yearbook (Guskey, Chapter 3, and Wiggins, Chapter 11) point out that grades often reflect a combination of achievement, progress, and other factors (e.g., effort, behavior, completing assignments on time). Though most secondary schools currently report using a single, holistic grade or number for subject area courses, experts express concern that this tendency to collapse several independent elements into a single grade may blur its meaning (Stiggins 1994, Wiggins 1994). As an alternative to the "single grade" approach, some schools have elected to disaggregate their reports to communicate their valued elements of learning more specifically. Wiggins provides examples in his chapter in this yearbook.

In addition to the content (the *what*) of grading and reporting, schools and districts have options regarding *how* they will communicate results. For example, grades and reports may be norm or standards/criterion referenced. In a *norm-referenced* system, a teacher determines a student's grades by comparing that student's performance with a norm group, typically the other members of a class. Norm-referenced grading and reporting are common practices in secondary schools, occurring when teachers "grade on the curve." Nevertheless, experts (Guskey 1994, Stiggins 1994, Wiggins 1994) caution against this approach because it pits students against one another rather than reflecting what a student has or has not learned.

In contrast, a *standards* or *criterion-referenced* approach calls for evaluating a student's performance according to established criteria or performance standards. Thus, criterion-referenced grading and reporting is more likely to effectively communicate a student's actual achievement.

Reporting Methods

A variety of reporting methods are available to secondary schools seeking to improve their communication about student learning. These methods include letter grades, numerical scores, developmental or proficiency scales, checklists, written narrative reports, portfolios, and verbal reports or conferences. In keeping with this chapter's focus on *how,* we briefly examine each reporting method and its benefits and limitations. We then show which of these methods, or combination of methods, was chosen by secondary schools wishing to improve their reporting systems.

Letter Grades

Letter grades on report cards constitute the most widely used method for reporting student learning in secondary schools. Letter grades are generally issued for subject area courses and presented on a five-point scale: *A* = excellent, *B* = good, *C* = fair, *D* = poor, *E* = failure. Some schools

Figure 10.2

WORK ETHIC CHECKLIST ACADEMY HIGH SCHOOL INTERNSHIP PREPARATION PROGRAM

Certain behaviors are representative of an extremely powerful and successful system of personal conduct which has come to be known as the American work ethic. It is the express intention of Academy High School's program to insure that all of its graduates demonstrate these behaviors because these behaviors lead directly to success in all areas of life.

This checklist is used to determine the degree to which a student has demonstrated the work ethics as described in the Work Ethic Standards. Successful demonstration over time of all of these standards is required before a student may be assigned to an internship program.

Student Name	Month		
Work Ethic Description	A Exceeds standards	B Meets standards	WP Below standards
1. Dresses and grooms in a manner which satisfies the school dress code			
2. Dresses and grooms in a manner which promotes a positive image of the student and school			
3. Comes to school on time each day, except for unavoidable personal emergencies and serious illness			
4. Notifies their advisor of an impending absence or tardy well in advance of the actual absence or tardy and arranges to minimize the impact this has on the school			
5. Makes personal appointments during off-hours only			
6. Is present and at work during all school hours			
7. Communicates in a positive, cheerful, and enthusiastic manner			
8. Accepts criticism and suggestions in a positive manner			
9. Seeks to constantly say and do things which improve the school and the school climate			
10. Focuses solely on school work during school hours so that personal situations never interfere with academic success			

FIGURE 10.2 (*continued*)

Student Name	Month		
Work Ethic Description	A Exceeds standards	B Meets standards	WP Below standards
11. Demonstrates socially-accepted patterns of courtesy and formality at all times, especially in the form of basic manners such as using words like "please," "thank you," and "you're welcome"			
12. Addresses adults with formal courtesy titles			
13. Makes decisions authorized to make and refers other decisions to the appropriate people			
14. Makes decisions in the best interests of the school			
15. Makes decisions based on facts, when such evidence is available			
16. Makes decisions quickly after due time is given to fact-finding and consideration of the alternatives			
17. Abides by decisions which have already been made			
18. Accepts responsibility for decisions			
19. Seeks harmony and success for groups in which they work			
20. Makes sure that everyone in their group expresses their opinion and listens carefully to the opinions of others			
21. When necessary, disagrees and debates with others in a professional respectful manner and always uses positive methods of persuasion			
22. Finds new opportunities for self-improvement			
23. Continuously learns new skills			
24. Displays the very highest standards of honesty, truthfulness, lawfulness, and decency			
25. Reports problems at once rather than concealing them			
26. Accepts responsibility for personal actions			
27. Fulfills obligations, contracts, and promises			
28. Uses facilities, equipment, and supplies belonging to the school for their intended purpose			

(Continued on the next page)

FIGURE 10.2 (*continued*)

Student Name	Month		
Work Ethic Description	A Exceeds standards	B Meets standards	WP Below standards
29. Accepts failure and disappointment as learning experiences and moves ahead with new plans and new solutions			
30. Seeks to solve difficult, long-term problems regardless of the number of previous failures			
31. Uses creativity to solve problems			
32. Works through the school's official hierarchy in search of solutions			
33. Uses evidence, research, expert opinions, and advisor instructions to solve problems			
34. Avoids solutions which simply cause different problem			
35. Strives for excellence in every task from the most mundane to the most important			
36. Completes all work on time, within budget, and with high quality			
37. Integrates the essential habits of the mind into school work			

Notes:
4. Unexpected absences or tardies should be avoided. Students who are absent or tardy without prior arrangement must telephone the Senior Portfolio Institute prior to 9:00 a.m. on the day of the absence or tardy.
6. Students should not sign out early without urgent need.
24. Referrals for any disciplinary infraction constitute a serious infraction of this work ethic. Students on contracts will not be provided with internships until the contracts are satisfied.

Comments ____________________

____

____

____

and districts have attempted to standardize the grading process by equating letter grades with numerical scores; for example, *A* = 99–93, *B* = 92–86, *C* = 85–78, *D* = 77–70, *E* = below 70.

Grades may be weighted to account for the additional challenges of specialized programs or honors courses. A variation on the typical five-point grading scale, the *A–B–I* model, has been tried in certain schools following a mastery learning approach. In such places, students are expected to reach an identified mastery level (*B*); otherwise, their learning is considered incomplete (*I*), and they must continue until the designated level is achieved.

Perhaps the most obvious benefit of using letter grades for reporting student achievement is that this system is familiar to nearly every person who has attended school. Thus, communication with students, parents, college admissions officers, and others would seemingly be easier for classroom teachers. In addition, classroom teachers comfortable with this system have developed streamlined recordkeeping systems to simplify the process of grade calculation and to justify the end results. Some schools are making effective use of computer technology to enable students to check their progress at any time. Finally, this type of system lends itself to student-to-student comparisons; in other words, students and their parents feel they are able to gauge their own progress against that of others in a class or grade using this simplified "yardstick."

Despite the time-honored tradition of using letter grades to report student learning, teachers, students, parents, and others have recognized limitations with this ubiquitous approach:

- The tendency to collapse several independent elements (achievement, progress, effort, behavior, attitude, completing assignments on time, etc.) into a single letter grade;
- The lack of specific and uniform performance standards; and
- A concern about reliable application of grading standards by different teachers within and across schools.

Numerical Scores

Like letter grades, numerical scores and percentages are commonly used for grading and reporting student achievement. The numbers allow for straightforward and defensible grade calculations. They may be readily converted to letter grades and lend an aura of objectivity to student evaluation. Moreover, numerical grading and reporting facilitate the selection of students for special programs and awards, such as class valedictorian.

Numerical scores and percentages are well suited to computing the results of tests and quizzes having single, correct answers; but these scores may be less appropriate for reporting on certain performance areas. For instance, the extent of understanding of scientific principles, effectiveness in writing and public speaking, or degree of physical fitness are less amenable to such precise quantifications.

Rating Scales

Developmental and proficiency rating scales contain descriptions of different levels of performance or degrees of proficiency. Such scales are generally more informative than numerical scores and grades because they tie student achievement or progress to specific performance criteria or developmental stages.

A scoring *rubric* is one type of proficiency scale being used with increasing frequency as a result of the expanded use of performance-based assessment methods. A scoring rubric consists of a fixed measurement scale (e.g., four or six points) and a set of criteria that describe the characteristics for each score point. Some schools are using scoring rubrics to both evaluate and report student learning. Information about student learning presented in terms of developmental or proficiency levels can be especially meaningful to parents. With this understanding, some schools and districts have revised their report cards, especially for the primary grades, to incorporate developmental and proficiency scales. In Chugach School District in Anchorage, Alaska, a student performance report contains evaluation of both academic and workplace skills (see Figure 10.3). This district's report makes use of a rubric and accompanying proficiency scale to evaluate work-related performance.

Rubrics are most effectively used for evaluation and communication purposes when they are accompanied by examples of responses for each of the score points. These examples, sometimes known as anchors, provide tangible illustrations of the criteria listed for the various points on the scale. These anchors not only assist teachers in more reliably applying the criteria when judging student work, they increase the clarity of communication to students, parents, and others. In Figure 10.3 (second page), for example, the rubric representing "Excellent" for the category "Learning Behavior" states: "Self-engages in classroom tasks." Other rubrics describe "Good," "Poor," and "Unacceptable" learning behaviors, citizenship, cooperation, and other work-related areas.

Despite their benefits, rubrics are time consuming to develop and to learn to apply reliably. Parents, students, and, sometimes, teachers may question whether the criteria in the rubrics are being applied consistently within and across schools. In addition, parents, colleges, and employers interested in comparing, sorting, or selecting students may become frustrated with this criterion-referenced approach to grading and reporting.

Checklists

Checklists consist of categories listing specific elements or traits and rating options for each category. The ratings may be as simple as "yes" or "no" to indicate the presence or absence of each trait, or presented as a scale, such as "never," "rarely," or "frequently." Checklists are easy-to-use, efficient tools for evaluation and communication, allowing teachers/schools to identify and report on specific aspects of knowledge and proficiency (see Figure 10.2.)

Though simple to use, checklists usually do not provide the detailed, explicit criteria found in scoring rubrics. Checklist developers, therefore, must be careful to avoid poorly defined or overly broad categories, such as "creativity," which are open to diverse interpretations.

The Chugach School District uses checklists of many kinds in its "Career and Vocational Kit," leading to its "Warranty of Employability" for seniors. For example, students must exhibit mastery of skills in problem solving; personal/social development; listening, speaking, reading, and writing; and work-related performance. Checklists of these skills, including criteria to be met and date mastered, are shown in Figure 10.4. The district's kit includes detailed checklists like this in many areas of work-related competencies, such as developing and using a resume, understanding and preparing income taxes, practicing with job applications and college applications, and community service. When students satisfactorily complete the kit, they receive the "Warranty," which guarantees them either an interview or a job with one of the district's business partners.

Narrative Reports (Written)

Written comments and narrative reports can be effective communication methods because they enable teachers to clearly and directly connect student effort and performance to elements of quality and standards of performance. They also allow for more individualized feedback than do other communication methods. Regrettably, the time-consuming nature of these methods often limits their

FIGURE 10.3

SUMMARY OF STUDENT PERFORMANCE
CHUGACH SCHOOL DISTRICT
STUDENT SKILLS

Student Name ______________________ Graduation Date ______________________

Entrance Date ______________________ Completion Date ______________________

Program Completion Requirements

The Chugach School District Performance Warranty requires the following:

Problem Solving & Personal/Social Development: The student must complete two tasks or projects per area.
Reading: The student must master critical reading skills as demonstrated in the Chugach School District Language Arts Curriculum Guides or is referred for remediation.
Listening and Speaking Skills: The student must master speech outcomes as demonstrated in the Chugach School District Language Arts Curriculum Guides.
Writing Skills: The student must master writing outcomes as demonstrated in the Chugach School District Language Arts Curriculum Guides.
Work Related Performance: The student must demonstrate a trend of improved performance or attain "good to excellent" ratings throughout.
Competencies: The student must successfully complete all five competencies.
Career Development: The student must complete all six areas.
Upon successful completion of the program requirements the student is awarded a "Warranty of Employability" along with his or her **High School Diploma.**

Program Requirement	Required	Completed
Problem Solving	2	
Personal/Social Development	2	
Reading Skills	Mastery	
Listening and Speaking Skills	Mastery	
Writing Skills	Mastery	
Work Related Performance	***	
Attendance Record	Good - Excellent	
Punctuality	Good - Excellent	
Completion of Work	Good - Excellent	
Paying Attention	Good - Excellent	
Following Directions	Good - Excellent	
Competencies	5	
Career Development	***	
Job Application	Yes	
Resume	Yes	
Career Exploration Event	Yes	
Vocational Interest Inventory	Yes	
Transition Plan	Yes	
Work Experience	Yes	

This certificate constitutes the official statement of student accomplishments for the Chugach School District Performance Warranty Program.

____
Program Administrator

(Continued on the next page)

FIGURE 10.3 (*continued*)

SEMESTER PROGRESS REPORT—WORK RELATED PERFORMANCE
CHUGACH SCHOOL DISTRICT

Student Name ______________________ Date ______________________

Key to Terms

	Excellent 4	Good 3	Poor 2	Unacceptable 1
Attendance	Perfect Attendance	Seldom Misses, Always Excused	Occasionally Absent	Misses Often, Affects Work
Punctuality	Never Tardy	One Tardy	Several Tardies	Habitually Tardy
Preparedness	Always Brings Materials and Work	Consistently Brings Materials and Work	Occasionally Lacks Materials and Work	Habitually Lacks Materials and Work
Learning Behavior	Self-Engages in Classroom Tasks	Needs Support to Become Engaged	Will Not Stay Engaged	Disrupts Other Engaged Learners
Citizenship	Respects the Rights of Others	Has to Be Reminded of Classroom Rules	Needs Teacher Guidance	Disregards the Rights of Others
Cooperation	Contributes Well in Group Processing	Participates in Group after Encouragement	Does Not Participate in Group Activities	Disrupts Others in Group Activity
Work Closure	Never Misses Work or Tests	Immediately Makes up Work or Tests	Makes up Work or Tests with Reminders	Has Little Interest in Task Completion

Student Evaluation

	Grade 9		Grade 10		Grade 11		Grade 12	
	Qtr. 1	Qtr. 2	Qtr. 1	Qtr. 2	Qtr. 1	Qtr. 2	Qtr. 1	Qtr. 2
Attendance	4 3 2 1	4 3 2 1	4 3 2 1	4 3 2 1	4 3 2 1	4 3 2 1	4 3 2 1	4 3 2 1
Punctuality	4 3 2 1	4 3 2 1	4 3 2 1	4 3 2 1	4 3 2 1	4 3 2 1	4 3 2 1	4 3 2 1
Preparedness	4 3 2 1	4 3 2 1	4 3 2 1	4 3 2 1	4 3 2 1	4 3 2 1	4 3 2 1	4 3 2 1
Learning Behavior	4 3 2 1	4 3 2 1	4 3 2 1	4 3 2 1	4 3 2 1	4 3 2 1	4 3 2 1	4 3 2 1
Citizenship	4 3 2 1	4 3 2 1	4 3 2 1	4 3 2 1	4 3 2 1	4 3 2 1	4 3 2 1	4 3 2 1
Cooperation	4 3 2 1	4 3 2 1	4 3 2 1	4 3 2 1	4 3 2 1	4 3 2 1	4 3 2 1	4 3 2 1
Work Closure	4 3 2 1	4 3 2 1	4 3 2 1	4 3 2 1	4 3 2 1	4 3 2 1	4 3 2 1	4 3 2 1

Annual Teacher Comments

Grade 9 ____

Grade 10 ____

Grade 11 ____

Grade 12 ____

FIGURE 10.4

STUDENT SKILLS SUMMARY
CHUGACH SCHOOL DISTRICT
STUDENT SKILLS

Student Name ______________________ Date ______________________

The student is required to demonstrate successful completion of each area to the satisfaction of the school principal. Documentation of service organization, church, or special training activities may be used to satisfy requirements.

Skill Area/Content Description	Task or Project Title and Teacher Verification
Problem Solving Skills: The student must complete two projects or tasks. Each one must be in a different subject area. The student will apply a critical thinking process by identifying a problem or issue, gathering and sorting information related to the issue, interpreting the information, developing alternative solutions and choosing a course of action, evaluating the results, and if necessary choosing an alternative course of action.	**Title of Project #1:** ______ Verified by: ______ **Title of Project #2:** ______ Verified by: ______
Personal/Social Development: The student must complete two projects or tasks. Each one must be in a different subject area. Projects or tasks will include experiences that increase the ability to understand self, demonstrate self-direction and responsibility, and initiate and mainstream effective interpersonal relationships.	**Title of Project #1:** ______ Verified by: ______ **Title of Project #2:** ______ Verified by: ______
Listening and Speaking Skills: The student must successfully master listening and speaking outcomes as indicated in the Chugach School District Curriculum Guides.	**Date Mastery Accomplished:** ______ Verified by: ______
Reading Skills: Students must successfully master the ability to read for information as appropriate in the workplace.	**Date Mastery Accomplished:** ______ Verified by: ______
Writing Skills: The student must successfully master writing outcomes as demonstrated in the Chugach School District Curriculum Guides.	**Date Mastery Accomplished:** ______ Verified by: ______
Work-Related Performance: The student must perform satisfactorily in all five of the personal characteristics required with a rating of at least Good in all five characteristics.	**Date All Five Characteristics Mastered:** ______ Verified by: ______

use, especially for teachers at the secondary level because of the greater student-to-teacher ratio. Technology offers some promise in this regard. For example, Edmonton (Alberta) Public Schools, a large Canadian district, uses computer-generated report card "templates" and a large database of teacher comments to enable teachers to efficiently generate "personalized" reports detailing student achievement and progress in courses (see Figure 10.5). To further personalize their reports, Edmonton secondary schools include scanned photographs of each of the students and their teachers. The first page of the report includes a photo of the student and information about him, as well as information about the school. The next page (or pages) includes photos of his teachers; their comments on his achievements; and cumulative marks, attendance reports, and "effort" ratings. The last page of the Edmonton report (not shown) presents a written student self-assessment. On this page, the student, in consultation with his teacher-advisor, writes about his accomplishments, goals, and action plans. There is a place for parents to signify their support.

Portfolios

Assessment expert Rick Stiggins offers one definition of a portfolio: "a purposeful collection of student work that tells the story of a student's efforts, progress or achievement in a given area" (Stiggins 1992). Portfolios can present a more thorough and accurate view of a student's progress than a single letter grade, teacher narrative, or numerical score because they offer a multidimensional view of a student. Sandra Murphy and Mary Ann Smith state, "The benefits of portfolios lie as much in the discussions they generate among teachers—and between teachers and students—as in the wealth of information they provide" (Murphy and Smith 1990, p. 26). Bena Kallick points out that "a portfolio is initially a *collection,* which over time is reduced to a *selection,* which then becomes a *reflection* of the learner. The power is in the reflective process" (Kallick 1993). These experts agree that one of the greatest benefits of portfolios is student ownership and involvement in the portfolio process.

Of the secondary reporting systems discussed here, perhaps no other has as much power as portfolios to foster student participation and responsibility, as well as to communicate what and how well students are learning, by presenting actual samples of work as evidence of achievement. Since portfolios contain work systematically collected over time, this method is particularly effective for documenting progress. Academy High School has designed an assessment report for its core portfolio program. Figure 10.6 shows an example of a completed portfolio report; Figure 10.7 shows an example of portfolio standards—in this case, a portfolio showing a student's preparation for careers. The high school provides portfolio standards in the following areas:

1. Careers
2. Communications
3. Diversity
4. Human Relations
5. Information
6. Mathematics
7. Resources
8. Systems
9. Technology
10. Thinking

At Academy High School, students must provide at least 85 percent of the items in all 10 portfolios to advance to "senior" status.

Portfolios can fit into the existing grading system used by a school district even as they offer a richer, fuller description of student achievement than a letter grade or numerical score. Teacher Mark Carter notes:

FIGURE 10.5

PERSONAL EXCELLENCE REPORT, 1992–93

W.P. Wagner School

6310 Wagner Road, Edmonton, Alberta T6E 4N5 FAX 466-6748 Telephone 469-1315

Student: MANDER MAH
Address:
Phone:

E.P.S. Number: 11988526 (920248)
Teacher Advisor: Mrs. J. Miskew
Principal: Mr R. McPhee
Date of Report: February 12, 1993

Communicating Student Growth

Edmonton Public Schools are committed to maintaining close contact between the home and the school. To this end, it is our hope that this report will present parents with an accurate interpretation of your child's progress and development.

Should more detailed information on school programs or student progress be desired, I sincerely urge you to make personal contact with your child's teacher or teachers at your earliest opportunity.

MICHAEL A. STREMBITSKY
Superintendent of Schools

W. P. Wagner School is committed to teaching students to be members of society, able to meet the challenges of a changing future. Personal excellence reports will communicate student success in relation to the curriculum. Each student and his or her parents can then establish a plan that will enable the student to achieve personal excellence.

W. P. Wagner Mission Statement

Upon graduation each of our students will:

- **have achieved personal excellence through broad and challenging opportunities**
- **have the abilities, attitudes, and opportunities to continue pursuing excellence and learning in a variety of settings throughout life**
- **accept rights and responsibilities for themselves and others within society and the global environment**
- **have the creative and critical abilities to deal with a changing future**
- **be able to use leisure time successfully**
- **have the ability to form ongoing and meaningful personal relationships**

Note: Mander Mah has graciously permitted us to use his report here.

(Continued on the next page)

FIGURE 10.5 (*continued*)

ALL MARKS REPORTED ARE CUMULATIVE

1100-5/03
ENGLISH 10

Picture to be shown here

Ms. T. Dobson

In English 10, the class has just completed a unit on poetry which focused on developing an appreciation and understanding of this literary form. Students continue to use exploratory writing to respond to literature read in class. Mander failed to complete two assignments worth 25% collectively this term. This has significantly affected his overall mark. Mander can improve his performance by insuring assignments are completed and handed in on time.

Mark to Date:	70
Previous Mark:	80
Effort:	
excellent	
satisfactory	✓
needs improvement	
Final Mark:	•••
Credits Earned:	••
Periods Absent Since Beginning Of Course:	4
Periods Late Since Beginning Of Course:	6

1150-5/02
SOCIAL 10

Picture to be shown here

Mrs. V. Fuchshuber

In Social Studies, Mander has been studying Canadian identity by focusing on regionalism and its associated factors such as geography, climate, provincial governments, traditions, and economics. There have been eight regional assignments given and Mander did an excellent job on all of these! He works very well in group settings and shows a commitment and dedication to doing well in Social Studies. He is a terrific student ot have in class! Keep up the fine work, Mander!

Mark to Date:	86
Previous Mark:	81
Effort:	
excellent	✓
satisfactory	
needs improvement	
Final Mark:	•••
Credits Earned:	••
Periods Absent Since Beginning Of Course:	6
Periods Late Since Beginning Of Course:	7

1200-5/10
MATH 10

Picture to be shown here

Mr. R. Evans

This term Mander has studied the basic skills of algebra. In particular, he has studied units on the operations of polynomials, equation solving and factoring polynomials. Class time is used wisely. He organizes work effectively. He aims for excellence. Keep up the good work Mander!

Mark to Date:	90
Previous Mark:	•••
Effort:	
excellent	✓
satisfactory	
needs improvement	
Final Mark:	•••
Credits Earned:	••
Periods Absent Since Beginning Of Course:	None
Periods Late Since Beginning Of Course:	None

ALL MARKS REPORTED ARE CUMULATIVE

1270-5/02 SCIENCE 10 Picture to be shown here Mr. G. Berge	Mander is currently working on the Science 10 Unit "Matter and Energy in Living Systems" reviewing cells as the basic unit of life: covering cell function, growth, comparing single and multi-cellular organisms, differentiation and cell transportation. Mander has completed THREE of FIVE MAJOR PROJECTS this year. Completing current event assignments will improve mark. Mander is showing greater initiative this term.	**Mark to Date:**	70
		Previous Mark:	80
		Effort:	
		excellent	
		satisfactory	✓
		needs improvement	
		Final Mark:	•••
		Credits Earned:	••
		Periods Absent Since Beginning Of Course:	8
		Periods Late Since Beginning Of Course:	1
1345-5/01 SPANISH 10 Picture to be shown here Mr. D. Barrales	In our Spanish class we have been studying basic concepts of grammar and syntax. We have continued working on building a basic vocabulary to be used for meaningful oral and written expression. We have researched and discussed some cultural traits of various Spanish speaking countries. Mander has had the opportunity to participate in a variety of activities designed to enhance his appreciation and ability to communicate in Spanish. He makes a positive contribution to the class. Mander is always willing to participate and help his peers in class. Caramba, hombre, que bien!	**Mark to Date:**	81
		Previous Mark:	91
		Effort:	
		excellent	✓
		satisfactory	
		needs improvement	
		Final Mark:	•••
		Credits Earned:	••
		Periods Absent Since Beginning Of Course:	3
		Periods Late Since Beginning Of Course:	2
1400-5/02 ART 10 Picture to be shown here Mrs. K. Hula-Hetu	In Art 10, Mander developed techniques in watercolor and acrylic painting. He applied knowledge of color theory and painting techniques in several compositions. We also had a guest artist visit us. Next term's projects will include stretching a canvas and creating a composition in acrylics. Mander is improving in the area of acrylic color blending and should concentrate on brush technique and careful attention to assignment requirements and problem solving. Mander is a talented artist and is enjoyable to have in class.	**Mark to Date:**	85
		Previous Mark:	90
		Effort:	
		excellent	✓
		satisfactory	
		needs improvement	
		Final Mark:	•••
		Credits Earned:	••
		Periods Absent Since Beginning Of Course:	6
		Periods Late Since Beginning Of Course:	None

(Continued on the next page.)

FIGURE 10.5 (*continued*)

ALL MARKS REPORTED ARE CUMULATIVE

<table>
<tr><td rowspan="10">1527-3/04
INTR. TECH 10A

Picture to be shown here

Mr. D. McDonald</td><td rowspan="10">This term Mander has been working with the Microsoft Word, word processor. He has been working with documents in columns, importing pictures, and using bullets and numbering systems, and developing charts. He extends learning beyond expectations. He demonstrates responsibility in completing assignments.</td><td>Mark to Date:</td><td>96</td></tr>
<tr><td>Previous Mark:</td><td>95</td></tr>
<tr><td>Effort:</td><td></td></tr>
<tr><td>excellent</td><td></td></tr>
<tr><td>satisfactory</td><td>✓</td></tr>
<tr><td>needs improvement</td><td></td></tr>
<tr><td>Final Mark:</td><td>•••</td></tr>
<tr><td>Credits Earned:</td><td>••</td></tr>
<tr><td>Periods Absent Since Beginning Of Course:</td><td>7</td></tr>
<tr><td>Periods Late Since Beginning Of Course:</td><td>None</td></tr>
<tr><td rowspan="10">1611-5/04
FOOD STUDY 10

Picture to be shown here

Mrs. J. Miskew</td><td rowspan="10">The topics studied this term include grains and grain products, including yeastbreads, past, and cake decorating. Mander has completed *1* of the *3* assignments given this term. With regular attendance, Mander's performance will improve.</td><td>Mark to Date:</td><td>70</td></tr>
<tr><td>Previous Mark:</td><td>90</td></tr>
<tr><td>Effort:</td><td></td></tr>
<tr><td>excellent</td><td>✓</td></tr>
<tr><td>satisfactory</td><td></td></tr>
<tr><td>needs improvement</td><td></td></tr>
<tr><td>Final Mark:</td><td>•••</td></tr>
<tr><td>Credits Earned:</td><td>••</td></tr>
<tr><td>Periods Absent Since Beginning Of Course:</td><td>14</td></tr>
<tr><td>Periods Late Since Beginning Of Course:</td><td>2</td></tr>
</table>

TEACHER ADVISOR COMMENTS

Advisor Signature: ____________________________

FIGURE 10.6

ACADEMY HIGH SCHOOL CORE PORTFOLIO ASSESSMENT REPORT

Student Name: Jane Doe
Advisor Name: Horace Smith
Assessment Date: October 17, 1994

Total Artifacts	Standard I	Standard II	Standard III	Standard IV	Standard V	Standard VI	Standard VII	Standard VIII	Standard IX	Standard X
Total Artifacts Presented	14	30	20	25	12	12	12	31	2	13
Total Artifacts Required	15	42	24	27	15	42	12	31	31	15
Percentage Completed	93%	71%	83%	93%	80%	29%	100%	100%	6%	87%
	Careers	Communications	Human Diversity	Human Relations	Information	Mathematics	Resources	Systems	Technology	Thinking

Advisor's Recommendations and Comments:

Jane has been working hard this quarter to qualify for the Senior Portfolio Institute and she has made considerable progress since our last assessment. She has completed her Core Portfolio requirements for Standards I, IV, VII, VIII, and X. She should now concentrate on those standards below the 85% mark. In particular, Jane should try to focus on mathematics and technology during the next quarter. Jane's communication artifacts show excellent growth—she should soon complete this area of study. Good work, Jane.

Student's Recommendations and Comments:

I don't have too many items in mathematics or technology because I was in the Language Arts/Social Studies division this quarter. My goal is to complete either the mathematics or the technology standard before our next assessment. I really worked hard in my communications standard, and I'm not sure why I still don't have enough artifacts. I plan to do more of my work this time (I know I said that last time, but this time I really mean it!)

> If a school district uses *A, B, C, D,* they can use the same kind of criteria to grade portfolios if they need to do that. At the same time what we've seen happen, probably with all the teachers that we've worked with is, as they work with portfolios, they see the value in a more descriptive form of assessment (Tierney, Carter, and Desai 1991, p. 15).

Portfolios present special challenges to secondary teachers working within a typical setting with responsibility for 120 to 150 students. Find-

FIGURE 10.7

PORTFOLIO STANDARD 1: CAREERS

Academy High School students will prepare for careers of their own choosing.

While performing individual or group tasks, Academy High School students will:

1.01 Demonstrate awareness of a variety of career options;

1.02 Demonstrate awareness of the changing qualifications necessary for a variety of career options;

1.03 Maintain an accurate personal resume;

1.04 Demonstrate skills and knowledge necessary to accurately complete a variety of application forms for jobs, schools, colleges, and universities;

1.05 Demonstrate effective interviewing skills,

1.06 Demonstrate mastery of essential career skills, including:
  a. verification of mastery by CTBS;
  b. verification of mastery by HSCT.

ing the time for dialogue with individual students—one of the most important parts of maintaining a quality portfolio—is a challenge. In addition, teachers must find time with colleagues to discuss and agree on the portfolio's purpose and use, especially if a portfolio is to be used across different grade levels and subject areas. As mentioned with other reporting methods, the portfolio can effectively show the student's growth as an individual, but it doesn't satisfy a parent's or student's need to see achievement compared to that of other students.

CONFERENCES

Traditional parent-teacher conferences are common ways of reporting student progress. The benefits of a face-to-face conference include the opportunity to establish rapport and begin a relationship with parents. The conference format also is useful for conveying information that is confidential or difficult to capture through other reporting methods. Yet, teachers often see conference and report card time as added scheduling and paperwork burdens in an already demanding teaching job (Little and Allan 1989). Thus, some educators are using a different type of conference, the *student-led* conference. Students take responsibility for directly reporting their own progress to parents through the use of a portfolio. The teacher then becomes a facilitator. One goal of the student-led conference is to encourage students to take responsibility for their own learning (Little and Allan 1989, Strom 1989). In addition, students learn new skills in preparing for the conference (self-evaluating, interviewing, and role playing), and they can feel a sense of pride and achievement in what they have accomplished. Students have reported feeling very proud of their accomplishments, while parents often respond with comments similar to this one:

> I didn't really know what my son was doing in school. I knew he was taking the required set of classes, but I had no idea how much he was learning in certain areas. I also didn't know that my son would ever be able to explain his work to me like he did. It was a wonderful experience for both of us!

As with other innovations, student-led conferences have limitations—and the most important is time, particularly at the secondary level. Teachers working in a traditional secondary school schedule have difficulty scheduling conferences for individual students. To overcome this challenge, teachers have used homeroom or advisor/advisee periods (if available) as the main vehicle for scheduling conferences. Teachers are then responsible only for helping students in the homeroom or advisor period to prepare a portfolio or other materials for the conference, to role-play, and to complete forms. Students are provided with a checklist to ensure that work from all subject areas or classes is included in the portfolio. Homeroom teachers or advisors then schedule and facilitate student-led conferences for 20 to 35 students. Typically, conferences are held with four families at a time in a room for approximately one-half hour per time slot. This same structure could be used in schools without a homeroom by scheduling conferences for all students in one required subject area, such as "all 9th grade English classes."

Another concern with student-led conferences expressed by teachers and parents is the need for private time between the teacher and parents to discuss confidential concerns without the student being present. Many teachers who have implemented student-led conferences have also offered parents an additional scheduled appointment on request. This assures parents that teachers are always available to discuss concerns or problems. Teachers using a system of student-led conferences often recommend that the fall (or first) conference be "parent-to-teacher," with student-led conferences scheduled for later in the school year when more work samples have been collected and after teachers have met separately with parents. Overall, teachers, students, and parents with whom we work report that the benefits of student-led conferences far outweigh the limitations.

Teachers in a Charlevoix-Emmet Intermediate School District training project in northern Michigan developed several letters and forms that they believe were helpful in organizing a system of student-led conferences. Figure 10.8 shows a sample letter to parents, setting up student-led conferences in the Public Schools of Petoskey, Michigan; Figure 10.9 provides a checklist or outline for students to use in preparing for the conference. Note that the checklist contains items to be included in the student's portfolio—from subject-matter areas such as reading, math, and science, as well as problem-solving, behavior, and teamwork skills.

* * *

We have found no single "best method for reporting student learning." The most effective communication system *(how)* is determined by the content *(what* is being communicated), purpose(s) *(why* it is being communicated), and audiences *(for whom* it is being communicated). Practical considerations, such as the time required for preparation and student/teacher ratios, will influence the nature and breadth of the reporting system. Nonetheless, as illustrated by the examples provided in this chapter, secondary schools will likely use a combination of methods to improve their communication with students, parents, post-secondary institutions, and employers.

FIGURE 10.8

SAMPLE LETTER TO PARENTS

Public Schools of Petoskey
1130 Howard Street
Petoskey, Michigan 49770
(616) 348-0150
FAX (616) 348-0165

March 1995

Dear Parent/Parents,

I want to try a new format for conferences with parents this spring that I believe will have much more meaning for students. I also believe that this new format will give you as parents much more information on what your child has learned this year.

The new format is called Student-Led Conferences. This means that your child will be leading a conference with you to show you the work that I feel best represents what your child has learned and what growth your child has made over this school year. I will meet with each student and his/her parents for a short time. Most of the conference, however, will be a time for you to see many examples of your child's accomplishments. Please do not bring siblings.

The format is this: at each scheduled time, four students and their parents will be in the room for conferences. You will sit in a private space with your child to see his/her work. I will be available to talk with you to answer questions and to help explain your child's progress. The rest of the time will be yours. At the end of the scheduled time, a new group of students and parents will enter the room.

I believe that this will be a time for your child to share work that he/she is most proud of, and it is a time for you to ask some questions of your child about school. To help you as a parent prepare for this conference, on the back of this letter I have included suggested questions you might want to ask your son or daughter. I hope that you will see this as an opportunity to learn more about our classroom and about your child's progress. Please note that report cards will not be sent home until Thursday, April 13th.

If you have any questions or concerns, please feel free to call me. After conferences are complete. I will be asking for your opinion about the whole experience. I want to make this a great experience for everyone involved.

Thanks for your help! I'll see you soon!

Sincerely,

- -

Child's Name ______________________ Conference Date ______________________

Parent's Signature ______________________ Conference Time ______________________

FIGURE 10.9

STUDENT-LED CONFERENCE ORGANIZER

Procedures/Things to Do Before Conference:

1. Make invitation with time and date of conference.
2. Organize portfolio.
3. Practice introductions.
4. Role-play to practice for conference.
5. Set up room.

Procedures/Things to Do at Conference:

1. Find portfolio.
2. Go to designated spot.
3. Review all parts of portfolio with parents.
4. When teacher arrives, introduce teacher to parents.
5. Ask parents to write a comment.
6. Ask parents to sign guest book. (Do they want another appointment with the teacher?)
7. Return portfolio.
8. Remind parents to fill out evaluation in hallway.

____

Student Signature

____

Parent Signature

____

Portfolio Checklist

Portfolio Subjects to Review:

- ❑ Reading
- ❑ Writing
- ❑ Math
- ❑ P.E.
- ❑ Science
- ❑ Social Studies
- ❑ Cooperative Work or Team Work
- ❑ Behavioral Checklist
- ❑ Problem Solving
- ❑ Special Projects
- ❑ Other

These are the things I think I do well:

Would you please write a comment after you have seen my work?

Participating Schools and Districts

Academy High School
at New Directions Center
3650 Michigan Ave.
Fort Myers, FL 33916-2202
Phone: (813) 334-3416; Fax: (813) 332-7772

Charlevoix-Emmet Intermediate School District
08568 Mercer Boulevard
P.O. Box 318
Charlevoix, MI 49720-0318
Phone: (616) 547-9947; Fax: (616) 547-5621

Chugach School District
165 E. 56th Ave., Suite D
Anchorage, AK 99518
Phone: (907) 561-3666; Fax: (907) 561-8659

Edmonton Public Schools
One Kingsway
Edmonton, Alberta T5H 4G9
Phone: (403) 425-3195

Public Schools of Petoskey
1130 Howard Street
Petoskey, MI 49770
Phone: (616) 348-0150; Fax: (616) 348-0165

W.P. Wagner School
6310 Wagner Rd.
Edmonton, Alberta T6E 4N5
Phone: (403) 469-1315; Fax: (403) 466-6748

References

Glickman, C. (1993). *Renewing America's Schools.* San Francisco: Jossey-Bass.

Guskey, T. (1994). "Making the Grade: What Benefits Students?" *Educational Leadership* 52, 2: 14–20.

Kallick, B. (1993). "Portfolio Assessment." *The Video Journal of Education* [video], Vol. 3, No. 4. (Salt Lake City, UT: Linton Productions).

Kohn, A. (1994). "Grading: The Issue Is Not How But Why." *Educational Leadership* 52, 2: 38–41.

Little, A.W., and J. Allan. (1989). "Student-Led Parent-Teacher Conferences." *Elementary School Guidance and Counseling* 23: 210–218.

Marzano, R., D. Pickering, and J. McTighe. (1993). *Assessing Outcomes: Performance Assessment Using Dimensions of Learning.* Alexandria, VA: Association for Supervision and Curriculum Development.

Murphy, S., and M.A. Smith. (1990). "Talking About Portfolios." *Quarterly of the National Writing Project and the Center for the Study of Writing* 12: 1–3, 24–27.

Secretary's Commission on Achieving Necessary Skills (SCANS). (1991). *What Work Requires of Schools.* Washington, D.C.: U.S. Department of Labor.

Stiggins, R. (1992). *Classroom Assessment Video Training Program: Using Portfolios in Assessment and Instruction* [video]. Portland, Ore.: Northwest Regional Educational Laboratory.

Stiggins, R. (1994). *Student-Centered Classroom Assessment.* New York: Macmillan.

Strom, R. (1989). "Expectations for Learning in the Future." *The Journal of Creative Behavior* 23, 2: 121–135.

Tierney, R., M. Carter, and L. Desai. (1991). *Portfolio Assessment in the Reading-Writing Classroom.* Norwood, MA: Christopher-Gordon Publishers, Inc.

Wiggins, G. (1994). "Toward Better Report Cards." *Educational Leadership* 52, 2: 28–37.

11

Honesty and Fairness: Toward Better Grading and Reporting

GRANT WIGGINS

I have heard the following story, in various forms, many times over the past decade.[1] A faculty rethinks its report card, trying to provide more helpful information to students and parents alike, while playing down the more harmful aspects of grades based on crude comparisons of students only. They develop a more narrative-based reporting system, one that costs them many more hours but that seems well worth the effort. Yet, at the first parent conference, parents invariably ask, "OK, but how is she doing?"

The question reveals that reports must do more than highlight the positive or unique accomplishments of a student if they are to have meaning. In fact, this vignette has three vital implications for report card reform:

1. Clients typically require a frame of reference to make sense of individual results.
2. Judgments require data to make them meaningful to readers.
3. The client for the information is almost always more astute about what should be reported than is the purveyor of the information.

Revising report cards is thus not merely a matter of solving a graphics-design problem. To improve our reports, we must start anew by asking the "writing process" questions used by teachers to guide student writers: Who is the audience and what is the purpose of the writing? *The clients are the audience, and the aim is to inform them about student performance.* This answer seems straightforward enough. Yet many well-intentioned faculties keep inventing reporting systems based more on their own interests than those of their various cli-

[1] This essay is a greatly revised version of an article that appeared in *Educational Leadership* (Wiggins 1994).

ents (students, parents, school boards, and receiving institutions or teachers). Report card redesign follows from a more careful study of client needs for information. To honor the clients' needs, I believe reports should be more thorough, honest and fair about all aspects of student performance so that we not only know how the child is doing but we can verify it.

Toward More Context in Reporting

An isolated narrative can never tell us whether laudatory or critical language in the report represents *absolute, relative,* or *idiosyncratic* achievement. Maybe *all* students "work hard" and "do well on multivariable math problems," as Susan's narrative says of her; who knows other than the teacher? Maybe what is "good" performance in Susan's class is mediocre in the school as a whole and poor in the region. Maybe the teacher is setting different standards for each student. How would we know without some information about the performance context?

Comparisons provide one such frame of reference, as the parent comment shows. Joe is successful only 3 times out of 10 at his performance tasks: That certainly seems like a poor achievement. But not if Joe is a Major-League outfielder batting .300: Historical norms reveal he is a far better hitter than most of his peers. Yet, in Little League, the .300 performance is often only average. Context matters; expectations change over time and as the student performs at higher levels. A reporter trying to provide more honest and fair information would not shy away from helpful data comparisons and more meaningful reports for gauging progress.

But when are comparisons helpful and when are they harmful? Merely comparing performers can be misleading at best and hurtfully unfair at worst. To give a single low grade to a recently mainstreamed student simply because her recent performance was not as good as that of her classmates; to give a *B* to a student who happens merely to be the most experienced student in an otherwise novice-filled class; to give *A*'s to our best students even though they are performing in the 20th percentile on nationally normed tests; or to grade on a curve in the most demanding schools, and thus give *C*'s to students who would get *A*'s if judged on their level of achievement—all such decisions are unfair and misleading. Honesty requires that we report apt comparative data. Fairness demands that we factor in apt extenuating circumstances when giving grades.

Comparisons best serve the performer and school clients if what is also compared is performance against *standards*, not merely norms. Standard-referenced information is what clients most want: How is the student doing—in absolute terms, against credible tasks and standards? Just what did the student actually do or not do, and how do those achievements relate to exit standards? How do school evaluations relate to meaningful real-world performance benchmarks? Without a frame of reference whereby educators employ credible standards in their assessments, local reports won't be very helpful. Over time what matters is whether Johnny can make discernible progress toward authentic standards, irrespective of the grades teachers are most comfortable giving.

But a *single* score, like a single grade, is inadequate feedback. A more helpful report would disaggregate complex performance into its many separate elements: Susan is thorough and accurate at laboratory work, though weak on tests; she is very conscientious and accurate in her homework problems. Jamie's labwork is spotty but indicative of understanding; he does extremely well on tests; and his homework, when done, is excellent—but it isn't always turned in on time, and careless mistakes are made in it. Why merely give them both the same *B*? What have we hidden from the performer and the clients of schools in so reporting?

Providing more data, however, does not necessarily mean more information, however. Data that are not made intelligible to laypersons are as unhelpful as being told that a pitcher had an ERA of 3.78, a strike-out–to-walk ratio of two-to-one, and 24 saves when one is not a baseball fan. We need to do a better job of making clients understand grades and scores. Beyond comparative data, clients need evidence that *justifies* grades, scores, and comments. Substantiation of all reports would make grades not merely meaningful but valid to the report reader, not just the writer. We should therefore supply clients with a set of background materials, including such artifacts as anchor papers/performance samples, rubrics, and teacher commentaries on the sample products. Personalized narratives are not enough.

Criteria and Guidelines for Report Card Reform

These introductory ideas suggest a set of criteria for building better student performance reports. Greater thoroughness and disinterested data are required in our reports. Our reports need to be more honest, so that we answer the question: *What were the student's achievements, irrespective of capacity, effort, and attitude?* But they should also be more fair and helpful (as our narrative writers wished to be), so that we also ask and answer: *Were reasonable expectations set and met for each child?*

Current reports err on one side or the other. They either are typically based on glib and unfair comparisons, or the grades and comments sugarcoat bad news. Comparing students to each other in crude terms tells us little about what the student can do. Yet, even for students who are scoring very low in absolute terms, it is in their (and their parents') interest to know how low, and whether such low scores are worrisome. Such knowledge is the only hope all parties have of helping students meet worthy standards, helping teachers avoid inappropriately low or capricious expectations, and of ensuring that student performance is judged wisely by the public—even as we also note, in fairness, any personal gains made.

Based on the criteria of honesty and fairness, I offer five complementary approaches to better reporting:

1. *Many more "subscores" of performance reported in summarizing performance data.* "Math" or "reading" is not one unitary performance but many (just as baseball hitting is runs, hits, average, home runs, walks, etc.) The performance report should be organized in categories that highlight the many key curricular goals and performance aspects used to analyze complex performance (such as identified in the National Council of Teachers of Mathematics (NCTM 1989) *Standards* in mathematics and the American Association for the Advancement of Science (AAAS 1993) "Project 2061" *Benchmarks* in science).

2. *An explicit distinction between achievement data and expectation-based evaluation, symbolized as scores and grades. Scores* would refer to performance measured against valid performance standards. *Grades* would refer to the judgments made by teachers about the performance, measured against "expectations."

3. *Expectation-referenced grades of two kinds exist and would be reported:* expectations of the student measured against benchmarks for their "cohort" (age group, class, developmental level, experience level), and expectations measured against the teacher's judgment of each individual's expected growth versus actual growth. The former kind of grade would be deemed "normed," and the latter kind would be termed "individual growth." Both would be reported, irrespective of

what symbol system we might choose for the reports—even including when our reports are narratives, woven into the discussion of results.

4. *A reporting system that analyzes student academic achievements in three kinds of data:* level of achievement, quality of work, and progress against standards. *Achievement levels* refer to exit-level standards of performance sophistication. *Work quality* refers to the caliber of the products produced, at any level (thus allowing us to make the kind of apt distinction made in diving, figure skating, and music competition: degree of difficulty vs. quality points). Progress is measured backwards from exit standards. *Progress* would thus be charted along multiyear continuums, so that a 3rd grader would know how she was doing against 5th grade and (sometimes) 12th grade standards, just as we find in performance areas like chess, diving, and band. Judgments would be made, based on these longitudinal data, about whether a student was on course to meet exit-level standards.

5. *An evaluation of the student's intellectual character—habits of mind and work—based on performance and products.* The report would highlight teacher judgments concerning the dispositions that are essential to higher-level work success and routinely found on college reference forms and personnel records (such as persistence, ability to work independently and with others, attention to detail, open-mindedness, etc.).

As these ideas suggest, our reports will only be as insightful, honest, and fair as the quality of local assessment. Yet, too often assessment systems are not built on credible standards and authentic measures. Faculties typically rely too greatly on local norms in giving a single grade per subject. Rarely are local achievements linked to valid external standards, and this failure makes reports suspect or opaque. The key to report card change, then, is to make sure that grades, scores, brief comments, and any other shorthand symbol system can be translated by parents into achievements they can understand as worthy. This requires far more authentic and detailed assessment than we now do.

Thus, the problem we need to solve is not the use of letter grades per se. The habit of using a *single grade,* with no clear, agreed-on, and stable meaning to summarize all aspects of complex performance, is at the core of our present difficulties.

Toward Better Grades and Grading Categories

A report card is designed to summarize students' performance in school. Grades or numbers, like all symbols, offer efficient ways of summarizing. Since the parent cannot be expected to wade through all the student's work and draw all apt meanings, *the educator's job is to make meaning of the performances and to present facts, judgments, diagnoses, and prescriptions in a concise, user-friendly form.*

What critics of grading must understand is that the symbol is not the problem; the lack of stable and clear points of reference in using symbols is the problem. Trying to get rid of familiar letter grades thus gets the matter backwards while also leading to needless political battles. We need more data, not less. And we need many different kinds of data. Parents have reason to be suspicious of educators who want to reduce the amount of available data (and tinker with a 120-year-old system that they think they understand)—even if we know that traditional grades are often of questionable worth.

Symbols, including letter grades, are not inherently misleading, after all. There is nothing ambiguous about a typing or Advanced Placement (AP) score; company logos, red traffic lights, and company stock prices and dividend rates have objective significance. Grades are clear if we use specific and stable standards and criteria when giving them. Grades are unclear if they represent murky and inconsistent intellectual values across teachers.

The problem with letter grades now is that teachers must use too few grades to accomplish too many—and too many different kinds of—reporting tasks. Effort, achievement, progress; class participation, quality of papers; the consistency with which homework was done: How can a single grade make sense of these distinct variables? Then the problem is compounded: The weighting of those different factors not only varies across teachers but even by the same teacher in considering different students. Too often, therefore, our current use of letter grades amounts to shifting praise and blame, based on rarely shared and sometimes unjustified personal values. The use of the standard curve for giving grades only exacerbates matters. Now, the grade is an artifact that bears no clear relation to valid standards (and is psychometrically indefensible at the classroom level, as Bloom, Madaus, and Hastings [1981] argued years ago).

Regardless of technical concerns, a common criticism of letter grades is that they lead the student to worry more about grades than learning. But 60 years ago, in an article in *Atlantic Monthly*, President Lowell of Harvard wisely argued the case for working for good grades where the grades stand for something of clear value and validity: "To chide a tennis player for training himself with a view to winning the match, instead of acquiring skill in the game, would be absurd. . . . If marks are not an adequate measure of what the course is intended to impart, then the examination is defective" (Lowell 1926, p. 61). If the grade summarizes results derived from performance results, with known and apt criteria in force (as in skating figures, or wine ratings), then motivation is not extrinsic or corrupted. Student grade-grubbing stems from capricious and mysterious grading, not grades themselves.

So, pity our teachers; don't blame them. Few principals or administrators devote energy, meeting time, and the political gumption to rationalize the grading and reporting procedure or to cajole faculty to solve these problems collectively. Teachers are typically left to sort this all out in private. For most, the giving of a (single) grade is always an ugly compromise—all the more so, as we move to greater heterogeneity in classes through mainstreaming and detracking. Without agreed-on program goals, assessment procedures, and performance standards, there is little the individual teacher can do beyond muddling through. And then we will likely see continued unfairness and well-meaning dishonesty in reports.

More Grades, and Many Different Types of Grades, Needed

A single grade hides more than it reveals. We wouldn't feel comfortable giving each teacher only a single letter grade in a district performance appraisal system; why do we allow it for students? Giving more separate grades for performances in subtopics and skills within a subject area is thus in everyone's interest. It is better measurement, it provides more helpful data, and it is more fair.

All subjects are composed of many different and independent topics, skills, and concepts. Being good in one area of a subject doesn't mean that one is good in another. Why, then, do we give a single score, considering the obvious performance variability within the subdomains of each subject? One student is great at using formulas and algorithms in textbook problems but miserable at applying math models to real-life situations. Another student has the exact opposite profile. Why do we persist in giving one grade to each, making the performances erroneously look equivalent? Teachers should agree on how to divide each subject into the many important yet distinct aspects of performance, and provide data for each.

We have a model for the type of report that summarizes performance data efficiently in many subcategories while also offering a brief narrative judgment about the meaning of the data: the baseball card that fans buy at the store checkout counter. For each baseball player, we get a brief description of their previous year's performance in data highlighting the *many* subdimensions of their performance over time. One batter hits for a low average but drives in many runs. And though he struck out a lot, he led his team in home runs. Another batter has a very different profile: high batting average but few extra-base hits and few runs driven in. Why reduce each profile to a single score? The *disaggregation* of data personalizes the report by doing a better job of showing specific strengths and weaknesses.

More than being unhelpful, a glib reduction to a single grade is arbitrary—even if computed "objectively"—whether in baseball or school. Why would it be arbitrary in baseball? Because runs batted in, runs, hits, strikeouts, and home runs are *independent* of one another. There is no simple or agreed-on formula for combining all the data. "Averaging" all scores to "objectively" compute a grade hides the fact that we have thus *arbitrarily* judged each category of performance to be equally valuable. Why, then, do we arbitrarily average grades and scores in school to come up with a single grade per subject, where the dimensions of performance are even more complex and diverse? (And why do we use earlier grades to compute an "average" if students are expected to perform at higher levels as they go?[2]) Problem solving is not research is not writing is not discussing is not accuracy is not thoroughness is not mastery of the facts. This makes clearer why parents need not only more data but also those normative comparisons—and also why they need teacher judgments about gains. Let us report complex performance by its major elements, and summarize the meaning of the data in a brief narrative—just as occurs on the back of a baseball card.

We might therefore build reports out of various performance subcategories, standards, and benchmarks, using the national standards now developed for most subjects.[3] In the NCTM *Standards,* for example, mathematical performance is divided into mathematical power, dispositions, problem solving, communication, and so forth. In addition, the document provides major content categories (e.g., synthetic geometry, analytic geometry), with subskills and concepts implied in each. Why not encourage all math teachers to disaggregate their letter grade into these separate categories, with rubrics for each Standard? Why not make sure that English teachers report each student's performance on different genres of writing and literature since performance across genres is not constant, as many large-scale assessments have shown? Why not use the AAAS Project 2061 *Benchmarks* to establish both reporting categories and longitudinal scales in science?

More disaggregated scoring, where achievements and progress are separated and where performance is separated into its many subscores,

[2] In a recent article, Russell Wright (1994) suggests that grades would be more valid if they were based on the *median* grade as opposed to the *mean*. This is a fine idea, given the inherent inconsistency of both performer and assessor, and the need to justify the judgment that a (relatively inconsistent student performer) can be said to achieve a specific level of performance. Note, though, that his proposal will work only if there are clear and stable performance standards and criteria against which grades are given.

[3] See Kendall and Marzano (1994) for an excellent cross-referenced compendium of all the national reports on standards and benchmarks. Note, though, that most of the reports focus on content standards, not performance standards.

would also improve the incentives for students, not just the clarity of the report for parents. No one is a standout or a failure at everything, so particular strengths are now more likely to be revealed; particular weaknesses are now more reliably identified so that improvement can be sought with a clearer focus on the problems to be solved.

If more data are desirable, then reducing grades to *A, B, INC* (Incomplete)—or dispensing with them altogether—is heading in the wrong direction. (These are grading systems widely used in outcome-based education [OBE] and Mastery Learning projects.) Getting rid of grades lower than a *B* makes as little sense as not reporting batting averages under .300. More important, such a system confuses valid standards with unfair expectations. Students may "not yet" meet our local expectations. But few students, by definition, will ever meet the highest possible standards (e.g., a four-minute mile, or perfect scores on national achievement tests). It doesn't follow, however, that it is unwise or unfair to write standard-referenced reports. On the contrary, such reporting supplies feedback that is the key to future mastery.

Use of the national standards also solves a key part of the problem of report card credibility as viewed by clients other than the student. Irrespective of how many grades we give, letter grades rarely represent what many clients seek: achievement per se, that is, performance measured against fixed standards. Honesty demands that we do a better job of reporting it, even if fairness requires that we show the performer's personal growth in a subject.

The criteria of honesty and fairness suggest the need for different kinds of grades, therefore, not just more data. How might different kinds of grades enable us to more accurately and helpfully report achievement? By distinguishing the two different criteria that get the grade-giver into trouble: performance measured against "standards" and performance measured against "reasonable expectations" for each student.

Distinguishing Between Standard-Referenced and Expectation-Referenced Reporting

The questions a report should address are of two kinds, then: How did each child do, given authentic and fixed standards? And how did each child do, given "reasonable expectations" for performance gains during the time period? I want to reserve the term *scores* for the former question and the term *grades* for the latter (irrespective of which symbol system we use to summarize these distinct measures of performance).

How do scores differ from grades? Think of scores as the pure performance data, such as the results of performance tests in writing, typing, diving, or music; and standardized criterion-referenced achievement tests (e.g., the College Board Achievement Tests, NAEP subject-area tests, or the Degrees of Reading Power Test). Scores are given in terms of performance standards. The standards are set by exemplary performers or perfect performance. A standard is a standard whether or not anyone in the school can meet it.

Scoring, whether by human judge or machine, must be done in a disinterested or "blind" way to be valid and credible. The judge considers no mitigating or extenuating factors in giving the score, such as age, history, or character. The judge simply scores the performance in reference to uniform criteria and standards, through rubrics and exemplars/anchors or specifications (e.g. 100 words per minute in typing; a raw Degrees of Reading Power score of 68; a four out of six on a state writing assessment that is anchored by papers from around the state, etc.). Any performance test (not just a multiple-choice test) should yield valid and reliable—i.e., comparable—scores. We are scoring performances, not performers.

Grades, on the other hand, represent a judgment about a unique performer's overall record in context—the meaning of scores. The teacher appraises the value of the aforementioned scores, taking into consideration "what it is reasonable to expect" from such a performer. Circumstances now appropriately influence our judgment: How good a performance is this for a student at this stage in a career? How good a performance is this for this particular student? We take the scores and "translate" them in various ways for report readers as we consider each of those questions. When it comes time to grade the performance, we are thus asking: To what extent did the student meet "reasonable expectations"? The answer will always be, in effect: Well, it depends. The same 4.5 diving score may well be a "good" performance or a "poor" one, depending on the diver, her prior experience, our sense of whether she worked to capacity, and our sense of the norms for her stage of development. This is why it is technically and pedagogically wrong to mechanically compute letter grades on the basis of scores—that is, turning a 6 into an *A*, a 5 into a *B*, and so forth, as some teachers and districts are now doing with performance assessments. This is as unwarranted as turning the diver's 4.5 into a *D*, irrespective of the diver's age, experience, and level of competition. The "translation" of scores into grades requires greater judgment and less mechanical computation since expectations properly vary from student to student.

But note that expectations are essentially of two kinds, and we will have to distinguish them in our reports. There are expectations of students, given the larger context of one's peer group (often cast in grade-level, developmental, or course-level terms); and expectations of the student, given each student's personal circumstances. In the former sense, we typically refer to or infer from local norms: "You earned a *B* in English this term because you met pretty well my general expectations for students in 9th grade English." This is the de facto meaning of a letter grade in many schools.

Another kind of expectation-based grade is more personalized: "You earned an *A*, given your improvement vis a vis my expectations of you personally, based on your past individual record and level of experience." We can refer to the former as a *normed* grade and the latter as a *growth* grade. A normed grade is based on expectations of a cohort, presumably linked to valid developmental data. A growth grade represents a rough assessment of whether personal potential was realized. To speak of "potential" here is to risk invoking bad psychology. I'm comfortable with the phrase as shorthand for the judgments teachers (and coaches and military and job recruiters make daily), but we should beware reifying the idea of potential or aptitude and being guilty of a false determinism about native capacity. Few psychologists today believe that there is any reality behind the conceptual construct termed *aptitude* or *potential*. All those ideas represent are merely generalizations induced from past predictions and actions. (That's one reason why the SAT is no longer called the Scholastic Aptitude Test.)

We should keep normed and growth grades separate and report both because they represent distinctly different judgments. Too often, teachers now seem to merge the two meanings of "expectation" as they assign single letter grades.

Some readers might think I am describing "effort" when I use the term *growth*, but growth is different from effort. Growth is measured in terms of performance standards, although it is determined mindful of the circumstances for that student. To assess growth, we ask: "Relative to your experience and history, how much improvement in performance (scores) can I reasonably expect you to make, and how much did you make?" This comparison of projected gains to actual gains yields the grade. (Note, however, that one could grow a great deal but make relatively little absolute progress. You may have moved from 1 to 2 on a scale of 10—great growth for you, but still a long way from the standard. See the later section "Longitudinal Assessing and Reporting.") Effort and other attitudinal traits are separate from any gains you may or may not have made in scores. Maybe great intentions yielded poor results. Maybe your hard work was ineffectual. There can be great effort with little or no gain in performance ability—and vice versa. These distinctions are rarely made despite the fact that these are critical distinctions for understanding a student's record.

In the West Windsor-Plainsboro schools in New Jersey, educators explicitly report growth against norms, as well as disaggregating literacy into many different subelements, each separately graded. For the various literacy behaviors (e.g., Uses Appropriate Comprehension Strategies, Writes Effective Responses to Literature, Participates Successfully in Sustained Short Reading), the report uses the following categories for assessment:

CO (*Consistently* demonstrates this behavior)
DE (Is *developing* this behavior as *expected*)
DD (Is experiencing *difficulty developing* this behavior)
NC (Is *not currently* demonstrating this behavior).

Teachers hold expectations constant across students when they are placed in a grade-level class.

A suburban Texas district not only reports performance against reasonable expectations but also translates the report into a visual record of individual performance compared against both norms and developmental criteria over the course of the year (see Figure 11.1). The graph is used six times and visually shows the gains made during the year toward grade-level expectations. (The second page of Figure 11.1 shows a continuum of "Communication" achievements.)

Though it is convenient bureaucratically to treat all kindergartners as the same type of student, such a view flies in the face of reality. At this age, the youngest and oldest students may be light years apart either developmentally or in terms of prior experience. Fairness requires, in addition to such a picture, that we look at whether the individual student was in the same place developmentally as her peers. That's why we also need a growth grade in addition to a normed report such as this.

If it is unreasonable to hold a group composed of diverse abilities to the same expectations, why do it? The answer takes us back to our opening story. The clients, in this case the parents, need to know the data about what is "typical" kindergarten performance if they are to understand the report. Reporting norms also ensures that our report is honest and that our expectations for each student are more reasonable and supported by data. If it is a fact that you "consistently demonstrate" the targeted literacy behaviors, but your performance scores put you in the 2nd quartile for your class, let's report both—and rethink our report language, as well as our local expectations. If it is a fact that only 14% of all 3rd graders received a 5 or a 6 out of 6 on their year-end writing portfolio, and your score was a 5, let's report it and appropriately give you a good growth grade. And if the top quartile and bottom quartile are composed of students from different racial, gender, or socioeconomic backgrounds, let's report that, too, and investigate whether our expectations are a function less of fairly factoring in performance histories or inappropriately biased expectations.

Note that the categories of reporting in literacy reports such as that shown in Figure 11.1 overlook the distinction between frequency of behavior and quality of performance: The student could be consistently demonstrating the "behaviors," but her work could be sloppy. We need to use the ath-

Figure 11.1

GRAPH OF ACHIEVEMENT
ROUND ROCK INDEPENDENT SCHOOL DISTRICT

		INTELLECTUAL DEVELOPMENT										PHYSICAL DEVELOPMENT			AESTHETIC DEVELOPMENT			
		COMMUNICATION				SCIENCE/SOCIAL SCIENCE			MATHEMATICS									
		Listening	Speaking	Writing	Pre-reading	Observes Identifies Predicts	Sequence & Order	Compare Contrast Classify	Observes Identifies Predicts	Sequence & Order	Compare Contrast Classify	Motor & Percep-tual Aware-ness	Wellness	Fine Motor	Singing Concepts	Compar-atives and Listening	Rhythm Movement Expres-sion	Visual Arts
	6																	
Performances beyond K Level	5																	
Exit Expectation	4																	
	3																	
Performance at K Level	2																	
Entry Level	1																	

Note: The <u>same</u> copy of the graph is used 6 times per year, with different colors used for showing growth for each marking period

FIGURE 11.1 (*continued*)

COMMUNICATION

WRITING

• Expresses ideas through drawing and painting • Uses writing materials • Random Scribbles	• Expresses ideas through drawing, painting, and dictating • Shows appropriate use of writing materials to communicate • Scribbles with meaning	• Expresses ideas using letter-like shapes • Demonstrates some knowledge of the alphabet • Associates print with spoken language • Shows awareness of left to right, top to bottom	• Expresses ideas and recognizes that experiences and stories can be written about • Uses letters to represent sound in words with some reversals • Understands that print conveys messages	• Uses temporary spelling to write ideas (some reversals) • Uses some conventions of capitalization and punctuation • Shows awareness of spaces between words • Works left to right, top to bottom • Begins to revise and edit work	• Attends to Purpose while writing • Extends and elaborates ideas • Applies many conventions: capitalization, punctuation, spacing • Demonstrates readiness for more direct spelling instruction

PRE-READING/READING

• Develops an awareness of printed materials and pictures	• Displays interest in print • Spends time looking at books and likes to have stories read	• Recognizes that print conveys meaning • Retells stories from pictures • Recognizes concepts of print • Displays developing fluency of language	• Follows print left to right • Identifies and connects sounds with letters • Recognizes some high frequency words or names in and out of context • Shows signs of becoming a beginning reader • Actively participates in shared reading	• Participates comfortably in reading activities • Follows print with 1-1 correspondence • Begins to use phonics, pictures, and language structure to read for meaning	• Reads for meaning, information • Uses reading strategies automatically • Is comfortable with a variety of literature

letic-competition distinction between "degree of difficulty and "quality" of performance. (See the later section, "Distinguishing Between Quality and Sophistication of Performance.")

At the very least, a report should explain obvious and inevitable discrepancies in data viewed from different perspectives. That may be the most important use of narrative comments.

Honesty Requires Standard-Referenced Reports

Local norms and clear, common expectations are not enough, however, to produce fully honest reports. The reader needs not only data on local norms, but a justification of local norms as—well, as "normal." Local norms might be uniformly too low. What is "normal" locally can be below average nationally. It certainly isn't wise or helpful to put in a report that a student "is developing" key literacy behaviors "as expected" while teachers know the student performs in the 29th percentile nationally—regardless of how one feels about standardized tests. And being "above normal" nationally can still be "unacceptable" when measured against valid standards—or elite norms. For example, the Educational Record Bureau (ERB) usefully reports three different kinds of percentile scores in its writing assessment results: national norms, suburban norms, and private school norms.

To avoid inappropriately provincial expectations, we should report performance against credible standards, as well as against valid norms. By "valid norms" I mean an apt and credible frame of reference. That may mean national norms or state norms—but in a good suburban district, those are absurd points of comparisons. (In New York State, suburban districts trumpet that they get 99% of their students above the state passing [or "cut"] score in reading—despite the fact that the cut score is set terribly low to deal with the much weaker performances in the five urban districts. One might, by contrast, deliberately compare local norms to private school norms or other suburban norms—as is available in the ERB writing assessment, for example.)

To illustrate the use of credible standards and valid norms: As part of Toronto's Benchmarks program, the following rubric was used on an 8th-grade oral performance task, and the summary data showing the percentage of students earning each score across the district was published:

8th Grade Oral Performance

LEVEL FIVE
8%

The student is aware of the importance of both content and delivery in giving a talk. The content is powerfully focused and informative. The issue is clearly defined, and detail is judiciously selected to support the issue. The talk is delivered in a style that interests and persuades the audience. Questions, eye contact, facial expressions and gesture engage the audience. The student displays evidence of social, moral and political responsibility, and offers creative solutions. Causes and effects are elaborated. The second version of the talk reveals significant changes based on revision after viewing. The student may make effective use of cue cards. The student is confident and takes risks.

LEVEL FOUR
20%

The student is aware of the importance of both content and delivery in giving a talk. The student's talk is well shaped and supported with pertinent information. The student supports conclusions with facts, and makes connections between cause and effect. The talk is delivered in a style that may interest and persuade the audience. Questions, eye contact, facial expressions, and gesture are used occasionally to engage the audience. Delivery is improved after viewing the first draft of the talk. The student is fairly confident and can self-evaluate.

LEVEL THREE
28%

The student is aware of the importance of both content and delivery in giving a talk. The talk displays a noticeable order and some organization, primarily through lists. The student includes some specific information, some of which supports or focuses on the topic. The conclusion may be weak. The student may show personal involvement with topic and concern about the consequences of not dealing with the issues. There is evidence of revision as a result of viewing the first version of the talk. The student is fairly confident and can self-evaluate.

LEVEL TWO
22%

The student's talk contains some specific information with some attempt at organization. The main idea is unclear and facts are disjointed. Some paraphrasing of text is evident. The student uses no persuasive devices, has little eye contact or voice inflection and does not take a clear stand on the issue. The delivery is hesitant and incoherent. Little improvement is shown in the talk after watching the first version. The student demonstrates little confidence.

LEVEL ONE
22%

The student chooses one or two details to talk about but the talk lacks coherence. The talk is confused and illogical. There may be no response.

The percentages to the left represent the number of Toronto 8th graders who received each score in the first year of the assessment. The rubric makes clear, however, that what is "normal" is *not* acceptable: To be performing at Levels One and Two is not good in absolute terms, even if many students are now there. Such criterion-referenced reports make clear the distance needed to meet truly high standards. To report only the percentages or normed letter grades without the rubric would make it appear as if being at Levels Two or Three were satisfactory. (The anchor performances used in Toronto are 8th grade ones, and the "anchors" were derived from local assessment only. This makes the results less standard referenced and more normed than they might be. Using validated exemplars from the best Canadian 8th graders, or using exemplars from adult professional life would no doubt lower the scores—but improve the credibility and usefulness of the results to clients.)

Yet fairness again requires that we judge these scores in context. These results were the very first results recorded for Toronto's oral assessment. We should "expect" low scores for a new, complex performance task never encountered by students, in both the normed-grade and growth-grade senses. Further, we know that more than half of Toronto's students have non-English-speaking parents. That fact alone makes it unlikely that most students would do well in early rounds of testing. These comments are not meant as excuses but as needed perspective: By reporting scores and percentages, in addition to giving personalized grades, we paint an honest yet fair picture; and we set the stage for later gains.

Longitudinal Assessing and Reporting

The difference between grades and scores makes it clear that "growth" is not the same as "progress." Regardless of growth, are Johnny or Denise making sufficient gains over time toward exit-level goals? Even if they are meeting our current (8th grade) expectations in oral proficiency, are they on track to meet a real-world standard by graduation? If there are no shared and validated scoring scales across grade levels, how will we know for sure whether each grade level's narrowly framed expectations align with valid benchmarks? To measure progress accurately requires a new approach to reporting, one that places key student performances on a standard-anchored continuum, and a new kind of grade whereby teachers judge the likelihood of the student's meeting exit standards at the current rate of progress.

We see the value of such a report clearly in the few areas where they now exist: the American Council on the Teaching of Foreign Languages (ACTFL) Proficiency Scales, the Degrees of Reading Power Test, and in such scoring systems as tennis ladders, chess master ratings, cross-country running times, karate belts, and computer game levels.

The need for such scales in academic areas and for caution about framing standards only in terms of a grade level are made clear by national test data and grade inflation. Consider the scale for charting mathematics progress used a few years ago by the National Assessment of Educational Progress (NAEP) (shown in Figure 11.2).

According to NAEP data, only 6% of U.S. students can perform at the highest level—despite the fact that these levels correspond to the content of algebra classes where more than half of American 18-year-olds will have earned passing grades. Local grading and reporting thus need to offer clearer links to credible national standards. We need to ensure that local grades relate to credible standards (as often happens in other countries where state or national test scores must be factored into local teacher grades—which can be as high as 50 percent of the grade in some places, e.g., Alberta, Canada).

How does this kind of "progress" scale differ from the two kinds of "growth" described previously? Progress is an objective measure of the gains made over time against a common desirable goal. It is measured "backwards" from a desired final destination: What percentage of a trip has been completed? How close are you to the goal from your starting point? How far and forward have you traveled, and what would such a trend extrapolate to in terms of reaching your goal? Is that progress normal, optimal, or worrisome? These questions are only answerable if we score backwards from a valid performance standard.

How might we modify the Texas graph of performance gains over the six marking periods (see Figure 11.1) to accommodate the idea of progress? First, we might extend the report to beyond kindergarten (as shown in South Brunswick's report system, described later in this section); second, we might explicitly equate where genuine performance standards can be found on our graph of local expectations (e.g., by equating local scores on the scale to Degrees of Reading Power scores or by using national achievement tests merely to calibrate local grading). Whatever method we choose, we must ensure that local norms can be more easily related by readers to credible standards.

Note, therefore, that the expectation score would *change* over time while the highest standard stays the same: We appropriately expect higher standard-referenced scores as the student ad-

FIGURE 11.2

NAEP SCORING SCALES: MATHEMATICS

Level 200—Beginning Skills and Understanding
Learners at this level have considerable understanding of two-digit numbers. They can add two-digit numbers but are still developing an ability to regroup in subtraction. They know some basic multiplication and division facts, recognize relations among coins, use simple measurement instruments. . . .

Level 250—Basic Operations and Beginning Problem Solving
Learners have an initial understanding of the four basic operations. They are able to apply whole number addition and subtraction skills to one-step word problems and money situations. In multiplication, they can find the product of a two-digit and a one-digit number. They can compare information from graphs and charts, and are developing an ability to analyze logical relations.

Level 300—Moderately Complex Procedures and Reasoning
Learners are developing an understanding of number systems. They can compute with decimals, simple fractions and commonly-encountered percents. They can identify geometric figures, measure lengths and angles, and calculate areas of rectangles. They are also able to interpret simple inequalities, evaluate formulas and solve simple linear equations. They can find averages . . . and are developing the skills to operate with signed numbers, exponents, and square roots.

Level 350—Multistep Problem Solving & Algebra
Learners can solve routine problems involving fractions and percents, recognize properties of geometric figures, and work with exponents and square roots. They can solve a variety of two-step problems using variables, identify equivalent algebraic expressions and solve linear equations and inequalities. . . .

vances through schooling, just as divers getting the same standard-referenced score might have those scores interpreted differently by their coaches.

There is a judgment dimension to measuring progress. In reporting progress data over time, we are objectively charting a trend, parallel to reporting norms: What is the graph of student progress over time along the same continuum, and how does that graph compare to the cohort's graph and to historical patterns of many cohorts over time? But a judgment must also be made for the reader of the data. The progress data should be evaluated as "exemplary," "on course," and "grounds for concern" or the like. These progress reports would be professional predictions, not unanchored value judgments, based on trend data. (We often talk about "developmentally appropriate assessment," but until we have such norms we have little right to make such claims without research).

Growth, by contrast, represents a judgment about whether you are making gains "for someone like you." It represents our assessment of the degree to which your work has improved, given where you started and given expectations for someone or some group who started where you started. But growth may not involve *adequate* progress. You and your peers may have grown a great deal over the years, but still not be on track to meet exit standards. Here is where current reports are most deficient. Parents and other clients outside the school typically cannot tell from reports in the early grades the severity of the student's performance progress since the grades are typically linked to grade-level norms, and each grade level has typically not justified its own tests and grades against exit-level standards. Reporting "growth" benefits not only low performers: Such a system would enable us to solve an evaluation weakness in our current system, namely, whether students of great abilities (and thus able to get perfectly fine scores as a result and make progress) are dogging it.

Many educators (especially those who worry about the fate of minority children) fear that greater judgment-based assessment about "expectations" will be derived from bias or prejudice, not data. The fear is that such a system will only formalize and dignify the establishing of lower expectations for students by ethnicity, race, gender, class, and so forth. Reporting progress rates and norms of performance (including norms and progress rates for subpopulations) should help prevent such abuses; but ultimately the remedy is an accountability system that requires a staff to track progress, and intervene when progress for a group slows or stops. A faculty's job, after all, is to maximize the performance of the entire cohort—and investigate any discrepancies in performance by any subgroups. (Routinely scoring student work "blind" and collaboratively also prevents such abuses.) Credible and effective local assessments demand that these steps be taken.

Such a longitudinal system is also more likely to provide incentives for less able learners. Just as runners begin to worry less about their finish in the race and more about their times and "personal bests," so too can students of all kinds gain motivational power from ongoing reports of steady gains. Students can be "slow" learners but see *sufficient* progress over time. As I have elsewhere argued, such a standard-referenced system used over the student's career is feasible, as has been proven in other countries, even if U.S. educators are not used to it (see Wiggins 1988, 1991, 1993 [Chapter 4]).

This, too, is hardly a new idea. Edward Thorndike (1913), one of the fathers of modern educational measurement, 80 years ago called for scores that "redirect [the incentive of] rivalry into tendencies to go higher on an objective scale of absolute achievement, to surpass one's own past performance" (p. 288). The vice of the "old" system of scoring Thorndike was critiquing and sought to change—our current system of letter grades—was not its detail but its "relativity and indefiniteness, the fact that a given mark did not mean any defined amount of knowledge or power or skill." Competing against "one's own past" or an "accepted standard" yields consistently greater motivation:

> To be 17th instead of 18th does not approach in moving force the zeal to beat one's own record, to see one's practice curve rise week by week, and to get up to the standard which permits one to advance to a new feat . . . in so far as excelling others would imply and emphasize making absolute progress upward on a scale of real achievement, even direct rivalry with others [and the motive power that comes from it] would be healthy (Thorndike 1913, pp. 288–289).

An example from the Cherry Creek, Colorado, schools (see Figure 11.3) shows how this measurement of progress can look, and how normative data can also be charted. (Note that in this example, though, the standards refer to *elementary* school exit-level standards).

Similar information is given on science performance, as well as normed information on a host of intellectual habits of mind and social conduct. And content standards are not lost or forgotten:

FIGURE 11.3

CHERRY CREEK SCHOOL DISTRICT
POLTON COMMUNITY ELEMENTARY SCHOOL
FAIRPLAY PROGRESS REPORT

Student Name ______________________ Grade 3 ____________ 4 ______________

Teacher ______________________ School Year ______________________

Performance-based graduation requirements focus on student mastery of the proficiencies. The curriculum and written progress report are geared toward preparing students for this task. A date (e.g., 11/93) indicates where a student is performing on a continuum of progress based on the fifth-grade exit standards.

Name ______________________ Grade 3 ____________ 4 ______________

Language Arts Proficiency 1
Listens, interpreting verbal and nonverbal cues to construct meaning.

Basic	Proficient	Advanced
Actively listens, demonstrates understanding and clarifies with questions and paraphrasing.	Actively listens for purpose, demonstrates understanding and clarifies with questions and paraphrasing.	Actively listens for purpose, demonstrates understanding, clarifies with questions and paraphrasing, and classifies, analyzes, and applies information.

Language Arts Proficiency 2
Conveys meaning clearly and coherently through speech in both formal and informal situations.

Basic	Proficient	Advanced
Appropriately speaks to inform, explain, demonstrate, or persuade. Organizes a speech and uses vocabulary to convey a message.	Appropriately speaks to inform, explain, demonstrate, or persuade. Organizes a formal speech and uses vocabulary to convey a message.	Appropriately speaks to inform, explain, demonstrate, or persuade. Organizes a formal speech with details and transitions adapting subject and vocabulary. Uses eye contact, gestures, suitable expression for an audience and topic.

Language Arts Proficiency 3
Reads to construct meaning by interacting with the text, by recognizing the different requirements of a variety of printed materials, and by using appropriate strategies to increase comprehension.

Basic	Proficient	Advanced
Reads varied material, comprehends at a literal level. Recalls and builds knowledge through related information. Begins to use strategies to develop fluency, adjusting rate when reading different material.	Reads varied material, comprehends and draws inferences, recalls and builds knowledge through related information. Applies strategies to increase fluency, adjusting rate when reading different material.	Reads varied material, comprehends literally and interpretively. Synthesizes and explores information, drawing, inferences. Critiques author's intent, analyzes material for meaning and value. Applies strategies to increase fluency, adjusting rate.

Language Arts Proficiency 4
Produces writing that conveys purpose and meaning, uses effective writing strategies, and incorporates the conventions of written language to communicate clearly.

Basic	Proficient	Advanced
Appropriately writes on assigned or self-selected topics. Clear main ideas, few details. Weak elements in the beginning, middle, end. Sentence structure lacks variety and contains errors.	Appropriately writes on assigned or self-selected topics. Clear main ideas, interesting details, clear organization, sequencing, varied sentence structure and edits to reduce errors. Appropriate voice and word choice.	Appropriately writes on assigned self-selected topics. Connects opinions, details, and examples. Effective organization and sequencing, meaningful sentence structure, edits to eliminate most errors. Appropriate voice and word choice.

(Continued on the following page.)

FIGURE 11.3 (*continued*)

As compared to their class in the area of Language Arts, your child

	1	2	3
Displays strong performance			
Demonstrates appropriate development			
Needs practice and support			

Name________________________ Grade 3______________4 ______________

Math Proficiency l

Uses **numbers** and **number relationships** to solve mathematical problems of increasing complexity and communicates results.

Basic	Proficient	Advanced
Demonstrates a basic understanding of number relationships by performing simple mathematical operations.	Demonstrates a comprehensive understanding of number relationships by selecting and using computation and reasoning skills to solve problems.	Demonstrates an advanced understanding of number relationships by applying number theory concepts to make predictions.

Math Proficiency 2

Uses **geometry** and **measurement** to solve problems of increasing complexity and communicates results.

Basic	Proficient	Advanced
Identifies simple shapes and demonstrates simple measurement skills.	Analyzes properties of various shapes and measures using different units and mathematical calculations.	Uses geometric shapes, calculations, and dates to solve problems logically.

Math Proficiency 3

Uses **probability, statistics**, and **data analysis** to solve mathematical problems of increasing complexity and communicates results.

Basic	Proficient	Advanced
Demonstrates a basic understanding of chance, graphs, and tables.	Uses the fundamentals of probability and data analysis to predict outcomes.	Demonstrates an advanced understanding of probability and data analysis to solve problems logically.

Math Proficiency 4

Uses the recognition and construction of **patterns** and **relationships** to solve mathematical problems of increasing complexity, and communicates results.

Basic	Proficient	Advanced
With teacher guidance, recognizes, creates, and extends simple patterns using shapes and numbers.	Uses the fundamentals of probability and data analysis to predict outcomes.	Demonstrates an advanced understanding of probability and data analysis to solve problems logically.

Math Proficiency 5

Uses **algebra** to solve mathematical problems of increasing complexity.

Basic	Proficient	Advanced
Demonstrates a basic understanding of mathematical sentences.	Demonstrates reasoning abilities when solving simple problems with one unknown variable.	Demonstrates an advanced understanding of algebraic methods used to solve problems by independently constructing formal equations.

Source: Polton Community Elementary School, Cherry Creek School District, Cherry Creek, Colorado. Adapted by permission.

The report describes the books read, specific performance tasks mastered, and course-specific major assignments completed.

Norms have their place here, too, as noted previously. The staff at Polton who devised the Cherry Creek report system found out that the opening story about the parent's question was not apocryphal ("OK, but how is she doing?"). In an early draft of the report card, the only thing they were going to report was the achievement level noted on each continuum. I suggested that they needed to think through both the issue of performance quality versus work sophistication (see the next section of this chapter) and the issue of norms. Sure enough, the parents demanded the latter: The box at the bottom of the Language Arts section of Figure 11.3, where the child's performance is compared to that of the class, was recently added to respond to the parent feedback.

The descriptors on the Cherry Creek report card—"Basic, Proficient, and Advanced"—are helpful but ultimately too broad for use over multiple years. We need finer distinctions in performance levels to get a clear sense of just what the child can and cannot do—without overwhelming the parent with data. Consider, for example, the report used in South Brunswick, New Jersey, to chart progress toward sophisticated literacy in reading in the early school years (see Figure 11.4).

As part of their developmental portfolio and assessment system in South Brunswick, there is even an approach to spelling assessment and reporting that honors this idea of reporting progress "backwards" from a standard. Words are not merely spelled correctly or incorrectly and reported as scores on spelling tests. With help from Ted Chittenden at the Educational Testing Service (ETS), the teachers in the district learned to chart the students' progress toward correct spelling over the K–2 grades using what they call a "Word Awareness Writing Activity" (WAWA; see Henderson 1990, pp. 194–199). The different levels are based on empirically grounded criteria by which levels of sophistication in spelling hunches are catalogued (using the research on spelling acquisition and "naive" or invented spelling). Figure 11.5 shows the criteria and the scoring chart.

Readers of this spelling report have a clear and verifiable perspective on the student's progress. Charting scores over time clearly highlights progress toward the standards of correct spelling.

Again, I would argue that we also gain insight by reporting the local norms as well (which South Brunswick does not now report to parents): Where are the student's peers on the same scale at this point in time? And for fairness I would also report "growth" by giving a letter grade summarizing the teacher's evaluation of the progress in light of reasonable expectations for that student. In South Brunswick they do not give such grades. (These kinds of assessments against a standard do not favor or undercut any particular teaching philosophy or program philosophy. There is nothing inherently at odds, for example, with a Whole Language approach to instruction and such developmental scoring scales, as too many educators mistakenly believe.)

The WAWA and its use of the ultimate standard for all spellers—that is, the correct spelling of complex words—should cause us to reconsider the Toronto oral assessment and the numerous other performance tasks with rubrics now in use in many school districts. We noted previously that the standard was set by the description of exemplary performance in the rubric at scale point 5. But this was not quite accurate. The specific performance standard is established by samples of work that we deem exemplary, samples that serve as instances of the descriptor for scale point 5. The next question should be: Which samples? The answer will affect the scores.

To measure progress accurately, we occasionally need to measure current performance against exit (or even adult) standards. If the best 8th grade performances from Toronto schools are used to an-

FIGURE 11.4

K-2 READING/WRITING SCALE DEVELOPMENT OF CHILDREN'S STRATEGIES FOR MAKING SENSE OF PRINT

1—EARLY EMERGENT
Displays an awareness of some conventions of reading, such as front/back of books, distinctions between print and pictures. Sees the construction of meaning from text as "magical" or exterior to the print. While the child may be interested in the contents of books, there is as yet little apparent attention to turning written marks into language. Is beginning to notice environmental print.

2—ADVANCED EMERGENT
Engages in pretend reading and writing. Uses reading-like ways that clearly approximate book language. Demonstrates a sense of the story being "read," using picture clues and recall of story line. May, draw on predictable language patterns in anticipating (and recalling) the story. Attempts to use letters in writing, sometimes in random or scribble fashion.

3—EARLY BEGINNING READER
Attempts to "really read." Indicates beginning sense of one-to-one correspondence and concept of word. Predicts actively, in new material, using syntax and story line. Small stable sight vocabulary is becoming established. Evidence of initial awareness of beginning and ending sounds, especially in invented spelling.

4—ADVANCED BEGINNING READER
Starts to draw on major cue systems: self-corrects or identifies words through use of letter-sound patterns, sense of story, or syntax. Reading may be laborious, especially new material, requiring considerable effort and some support. Writing and spelling reveal awareness of letter patterns. Conventions of writing such as capitalization and full stops are beginning to appear.

5—EARLY INDEPENDENT READER
Handles familiar material on own, but still needs some support with unfamiliar material. Figures out words and self-corrects by drawing on a combination of letter-sound relationships, word structure, story line, or syntax. Strategies of rereading or of guessing from larger chunks of text are becoming well established. Has a large stable sight vocabulary. Conventions of writing are understood.

6—ADVANCED INDEPENDENT READER
Reads independently, using multiple strategies flexibly. Monitors and self-corrects for meaning. Can read and understand most material when the content is appropriate. Conventions of writing and spelling are—for the most part—under control.

Note 1: The scale focuses on development of children's strategies for making sense of print. Evidence concerning children's strategies and knowledge about print may be revealed in both their reading and writing activities.

Note 2: The scale does not attempt to rate children's interest or attitudes regarding reading, nor does it attempt to summarize what literature may mean to the child. Such aspects of children's literacy development are summarized in other forms.

Source: Rating scale developed by South Brunswick teachers and Educational Testing Service staff January 1991.

FIGURE 11.5

SPELLING CRITERIA AND SCORING CHART

A scoring chart is provided below to help you analyze the spelling. Before going further, think about the features that you will look for at each developmental level:

1. Precommunicative spelling is the "babbling" stage of spelling. Children use letters for writing words but the letters are strung together randomly. The letters in precommunicative spelling does correspond to sounds.

2. Semiphonetic spellers know that letters represent sounds. They represent sounds with letters. Spellings are often abbreviated representing initial and/or final sounds. Example: E = eagle; A = eighty.

3. Phonetic spellers spell words like they sound. The speller perceives and represents all of the phonemes in a word, though spellings may be unconventional. Example: EGL = eagiel- ATE = eighty.

4. Transitional spellers think about how words appear visually; a visual memory of spelling patterns is apparent. Spellings exhibit conventions of English orthography like vowels in every syllable and vowel diagram patterns, correctly spelled inflection endings, and frequent English letter sequences. Example: EGUL = eagle; EIGHTEE eighty.

5. Correct spellers develop over years of word study and writing. Correct spelling can be categorized by instruction levels; for example, correct spelling for a body of words that can be spelled, the average fourth grader would be forth-grade level correct spelling.

Look at the child's list. Were most of the child's spellings Precommunicative, Semiphonetic, Phonetic, Transitional, or Correct? This is the child's probable developmental level. You might feel that a child truly falls between two of the categories, but try to put in just one check mark per child.

Words	1 Precommunicative	2 Semiphonetic	3 Phonetic	4 Transitional	5 Correct
bed	random	b	bd	behd	bed
truck	random	tk	trk	truhk	truck
letter	random	lt	ldr	ledder	letter
bumpy	random	bp	bmp	bumpee	bumpy
dress	random	js	jrs	dres	dress
jail	random	jl	gal	jale	jail
feet	random	ft	fet	fete	feet
shopping	random	sp	spen	shoping	shopping
monster	random	m	mnstr	monstur	monster
raced	random	r	rast	raist	raced
boat	random	b	bot	bote	boat
hide	random	hi	hid	hied	hide

chor the scoring system, that yields one set of results (the current practice). If we anchor the scoring system by the best possible 12th grade oral assessments, gathered from all over the province of Ontario, that yields a different (lower) set of scores for the same performances.

There are virtues in using *both* standards. Knowing how your work compared to exemplary 8th grade work is helpful but incomplete. Assessing 8th graders against *12th grade* standards gives students and teachers information en route, before it is too late. Such ongoing feedback (e.g., giving the same oral assessment each year, using 12th grade standards and grade-level expectation grades) makes it more likely that 12th grade standards are met. This would be easy to do in areas such as writing, reading, problem solving, and other recursive intellectual skills. Such a system would be closer to the 10-point scale used in Olympic competition or master points in chess. (These kinds of scores would help teachers engage in badly needed equating and recalibrating of local grading.)

As these examples suggest, grading at the "exit" level needs to mesh with standards at the next "entry" level—or our students are set up for confusion and difficulty. Some high schools now do this. At Heritage High School in Littleton, Colorado, the exit-level writing assessment task and standards (given in Grade 11) are borrowed from the local university, lending not only greater clarity to the report but greater credibility. Now, scores given locally match scores given at the university, since the papers are read blind using the previously evaluated anchor papers of college freshmen. Similarly, in most technical programs, the local standards are and must be the same as professional standards. Nor are there any obstacles to using AP papers as benchmarks for anchoring local scoring systems. Until faculties are required to link their grading standards to wider-world credible standards, reports and transcripts will remain of little value—the very reason that standardized testing gained in power over the years.

More than honesty and rigor are at stake here. Those who use the "developmental" argument as an excuse for not evaluating work against standards simply fail to grasp how learning works. We require feedback as performers, not just praise, to know what is both possible and desirable. Learning and successive approximations cause mastery. Feedback requires constantly comparing the actual to the ideal if our progress is to be optimized. We rob all children of a successful future if we lie to them about their absolute levels of performance. And we deceive parents and other readers of reports by making it appear as if low-performing students who are highly motivated and working hard will inevitably perform at high performance levels.

Distinguishing Between Quality and Sophistication of Performance

Performance can be crude or sophisticated; students can be novices or advanced performers. In either case, we know nothing about the quality of their work: We require a separate report for the quality. Though the developmental/longitudinal descriptors used in South Brunswick and elsewhere are helpful in reporting student achievement levels, these statements do not reveal the quality of work done at that level. We need to develop a reporting system like assessments used in the performing areas of music, figure skating, and gymnastics, where "degree of difficulty" and "quality" are properly distinguished and scores are given for each (and sometimes combined using a weighted factor system).

Years ago, Deborah Meier, the head of Central Park East Schools and MacArthur Fellow, related an anecdote that shows the rationale for honoring this distinction in our reports:

> When people say, "Joe is two grades below grade level," they usually *don't* make clear whether or not he's doing *A* work at that lower level. They typically mean it negatively, in fact: i.e., he's not doing well for someone at that lower level either.

But *slow* does not mean *incompetent*. We need to better distinguish the slowly developing, yet adequate, reader from the sophisticated but sloppy reader. Honesty and fairness demand it.

A closer look at the limits to the language of the NAEP or South Brunswick descriptors (see Figures 11.2, 11.4, and 11.5) shows how much we need indications of quality. The differences in levels relate to the sophistication and scope of the reading strategies employed, not the accuracy or effectiveness with which they are employed; the arithmetic student may make many fewer mistakes than the algebra student. Similarly, in the ACTFL foreign language proficiencies, we distinguish between novice and native speakers, but do not show which students are careful novices or careless native speakers.

A complex yet effective system for making this distinction is the New York State School Music Association (NYSSMA) assessment process. All pieces that might be played by any student, either as a soloist or as a member of small or large ensembles, have been previously ranked by degree of difficulty on a scale of one to six. Once the student or group has chosen the level of difficulty at which they wish to be judged, they are assessed in terms of the various qualities of performance (as in many athletic contests, such as diving, figure skating, and gymnastics). Novices can play low-level pieces well; experts can play complicated pieces with mistakes. The teacher's expectations help parents interpret the judge's scores and help the teacher know whether or not the piece was too easy or difficult for the student(s). And we appropriately expect scores in piece difficulty to increase over time, while quality scores might vary as we tackle a new level of difficulty. Similarly, maybe a speller or writer is more sophisticated than her peers, but is prone to careless mistakes; maybe a boy who is "slow" produces excellent work for his level of development or amount of prior experience. The one-room schoolhouse makes this a needed qualification.

The Rialto, California, school system has developed a new report card that incorporates many of these distinctions. Note that they report not only the student's performance level, but the quality of work against normed expectations at each level in question, three times each year, using letter grades (see Figure 11.6).

Too often, we try to factor in these distinctions about sophistication versus quality merely in our placement system, not our grading. This is fine in theory, but unfair and misleading in practice. Bureaucratic thinking causes us to treat students as the same if they inhabit the same room, even where students may differ greatly in prior experience. We should therefore distinguish course "level" within a classroom, as needed.

For example, we judge all French I or all 1st grade reading students against common benchmarks. But all too often students vary in their prior experience. Assuming that their work is of acceptable quality, why flunk some students in French I for merely being behind their class cohort? What is gained? Why not simply report where they began and where they ended on a continuum, along with normative information?

If the degree of difficulty is fairly applied through placement (or chosen, as in the athletic and artistic cases), then we can judge the quality of the work produced by students in each class through uniform assignments and tests. With increased heterogeneity, however, the variety of sophistication and prior experience increases and the fairness decreases. Mustn't we, then, conduct assessments that attempt to separate sophistication from work quality even after placement into classes has happened? This is of course what

Figure 11.6

RIALTO UNIFIED SCHOOL DISTRICT PUPIL PROGRESS REPORT K–6

Name: ____________________

Guardian: ____________________

Birthdate: ____________________

Teacher: ____________________

School/Year: ____________________

Gr: ____________________

ATTENDANCE

Days Enrolled:			
Days Absent:			
Days Tardy:			

❑ SARB Date: ____________________

Keys To Success:

This Pupil Progress Report (PPR) is one form of communication between school and home. Although growth occurs in a very predictable sequence, each child will have a very different profile which reflects his or her uniqueness. A parent should not feel that all children must show the same progress in each category to be successful. Developmental learning is affected by the age and maturity level of the child, his or her out of school experiences, as well as classroom learning.

Rialto Unified School District strives for all students to be responsible learners. A responsible learner exhibits the following behaviors:
• listens attentively • controls talking • follows directions • works independently • completes assignments on time • returns homework • works cooperatively with others • contributes positively to classroom discussions • demonstrates a positive attitude • produces accurate/legible work • demonstrates organizational skills • uses a range of critical thinking skills • enhances work with technology, resources, and/or creativity • respects others • follows classroom and school rules • takes care of school materials • practices the "A.R.T." of communication (i.e. Appreciation, Respect, and Trust).

STUDENT SERVICES

❑ Title 1
❑ Resource Specialist Program
❑ LEP (Level-Fall_____ Level-Spring_____)
❑ Adapted P.E
❑ Special Day Class
❑ Speech/Language
❑ GATE (Gifted/Talented Ed.)
❑ SST Dates______

STUDENT GOALS: Identify areas of focus or concentrated study during the next trimester. Special attention could be needed to further refine a skill area where success is experienced by your student or to apply extra effort to improve growth in an area of concern. (Use extra paper if necessary.)

Agreements: (Date and Initials of Teacher, Parent, and Student for each goal set.)

TEACHER COMMENTS: (Dated for each reporting period.)

FIGURE 11.6 (*continued*)

STAGES OF DEVELOPMENT

Subject	1	2	3	4	5	6	7	8
BEHAVIORAL	Begins to take turns and shares.	Practices self-responsibility for expected behavior/safety.	Begins to take responsibility for choices. Begins to accept and appreciate differences in others.	Works well independently. Accepts the feelings resulting from challenges and success in daily activities/outline.	Follows rules consistently and works in groups toward a common goal. Accepts responsibility for choices.	Willingness to be flexible to achieve fairness within the group/class.	Displays consistent cooperative effort toward a common goal.	Capable role model/leader. Respected by peers.
HEALTH	Recognizes foods from plants cr animals. Knows personal information—name, address, phone number, etc. Communicates daily needs to an adult.	Recognizes food groups. Identifies potentially dangerous situations. Seeks help from adults. Takes care of daily needs. (food/hygiene)	Recognizes differences between food groups and other food types. Understands safety rules. Shows respect for others. Expresses feelings.	Makes healthy choices regarding food, sleep and exercise. Describes major factors which influence growth. Makes responsible choices with friends. Demonstrates appropriate outlets for anger, disappointment, and disagreement.	Recognizes connection between dietary, sleep, and exercise habits. Describes how to protect themselves from environmental hazards. Describes feeling related to body changes. Shows respect for feelings of others.	Examines own eating, sleep, and exercise habits. Recognizes emergency situations and responds appropriately. Makes decisions about feelings, friends, and safety issues. Recognizes strategies to cope with changes.	Understands connection between healthy mind and body. Analyzes potentially dangerous situations and responds appropriately. Demonstrates positive, realistic body image appropriate to individual differences. Applies appropriate strategies to cope with change.	Uses universal precautions consistently. Analyzes situations to prevent and/or avoid potentially dangerous situations. Practices steps that promote healthy personal hygiene. Recognizes and manages fluctuations in emotions and feelings.
READING	ONLY with individual adult support: Attends to pictures in books. Demonstrates an interest in books or stories.	With guidance: Listens to books. Uses pictures to predict a story. Begins to look at words and letters.	Independently shows reading behavior. Independently uses pictures to gain meaning from reading material. Memorizes reading material to re-read. Knows some letter/sound relationships.	Reads with instruction. Describes and predicts story sequence. Begins to self-correct to make sense of reading material. Recognizes some frequently used words. Uses letter/sound relationships.	Reads grade-level texts with minimal assistance. Understands reading material. Self-corrects to make sense of reading material. Recognizes frequently used words.	Reads grade level texts independently. Predicts and summarizes reading material. Self-corrects consistently to make sense of reading material. Uses a variety of strategies to read new words.	Reads independently. Has insights about reading material. Questions, predicts, summarizes, draws conclusions from reading. Reads and understands a variety of increasingly difficult materials.	Reads independently for a variety of purposes. Has in-depth insights about multiple perspectives on advanced reading material.
WRITING	Uses pictures to create meaning. Orally assigns meaning to their pictures.	Uses scribble writing or letter-like forms. Orally assigns meaning to their own writing. Writing is clearly not pictorial.	Writes words in a left to right, top/bottom progression. Uses letters placed in random order to write text. May copy print without comprehension. Orally assigns meaning to text. Reads own writing sequentially and logically.	Uses sound/symbol relationship to invent spellings. Writes simple sentences. Reads writing to others.	Continues to invent spelling with close approximations. Many commonly used words appear correctly in writing. Begins to use punctuation, mechanics, and grammar. Begins to include details and expand thoughts in writing.	Most words are spelled correctly. Writing reflects logical sequence and meaning. Uses punctuation/mechanics of writing regularly. Includes details and thoughts in writing. Uses a variety of resources to enhance the written product.	Begins to use a variety of writing styles accurately. Writes with examples to support topic. Writer's voice is appropriate to the written task. Uses an expanded vocabulary in writing.	Consistently uses correct mechanics and grammar. Consistently includes relevant reasons or concrete examples to support topic. The target audience is always clear. Uses an expanded vocabulary with fluency.

Note: Boxes in groups of three represent trimester reports. See following "Assessment Marking System."

(Continued on the next page.)

FIGURE 11.6 (*continued*)

STAGES OF DEVELOPMENT

Subject	1	2	3	4	5	6	7	8
LISTEN/ SPEAKING	Listens to stories for a short time. Follows a single direction. Responds or reacts using simple words and phrases.	Listens for short periods when adults are speaking. Listens for enjoyment. Follows more than one oral direction. Expresses ideas using simple words and phrases.	Listens for short periods while peers/ classmates are speaking. Listens for information. Participates in group discussion upon request.	Listens attentively and makes relevant responses. Contributes in a group setting. Expresses ideas using simple sentences in language appropriate to the situation.	Listens to others without interrupting. Participates in discussion using language appropriate to the situation. Speaks confidently and effectively. Delivers simple oral presentations with sequence.	Listens and confidently expresses meaningful ideas that further communication. Voluntarily begins to make relevant contribution to a class discussion.	Adjusts speaking style to meet the needs of a situation. Analyzes and applies verbal information. Consistently makes meaningful contributions to class discussions.	Listens interactively with the focus on the speaker. Uses different oratorical styles appropriately. Uses complex speech structures (idioms, inference) to communicate.
MATH	Develops number sense using objects. Explores geometric shapes, figures and patterns using a variety of materials.	Explores basic understanding of operations using objects. Identifies geometric shapes in their world.	Demonstrates understanding of place value concepts. Shows understanding of operations, i.e., addition facts. Has basic spatial and measurement sense in geometry. Collects and organizes data. Solves everyday problems using basic operations.	Estimates quantities and measures accurately. Selects appropriate computational methods. Uses calculator for complex computation. Uses variables to express relationships. Applies problem-solving strategies accurately.	Demonstrates understanding of fractions, decimals, and thinking strategies for basic facts. Uses measurement and geometry ideas throughout curriculum. Demonstrates exploration of chance orally, in writing. Consistently uses clue words to determine which operation to use in problem solving.	Pursues open-ended problems and extended problem-solving projects. Discusses and writes about math clearly for audience. Understands variables, expressions, and equations of algebra.	Investigates and formulates questions from problem situations. Uses a variety of methods to solve linear equations in algebra. Uses statistical methods to describe, analyze, evaluate, and make decisions.	Represents situations verbally, numerically, graphically, geometrically, or symbolically. Creates experimental and theoretical models of situations involving probabilities.
SCIENCE	Observes daily science through all senses. Communicates pictorially about science.	Communicates orally about science ideas. Compares and orders scientific information.	Uses simple written communication to convey science ideas. Categorizes and labels scientific data.	Communicates about science concepts orally and/or in writing. Sequences and organizes scientific data.	Relates big ideas of science to everyday life orally and in writing.	Draws conclusions and inferences from science lessons and can communicate them to an audience clearly.	Shares accurate scientific understanding with others consistently. Communicates abstract ideas of science accurately using writing multimedia resources.	Sets up experiments based on validity and laws of science. Accurately records scientific experiments through written observations and mathematical constructs.
HISTORY/ SOCIAL STUDIES	Identifies self as a member of family/ class/group. Retells one event from a personal timeline.	Understands/acknowledges need for rules. Expresses own thoughts/ideas. Recognizes ideological and cultural differences. Draws a simple map of home/class/school.	Understands people live/work in communities for mutual benefit. Begins to describe basic elements of culture. Identifies physical characteristics of local region. Produces simple written reports.	Identifies geographic/ economic factors influencing location of settlements. Reads and creates compass rose, street maps, and physical maps. Reads graphs/ interprets single grid charts to explain data.	Understands and articulates concept of cultural diversity. Describes economics of local community. Understands and explains government levels. Reads political map, longitude/ latitude and uses landmarks to create own maps with legend.	Interprets cause/ effect and consequences of living in communities. Understands basic elements of democratic/ constitutional rule. Locates information from a variety of sources and creates more than one type of communication to report data, including timetables and diagrams	Makes reasonable hypothesis and predictions regarding societal change (future). Uses compromise to resolve conflicts.	Analyzes arguments/data to detect influence of bias, and social/class injustices on course history. Independently creates/analyzes/ interprets multigrid charts, graphs, models using multimedia/library resources.

FIGURE 11.6 (*continued*)

STAGES OF DEVELOPMENT

Subject	1	2	3	4	5	6	7	8
PHYS. ED	Hops and gallops on preferred foot. Moves in large group without bumping into others or falling. Explores bouncing, throwing, and catching with many objects.	Hops and gallops on nonpreferred foot, marches, and slides. Travels and changes directions quickly in response to a signal. Performs underhand toss, bounce and catch with two hands, stationary kick, and rolls a ball to objects or classmates.	Skips, hops, gallops, and slides at various speeds/directions. Jumps self-turned rope repeatedly. Throws overhand with side orientation and opposite and catches after one bounce (solo and with partner).	Uses movement skills appropriately in tag and relay games. Performs sequential movements in rhythmic activities. Throws accurately from short distances, catches bounced and aerial balls, and dribbles a ball continuously (hands or feet).	Able to jump and land for height and distance. Recognizes fundamental strategies in simple games. Shows accuracy in throwing and catching, striking with body parts and objects, and controls hand and foot dribbling.	Able to start, stop, dodge, and pivot while maintaining body control. Performs well in games with emphasis on more than two skills. Throws a variety of objects for accuracy and speed.	Proficient in performance of all types of movement skills. Able to combine sequences of movements in complex skills. Throws a variety of objects of accuracy and distance.	Demonstrates excellent skills in individual and team sports. With minimal instruction, reasons how to perform new skills. Able to design basic offensive and defensive strategies in games designed to keep objects away from others.
VISUAL ARTS	Experiments with art material.	Uses pencil and crayon lines. Experiments with color mixing. Begins using paper and clay.	Uses boarders, all-over design, and repeated design. Learns to draw people and illustrate. Prints using runnings, stencils, and gadgets. Develops pictures with stamping and sculpture through paper and clay.	Uses lines, colors, shapes, contrasts, and shading to direct attention to the subject matter. Develops skills with paint experimentation. Utilizes various techniques for graphics, sculpture, and architecture.	Uses concepts of space. Develops construction with various materials. Manipulates various painting techniques using watercolors.	Makes collages, weaves, and uses various media in design and drawing. Develops paper sculptures and mobiles. Paints with various media may include computer aided art.	Designs lettering and strengthens abstract and realistic drawing. Plans prints for stamping and may include computer aided art. Constructs sculpture with paper-mache and other materials.	Uses sketching for drawing and designs murals. Generates original prints for painting and may incorporate computer aided art. Develops sculpture through ceramics and carvings.
PERFORMING ARTS	Experiments with musical and dramatic activities in the spirit of play.	Begins to move to music. Participates in group drama activity.	Dances and is able to mirror another's movements. Sings with an awareness of loud/soft, fast/slow. Develops dramatization of stories.	Develops sense of simple dance patterns. Sings various songs by memory and follows music. Develops awareness of musical instruments.	Dances to rhythms of various cultures. Awareness of musical notation. Prepares original dramatizations.	Senses pulse, tempo, meter, and rhythm patterns of dance. Awareness of computerized and/or synthesized produced sounds and experiments with various recording equipment. Performs plays.	Understands choreography. Performs part singing involved in staged productions.	Expresses the character of the music through improvisational dance. Develops an understanding of various keys, rhythms, and syncopations that can be performed in large or small groups involved in full development of staged productions both in front and behind the scenes.

(Continued on the next page.)

FIGURE 11.6 (*continued*)

"Appropriate Stages of Development"

Student growth and development in academic and behavioral areas occurs in stages. In elementary school students pass though stages of development. Each stage represents a cluster of skills that are linked to each other such that level 1 must be learned before level 2, level 2 before level 3 and so on. Stages are not the same as grade levels but, rather, overlap a span of grades. Progress is measured by movement through stages, not grade levels. "Expected" stages of student growth at each grade level are provided as a guideline.

		Stages of Development							
	K	1	2						
	1	1	2	3					
	2	1	2	3	4				
Grade	3		2	3	4	5			
	4			3	4	5	6		
	5				4	5	6	7	
	6					5	6	7	8

Assessment Marking System:

K–3 Students: "X" in trimester box indicates which stage of development a child is <u>currently working</u>.

Example:

	1			2			3		
Reading									
Trimesters				X				X	X

(Primary student is working in Stage 2 first trimester, stage 3 in second and third trimesters.)

4–6 students: "A,B,C or M" in trimester box indicates working level within stage.

Example:

	3			4			5		
Reading									
Trimesters				B	A				B

(Intermediate student is producing above average work within stage 4 first trimester, outstanding work within stage 4 second trimester, and moved to stage 5 third trimester producing above average work.)

A= outstanding work within stage
C= average work within

B= above average work within stage
M= more growth needed within stage

special education and vocational teachers have done for years; we can learn from their reporting systems.

A legacy of this confusion between sophistication and quality is found in the troubled attempts to establish uniform weighting systems for letter grades—dependent on the "track" of the course. I know of one high school where there are four different academic tracks, and the weighting system multiplies each grade on a 100-point scale by 1.00, 1.10, 1.25, and 1.50, depending on the track. We may appreciate the intent, but the result is capricious. Is the English I course taught in each track in fact more difficult by the specific weighting factor? Who has actually run the experiment, using student papers from all tracks that are graded "blind," to validate the system, to show that the scores in the better class are half again as good on average as in the lower-level class? Mustn't the expectations stay the same across tracks even if the standards differ? How is that assessed? What role do varying content standards play in grading? Insofar as there are rarely clear principles or procedures for asking and answering such questions—and enforcing the system that results—how can such a system be fair or credible? In theory, weighted grades are fair; in practice, most schools do not have the governance structures and oversight policies to ensure that the system works. Better I think to aim over time to do what they do in sports: Multiply the course difficulty by the performance scores, and report progress as well as personal growth. Then, the colleges will have almost all the information they need, and we will stop reporting class rank as if it meant something valid and reliable.

Habits of Mind

Even knowing what Johnny knows and can do, judged against continua of performance progress, doesn't tell us what we should be valuing in the long run about a person's educational progress: Johnny's habits of mind. Despite the typical fuss about SAT scores and transcripts, college admissions officers (and employers) are interested in students' dispositions as learners. Do they persist with difficult work? Can they clarify a task and organize an agenda? Do they ferret out unstated or unexamined assumptions? Are they tolerant of ambiguity? Can they shift perspective and consider different points of view? These capacities are the hard-won fruits of a good education.

By definition, a mature habit of mind is developed only over a long time. Our penchant for one-shot, short-answer tests (and simplistic class ranks) is thus antithetical to the quest for information about habits across time and context. I may know lots of knowledge and quickly put down right answers, but assessors have learned nothing about my ability to ferret out possible solutions to murky complex problems, or whether I am capable of inquiring effectively into what I do not fully know or understand. Surely in the long run my capacities to be self-critical, self-motivated, and effective in gathering research or seeking help are more important to my later intellectual life than whether I can produce pat answers on cue.

We once did not shy away from making these kinds of assessments in schools. Consider the report card categories from a private school in the 1950s, shown in Figure 11.7.

(Note that both teacher and parents are expected to evaluate the habits, and compare their findings!)

Some of these habits are quaint, of course, and a certain docility was clearly valued—but these kinds of reports have their value. Recent data from employers and such reports as the *SCANS Report* (U.S. Department of Labor 1991) on necessary skills in the workplace reveal that employers clearly value certain habits and attitudes (e.g., "works with diversity, negotiates, teaches others" in the *SCANS Report*), they wish them evaluated and reported, and they sometimes

FIGURE 11.7

ASSESSMENT OF HABITS OF MIND

	G	S	F	Un	Sch	H
HABITS OF STUDY AND WORK						
Begins work promptly						
Knows how to utilize time						
Completes assignments on time						
Follows directions accurately						
Is attentive during class						
Takes part in class discussions						
GOOD SOCIAL LIVING						
Shows consideration by caring for personal belongings						
Shares graciously with others						
Cooperates cheerfully						
Is careful of things belonging to others						
Listens politely when others speak						
HABITS OF POLITE SPEECH						
Says "I beg your pardon" when wishing someone to repeat what has been said						
Says "Thank you" for compliments received						
Greets teachers, parents, and friends graciously						
Knows how to make and acknowledge an introduction						
HABITS OF PERSONAL DEVELOPMENT						
Is dependable and responsible						
Shows initiative						
Shows self-control						
Responds promptly and cheerfully to authority						
Is attentive to good posture						

Key: G = Good; S = Satisfactory; F = Failing; Un = Unknown
Sch = school; H = home

place more emphasis on such evaluations than school transcripts. Most technical high schools do report such information on work-related habits and attitudes. And they matter in the college admissions process. Consider, for example, the rating sheet to be filled out by a student's teachers, which is part of the admissions packet used by more than 100 private liberal arts colleges nationally (see Figure 11.8).

This rating sheet is a useful model for emulating in our local school reports, especially if what we do can be better justified by its alignment with competitive college admissions.

Yet there are flaws in this form if we follow the logic I previously laid out. Rarely does a teacher have to justify or defend his rating. And note that the form asks for local-norm-referenced data, not criterion-referenced data: Maybe "the best I have encountered in my career" is pretty mediocre in the grand scheme of competitive colleges. By what criteria and indicators are these judgments to be made? The colleges should provide better guidance, as well as some sample data or student profiles that fit each category.

Nor would I recommend that we rely solely on anecdotal evidence and casual observation in

FIGURE 11.8

COLLEGE ADMISSIONS RATING SHEET

Please feel free to write whatever you think is important about the applicant, including a description of academic and personal characteristics. We are particularly interested in the candidate's intellectual purpose, motivation, relative maturity, integrity, independence, originality, leadership potential, capacity for growth, special talents, and enthusiasm. We welcome information that will help us to differentiate this student from others.

RATINGS

No Basis	Academic Skills and Potential	Below Average	Average	Good	Very Good	One of the top few encountered in my career
	Creative, original thought					
	Motivation					
	Independence, initiative					
	Intellectual ability					
	Academic achievement					
	Written expression of ideas					
	Effective class discussion					
	Disciplined work habits					
	Potential for growth					
	SUMMARY EVALUATION					

making such assessments about a student's habits of mind. Rather, we should do a better job of deliberately designing assessment tasks that can be successfully completed only by students who persevere, who challenge false but plausible assumptions, and who know that key data are missing. A teacher I worked with once wisely said: "The trouble with kids today is they don't know what to do when they don't know what to do." Yes, but it's because we rarely devise formal assessments that routinely put them in such authentic messy contexts, with real problems (as opposed to contrived exercises)—what I am fond of calling "Intellectual Outward Bound" (Wiggins 1993, Chapters 2 and 6).

Verifying the Report: Providing Models

If we are going to provide more information of different kinds, there will be a pressing need for "decoding" mechanisms so that clients can understand why a score and grade were justified. Few parents understand what counts as exemplary performance, what it actually looks like. Why? Because few schools disseminate samples of excellent work to serve as a frame of reference for assessing a child's performance in context. It stands to reason, then, that parents can fully decode a report only if we provide them with the rubrics, sample products, and developmental descriptors that we use in student performance assessment. If parents are to find the report helpful and credible, we must give them the tools to verify and understand student scores—the anchor products and scoring guidelines.

At the Center on Learning, Assessment, and School Structure (CLASS), we have worked with a few districts to develop a document-backed reporting system, using as our guide the fine work done over the years by the Carleton School District in Ontario, Canada (and similar models found in the AP program through the booklets published for AP teachers). Carleton publishes "exemplar booklets" that provide students, parents, and teachers with the operational standards of assessment: samples of the range of papers, teacher commentaries on those papers, and the rubrics used to score them. Parents are then in a position to actually *verify* the grades given (or challenge them, in the worst-case—but also fair—scenario). The report card then actually informs and educates the parent. With this report, parents will more likely be educational partners because they will understand the aims of the school and any gap between student intent and effect.

We have also developed a mockup of a page from a parent report that provides most of the kinds of data we have considered here. There would be a page for each aspect of literacy (reading, writing, speaking, listening), as well as separate reports for math, science, and social studies. This report card also assumes district use of the Victoria, Australia, K–12 "English Profiles," a scale with descriptors for charting literacy growth over the student's entire career (Ministry of Education and Training 1991). Figure 11.9 provides excerpts from the scoring system for writing.

The report card shown in Figure 11.10 assumes that the parent has received the background documentation for writing (as excerpted in Figure 11.9); that is, each parent possesses the booklet describing each of the literacy "bands," with A through I symbolized only with a letter on the report card, and samples of assignments and student work that correspond to each level.

Feasibility

Several people who read the earlier article on which this essay is based (Wiggins 1994) commented that my proposals were interesting but impractical. This is an understandable comment—if

FIGURE 11.9

ENGLISH PROFILES IN WRITING

Writing Band A

Uses implements to make marks on paper.
Copies "words" from signs in immediate environment.
Explains the meaning of marks.
Writing shows understanding of difference between print and picture . . .

Writing Band B

Holds pencil/pen using satisfactory grip.
Writes own name.
Writing shows use of vocabulary of print.
Use of letters and other conventional symbols . . .

Writing Band F

Narratives contain introduction, complication, and resolution in logical order.
Complex sentences—principal and subordinate clauses; use of both active and passive voice.
Corrects most spelling, punctuation, grammatical errors in editing other's written work.
A range of vocabulary and grammatical structures.
Understanding of the difference between narrative and other forms of writing.
Consults available sources to improve or enhance writing.

Writing Band H

Vocabulary shows awareness of ambiguities and shades of meaning.
Meaning is expressed precisely.
Edits and revises own work to enhance effect of vocabulary, text organization, and layout.
Organization and layout or written text is accurate and appropriate for purpose, situation, and audience.
Figurative language, such as metaphor, is used to convey meaning.
Edits and revises others' writing, improving presentation and structure without losing meaning or message.

Writing Band I

Writes with ease in both short passages and extended writing on most familiar topics.
Extension beyond the conventions of standard English writing in a skillful and effective way.
Uses analogies, symbolism, and irony.
Structures a convincing argument in writing.

Source: Victoria, Australia, K–12 "English Profiles." Adapted by permission.

we assume that the current job descriptions, schedules, testing systems, and policies remain unchanged. But it is a sad and unfortunate comment if it means that educators will resist any idea that cannot be immediately used "on Monday" in their current school context.

"Restructuring" is not a mere buzzword, but a call for getting the policies and resources of schools to align with missions and purposes. And the most important structure in schools that needs alteration *right now* is the schedule: Our use of time makes thorough assessment and reporting impossible.

FIGURE 11.10

DEWEY LANGUAGE ARTS REPORT
DEWEY SCHOOL DISTRICT: LANGUAGE ARTS—WRITING

Student: John Doe

Level of Performance: Writing: semester (2/93–6/93)

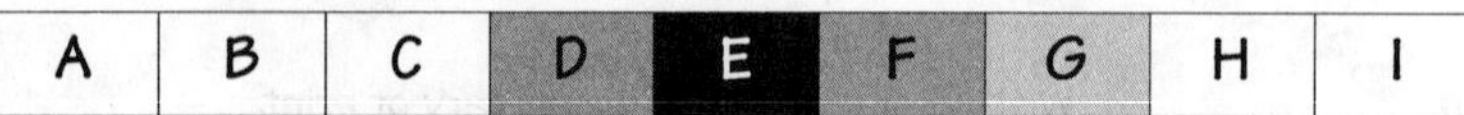

shading is proportional to frequency of scores

Level of Performance: Writing: year (9/92–6/93)

shading is proportional to frequency of scores

Progress in Writing: 4/5 (Good, relative to class)

Quality of Work Products: 3/5 (Satisfactory; slightly below average)

Consistency of Work Product Quality: 2/5 (well below average of class)

Class Data: Writing

Class Range: Writing 5/93

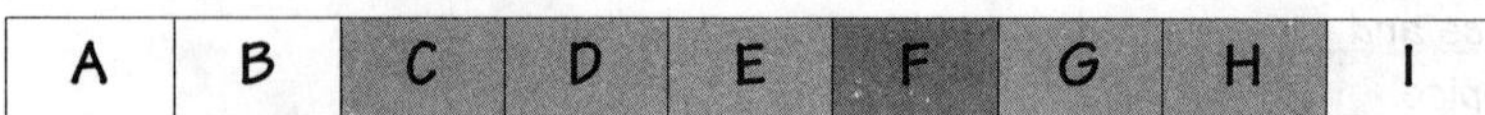

Class Performance: Writing 5/93

1. criteria scores (average of scores on all five leading criteria): **3.6** (out of 5)
2. most difficult criterion: "revision leading to polished work": **2.6** (out of 5)

Work This Quarter

4 stories, poems
6 analytic papers
1 formal reseach paper
reflection journal
4 tests on books read

Writing Profile

Genres of writing
strength: persuasive
weakness: analytic
most progress: description

Criteria scores
strength: vitality of ideas (**3.6**)
weakness: mechanics (**2.3**)
greatest gain:
focus (**2.4 -> 3.2**)

Each criterion is judged using a 5-point scale:
5 = top score

Score in parentheses = student's average score

Please refer to exemplar book for samples of student papers for each level of performance and quality of work, summary of the six genres of writing and five criteria used in scoring, and description of performance levels.

An old architectural aphorism tells us how to judge school structures: Form Follows Function in good design. But in schools, the opposite conditions exist. All functions must adapt to the (often dysfunctional) forms that are the hallmarks of bureaucratized schoolkeeping. Here are our usual, unfortunate responses to the things we wish we could do: *The schedule prohibits the doing of real lab science.* Sorry: Change your science teaching, not the schedule. *The job description of principals leaves no time to manage ongoing inquiry and discussion of student performance.* Too bad: Postpone the crucial conversations and stick to buses and fights in the halls. *Teacher jobs are defined in terms of contact hours with kids.* Can't help you: Do quality assessment in your free time.

These conditions persist only because we allow them to. Assessment and report card reform can occur only if we make our schedules adapt to our needs instead of the reverse.

The key question is simple enough: What time do faculties need to do quality ongoing assessment and thorough report writing? Let's alter the schedule, incrementally, to make that possible. What we will discover if we clarify our assessment and reporting needs is that we must keep asking an atypical next question that challenges a key unexamined assumption about scheduling: What kinds of yearly and monthly changes in the schedule—not weekly schedules—are necessary for quality assessment and reporting? We must stop thoughtlessly assuming, therefore, that changing the schedule means changing the weekly schedule; we must stop trying to make every week look like every other week.

Why? Because assessment and reporting come in cycles of about 4–8 weeks; why not free people up for a day a month to read portfolios, administer assessment tasks, do collaborative scoring, and write reports? (Either build in a noncontact day, rotate the day across teams/departments with the other teams covering, use aides/parents to cover the time needed, use early-release days, or plan special programs that use special or external teachers to cover the day.) This is not impractical; many schools now free up such time for team planning and committee work. Why do we continue to falsely assume that school boards and parents won't grasp the importance of noncontact time for the careful evaluation of children? A request for assessment time is *very* different from asking for "professional development" time: Why should the public pay for our education?

The other criticism often made of these ideas is that they won't work because they demand too much of teachers, and that there is little incentive to persist with such systems. The recent complaints in Great Britain about the new assessment system tend to bear this out; so does the experience of recent converts to portfolios. But the problem in both cases, I think, has been not only the failure to free up teacher time but also the failure to adequately sell parents, board members, and skeptical teachers on the need for the changes. Once the clients of schools see that they can get better information, they will demand it and support changes to get it. (And once we stop calling this noncontact time "professional development" time—as if the Board should underwrite our education—and calling it "quality evaluation and reporting:" time, we will see political battles ease.) Put differently, the incentives for change must not be derived only from teacher interests; they must be derived from what is in the clients' interests. If clients of schools do not see your new assessments and reports as more helpful, more informative, and thus worth the extra time and effort, then someone has failed to do a basic public relations job.

A fine way to begin such a public relations effort is with carefully run focus groups of representatives from each client group (parents, board members, colleges, employers, etc.) in which the sole purpose of the meetings is to hear out the clients on what they like and dislike about grades, tests, and reports—followed up by a discussion and rating of different possible reports (including the draft of the proposed new report your folks are working on, without the group knowing its origin). The focus group discussions should be videotaped, edited, and distributed to every school team or department. Until teachers are in the habit of considering real, diverse clients (as opposed to idealized clients—as if "the parents" were a unitary thing), the energy required to sustain the reform will not be forthcoming.

This brings us back to using narratives as a part of assessments. They have their value; they are worth the effort as part of a more comprehensive and data-filled report. I worked in a boarding school where each student we taught, each athlete we coached, and each person we counseled/advised received a written half-page of comments along with their grades—three times a year. It was a huge burden, but it was rarely begrudged. The parents—and the other faculty advisors—were invariably generous in their praise when reports were informative, and they really did grasp that the grade minus the comment was a poor substitute. The college guidance people routinely drew heavily on those reports. Students always appreciated reports that were thorough and helpful. And these reports were ideal for describing the students' habits of mind in context in a way that avoided the seeming arbitrariness of scores or grades for such achievements. (As an advisor, I also saw how bad it looked when one had to share glib or inarticulate teacher comments with advisees.) All of these facts were incentive enough for me to give my time over to writing narratives well.

Criteria for Effective Reports

We can summarize the points in this chapter as a set of criteria for judging reports:

1. The clients for the information are always the final judge of the report's value.
2. There are multiple clients with differing needs for information.
3. Reports should justify and substantiate data and judgments wherever possible, so that the readers have the resources to easily verify the report if they so choose.
4. The report should paint a rich, accurate, and honest profile of achievement, progress, and growth.
5. The assessments used to generate the report should be credible and fair.
6. Performance should be divided into major subcomponents, with separate scores/grades.
7. Performance scores should not be arbitrarily translated into letter grades. To summarize the differences:

"Performance Scores" are:	**"Letter Grades" are typically:**
• Absolute (judged against fixed exemplars, hence linked to standards)	• Relative (to the individual's best work or the norms of the local cohorts, hence linked to expectations)
• Criterion-referenced (dependent on adherence to criteria, and a disinterested scoring process focused on achievement only)	• Related to attitude and effort, not just achievement
• Standard-Referenced (scores in reference to validated exemplars; score ranges are unpredictable)	• Norm-Referenced and individual-referenced (scores based on past patterns for cohorts and the individual)
• Not age or experience dependent	• Context-dependent

As noted throughout this chapter, all my suggestions stem from trying to honor the core values of honesty and fairness in assessment and reporting. It matters little whether the specific ideas for reform proposed here are implemented. It matters a great deal if we fail to use honesty and fairness as the criteria against which any report card reforms are judged.

References

American Association for the Advancement of Science. (1993). *Benchmarks for Science Literacy: Project 2061.* New York: Oxford Press.

Bloom, B.S., G.F. Madaus, and J.T. Hastings. (1981). *Evaluation to Improve Learning.* New York: McGraw Hill.

Henderson, E.H. (1990). *Teaching Spelling.* 2nd ed. Boston: Houghton Mifflin.

Kendall, J.S., and R.J. Marzano (1994). *The Systematic Identification and Articulation of Content Standards and Benchmarks—Update.* Aurora, Colo.: Mid-Continent Regional Educational Laboratory.

Lowell, A.L. (January 1926). "The Art of Examination." *Atlantic Monthly* 137, 1: 58–66.

Ministry of Education and Training, Victoria, Australia. (1991). *English Profiles, Victoria Australia* (formerly the *Literacy Profiles*). Available through Touchstone Applied Science Associates (TASA), Brewster, N.Y.

National Council of Teachers of Mathematics. (1989). *Curriculum and Evaluation Standards for School Mathematics.* Reston, Va.: Author.

Thorndike, E. (1913) *Educational Psychology.* Vol. 1. New York: Teachers College Press.

U.S. Department of Labor. (1991). *What Work Requires of Schools: A SCANS Report for America 2000.* Washington, D.C.: U.S. Government Printing Office.

Wiggins, G. (Winter 1988). "Rational Numbers: Scoring and Grading That Helps Rather Than Hurts Learning." *American Educator* 12, 4: 20–48.

Wiggins, G. (February 1991). "Standards, Not Standardization: Evoking Quality Student Work." *Educational Leadership* 48, 5: 18–25.

Wiggins, G. (1993). *Assessing Student Performance: Exploring the Purpose and Limits of Testing.* San Francisco: Jossey-Bass.

Wiggins, G. (1994). "Toward Better Report Cards." *Educational Leadership* 50, 2: 28–37.

Wright, R.G. (May 1994). "Success For All: The Median Is the Key." *Phi Delta Kappa* 75, 9: 723–725.

12

Technology's Promise for Reporting Student Learning

W. Ross Brewer and Bena Kallick

Let's imagine a high school sophomore named Rachel who lives in Vermont. She has a videotape of her social studies research exhibition in which she has debated herself from two perspectives:

- There is no such thing as a "good" war; war is never a reasonable answer.
- The American Revolution was a "good" war; there is justification for war.

Rachel transfers the video to the school's computer and also scans in the text of her report. She will be evaluated on her presentation and the quality of her report by a panel of judges that includes community members and her teacher.

In art and mathematics, Rachel photographs her projects with a digital camera and uploads the pictures to her file on the computer. Her reading of Moliere in French is taped and added to the collection, along with her physics experiments. Rachel's digital portfolio contains examples of her work from throughout the year, along with pieces she and her teachers have decided should be kept from earlier years.

Rachel's activities are nothing new. They are happening in schools across the United States today. What is new is how people may use this information. For example, after dinner, Rachel's mother dials the school's computer from her television set. After entering Rachel's security code, she opens her daughter's portfolio and reviews her work over the semester. She also reviews teachers' evaluations of each project. When she has questions, she enters them for the teacher's consideration. She also switches to the standards used to evaluate Rachel's efforts and views benchmark work that is an example of how the scoring system operates. She sends comments about the portfolio pieces to Rachel, her teachers, and her advisor. On another evening, Rachel's father, who lives in California, dials the school's computer and goes through the same process.

At the end of the year, Rachel's work is stored in the district's computer archives after she selects the pieces she wants to add to her personal digital portfolio. This portfolio will be accessible only to Rachel, her parents, and school personnel. In her senior year, it will serve as the basis for a résumé if she decides to seek employment or an application if she decides to continue her education.

Wendell is a senior citizen in Rachel's hometown who has raised a question about his taxes. He is concerned with the amount of money being spent on education and believes that students are not producing high-quality work. He says schools aren't "doing the job."

Wendell can dial the district's computer from his living room TV and review the standards used to evaluate students along with benchmark work at each level of performance. He can read the records regarding student performance from the perspective of state measures, standardized measures, and qualitative measures of student work in the classroom. Also using his TV, he can send comments and questions to the board of education on the school's computer.

Although Rachel and Wendell are fictional characters, they symbolize the way technology will revolutionize our reporting system. The process will be propelled by the changing nature of society, the needs of schools, and advances in technology. Assessment will be more open and will provide much richer information to parents, teachers, school leaders, school board members, community members, employers, college admissions personnel, legislators, and other key state and federal officials.

A Vision for Reporting Student Learning

Early in the next century, parents will be able to dial schools from their TVs anywhere in the country and review their children's work. Upon request, the school's computer will collect relevant information and send it to parents for viewing at their leisure. Parents will be able to watch their children's performances in gymnastics, dance, or theater; see exhibitions of their work including reading and painting; review their papers; and see 3-D models of their mathematics and science projects. Also, parents—along with community members—will be able to examine the standards used to assess their child's work and to compare that work to benchmark performances exemplifying different levels of achievement.

Even before that scenario becomes reality, students will lead student-parent-teacher conferences. There they will explain their work using multimedia portfolios featuring models, exhibitions, and performances along with papers and projects. In the future, these might be video conferences connecting school and work or home. The teacher's role will be to answer parents' questions. At exit meetings with peers, parents, members of the community, and teachers, students will use their own digital portfolios to reflect on their accomplishments in school within and across disciplines.

Teachers from across a district or state will work together to establish benchmarks and assess student work without having to attend endless meetings. Instead, they will send student work and their responses to it from one computer to another, discussing their views online or in video conferences. Schools will send work that has been assessed to district offices where results from across the district can be compiled. Summary reports, along with student benchmark papers, will then be sent back to the school.

Catalysts for Change

Changes in society and technology will push schools toward the vision described here. Because fewer and fewer children live with both their birth parents, giving and getting information about student achievement is becoming more difficult. Where the original family is still intact, both parents are in all likelihood working outside the home. They have less time to visit schools, take part in conferences, or talk to teachers about their child's achievement.

In an Information Age, we can fully expect that school reporting systems will increasingly reflect what we have become accustomed to outside of school life. Technology makes it possible to satisfy our needs almost immediately through the use of fax machines and computers. You can order lunch or dinner using a fax machine and have it delivered at your convenience. You can even order pizza online. You can shop on TV using the Internet or many of the commercial online services. You can bank, get medical advice, read a newspaper or magazine, and even start dating online. In some parts of the country, you can order a movie to be viewed on your television at home, when you want to see it.

We are in an age of customer service, as well. Remember the days when you took your car in for repair, picked it up, then two days later it broke down again? What was the mechanic's response? Too bad! Bring it back. Today, when your car goes in for repair, you will receive a call one day later from the manager. How was the service? Were you satisfied? Is there anything more that we can do for you? Look on the top of the dresser in the next motel you visit. Most likely you will find a "report card" asking you to evaluate the services, the room, and the hotel in general.

Customer service means a high degree of accountability for services. It implies a feedback loop to the people who are serving you. As we become more accustomed to this level of responsive services, we will demand a similar orientation from schools. Parents will expect to be asked, "How is the school doing for your child?" They will expect to be part of a feedback loop in which their child's performance is reported with a sufficient amount of frequency so they can join the school's effort to improve learning. In addition, they will expect to see the school respond to their feedback.

In this age of accountability, products are continuously evaluated for their quality, companies for their performance, and public figures for their popularity. Society will demand more and more information about student performance in schools; and as people become more knowledgeable, they will want more complex information.

It is clear that parents and large percentages of community members care about how well students and schools are performing and want to know more. In the past several years, the Phi Delta Kappa/Gallup Polls have indicated the following trends:

- Interest in and contact with public schools has been increasing on the part of parents and the public (Elam, Rose, and Gallup 1991, 1994).
- Significant groups of parents, particularly those of high school students and students who are not doing well in school, would like better information about how well their children are performing (Elam, Rose, and Gallup 1992).
- Parents would like different, more informative formats for reporting about their children's progress (Elam, Rose, and Gallup 1994).
- Parents would like to use this information to understand the strengths and shortcomings of

both students and schools. Parent involvement varies along demographic dimensions and the characteristics of the school their children attend (Bauch and Goldring 1995).

A recent report of a survey released by the Center on Families, Communities, Schools, and Children's Learning noted that 80 percent of parents of high school students said they wanted to be more involved than they currently were in the school and with their children's work, and 77 percent wanted ideas on how to monitor homework and talk to their children about it (Connors and Epstein 1994).

The system, as it currently works, cannot supply sufficient and frequent enough information to satisfy the public. We are pushing the outer limits of what is possible given the limited amount of time and energy teachers have to do this work. Technology can provide useful tools for doing the work of reporting with greater breadth, depth, and efficiency.

Technology's New Promise

Time and again, technology's promise to schools has been exaggerated leaving educators, students, and parents disappointed. What is different now? How can technology make teachers' work easier and the information parents and the community receives better? What is it about technology that offers so much potential for improving how we report student performance?

Unlike some of the early work with schools and computers, technology for reporting offers a natural fit between the need and the medium. Consider, for example, the following:

1. *Technology can make information available anytime, anywhere.* Computers and telephone lines are accessible 24 hours a day so users are not limited by school hours or location. Rachel's mother does not need to take time from work to go to school for a conference. If Rachel's father arrives home at 9 p.m. in California (midnight in the Vermont), he will still be able to look at and comment on Rachel's work.

2. *Because computers can collect and store vast amounts of information—as well as process and retrieve it quickly and accurately—they put users in charge of information they want to review.* Information based on student work can be arranged, rearranged, and reported to meet the needs of different consumers. For example, Rachel's French teacher can review Rachel's reading performances in September, December, and May. Her principal can find out at what level students in his school are reading in French at the end of the year. The district office can determine how well students across the district are reading French. The district assessment committee can gather benchmark performances to guide future assessments and review how consistently teachers across the district are assessing student work. Rachel's mother can study only the work that Rachel has done since her last review. Rachel can arrange her work in a portfolio, selecting the best pieces of reading and composition to send to a statewide contest sponsored by the state foreign language teachers' association. All these needs can be met by one system.

3. *We value what we assess, but we can only assess what we see or hear.* Technology will make student achievement more visible. For a long time, student performances were available only to the few who happened to be in the classroom or auditorium. The performances that could be exhibited to a wider audience were limited and not widely accessible, such as art shows and science fairs. Even these events were rarely judged against a set of easily understood performance standards. Technology makes it possible to record and retain virtually all performances and to make them available to all who are interested. These performances can be compared directly to standards such as graduation requirements and building-level exit criteria. Everyone in the community

can become the assessor of the school's achievements.

4. *Technology also makes it possible to use time as a different dimension of assessment.* Today, we summarize students' achievement at year's end by reporting whether each student has passed the threshold for the current year—1 of 13 thresholds to be crossed on the journey to graduation. Technology allows us to review earlier performances any time—weeks, months, or years earlier. When used with standards related to graduation, performances can be seen as milestones toward achieving those goals. We can analyze achievement developmentally over one year or over several years and report the results in terms of progress toward achieving the graduation standard. Students do not need to be marched across 13 thresholds, 1 year at a time.

Tools Already Available

Everything we have described exists somewhere in the United States today. Teachers are using hand-held personal digital assistants to record information about their students as they work in their classrooms, downloading it to their computers when it is convenient, and assessing students based on that information. Students are preparing electronic portfolios. Now on the market are digital cameras costing less than $100 that can take both video and still images to record exhibits and performances. In more and more schools, classrooms are networked and schools are connected to the central office so that information can be shared conveniently.

Digital portfolios are a reality in many schools. With a grant from IBM, Croton-Harmon Public Schools are in the process of developing digital portfolios K–12. Each school has involved its building planning team—which includes parents, teachers, and administrators—in a process to determine the focus of the portfolios. In addition, each school has an action research team that is working out the practicalities of the portfolios. The elementary school is focusing its primary portfolios on emerging literacy. The upper elementary school is focusing on evidence from the academic and artistic life of students. These portfolios will include examples of problem solving, communication, and work in a team. The emphasis will be on developing students' capacity to be self-directed, reflective, and self-evaluative.

Students will enter the middle school prepared to focus on the next developmental stage of work: research, response to text, artistic and kinesthetic responses, and observation. The evidence will be organized according to eight themes: life cycles, symbols, aesthetics, time and space, social web, producing, and consuming and connection to nature. The students will prepare their portfolios and present them to their parents, community members, and members of the board of education.

Students also will present their work to their high school guidance teachers and will continue to build their digital portfolios by focusing on research, communication, and problem solving. By the end of their senior year, students will have portfolios to provide information for college admissions or employment applications. The students engaged in this process are not thinking about these portfolios as a replacement of present admissions requirements such as SAT test scores or grades. Instead, the portfolios are another way of demonstrating who they are as learners and what they are capable of doing with examples of their work and reflections about its meaning.

In Swift House, one of the learning units in Williston, Vermont's only public school, every student's learning plan is online on the school's computer. The learning plan includes broad goals, objectives, scoring rubrics for four levels of performance (novice, apprentice, practitioner, and scholar), and the projects and achievement levels for goal areas that have been met. The learning plan is reviewed regularly by teachers (who call themselves facilitators) and by students. Every eight weeks, students' portfolios are sent home so that students can explain their achievements to their parents who then attend a meeting with the student and facilitator to discuss progress and to select new goals. By next year, each student's portfolio will be on CD-ROM and linked to the learning plan so that all will be able to view the work and relate it to the achievement of goals.

At the Burris Laboratory School at Ball State University, each 3rd grade student receives a video report card at the end of the year. The videos run between 20 minutes and 1 hour, depending on how long the interviews with each student last. They include teacher comments personalized to each child; achievement modules depicting students' academic progress in math, reading, language arts, and spelling; special events and visits to the classroom; and interviews with students to discuss their accomplishments for the year. In a follow-up survey, 97 percent of parents reported that the video was more effective than traditional report cards, and 84 percent said that the video stimulated more discussion. Some viewed the video at least seven times (Greenwood 1995).

Technology is advancing at an exponential rate. Computers are becoming faster, larger, and cheaper, all at the same time. New and more sophisticated recording equipment appears on the market weekly. Software that allows users to describe the information they want to receive from a database on a regular basis exists in rudimentary form today. The capacity to link homes and schools grows rapidly. As budgets continue to shrink, the question of equal access to technology's tools will become increasingly more apparent. A crucial issue for the Information Age will be how to create a toll-free Information Highway.

Making the Vision a Reality

Even though the technology exists today, it is far from certain that schools or communities can make our vision a reality. For most school districts and parents, the Information Superhighway is a mysterious and untested place. Most teachers have only a nodding acquaintance with computers, and many parents still have VCRs flashing "12:00" because they have not learned how to use its features.

A variety of equipment will be needed: computers, scanners, VCRs, personal digital assistants, digital cameras, modems, and telephone lines. Careful planning will be required to establish priorities and a schedule for adding equipment. Easy-to-use software to weave the pieces together is critical to the process. Some technology must be improved and become cheaper before it can be used to achieve the vision. And while all of the technology we describe exists today, it is not all widely available. If he lives in the right community, Rachel's father can download a movie to his television, but he cannot dial into the school's computer with it.

Equally as important, few students, parents, teachers, or community members have experience with the substantive conversations about student learning that were described earlier. It is easy to be seduced by the promise of technology when many of the changes that need to be made have little or nothing to do with technology itself. Technology is a vehicle. Alone, it will not lead to achieving the vision. What nontechnological elements will help make the vision possible? There are two. The first has to do with how we organize our schools and interact with the community. The second is related to people and how we support them.

School Organization and Community Interaction

Most schools are not organized to engage in substantive conversations about how to assess and discuss student achievement. So a starting point is to have parents and community members who have worked with teachers and others in the educational community arrive at a common understanding of the important knowledge, skills, and habits of mind that are sufficiently important to be reported to all of the audiences described earlier.

Schools that put effective and lasting reporting systems in place spend a great deal of time listening to and working with community members and parents, finding out what they believe is important and how they think the information would be best reported. Each year, teachers in Swift House in Williston, Vermont, go on a retreat with a group of parents to review last year's program and explore and plan for changes for the coming year. Teachers in the group spend a great deal of time working with parents so they understand what the team is trying to accomplish and can contribute their own thinking. As one of the teachers on the team said, "We win over parents one at a time."

Years ago when they began planning, the school district's first action was to convene a community meeting to decide what children should be able to do as a result of attending school in Williston. Over the years, this document has evolved into a set of exit outcomes for 4th and 8th grade students. Teachers must be committed to and capable of teaching, assessing, and reporting the knowledge, skills, and habits of mind that they and their partners in the community have agreed on.

Results cannot be reported publicly using standards and benchmarks unless teachers have common expectations for their students and assess student work consistently. At a high school where one of the authors has worked, the faculty developed a set of standards for assessing student achievement and agreed to use portfolios as part of the assessment. However, teachers across different houses in the school did not agree on the contents of a portfolio and did not use portfolios in the same way, though they did score student work together to assure that they were applying and communicating the same expectations. At a community-school meeting to discuss expectations for students, parents with children attending different houses were surprised and somewhat discomfited to learn that assessment and evaluation practices differed. Before students can produce the kind of work that will be exposed to public scrutiny, they must have a clear understanding of the standards by which they will be assessed and the opportunity to develop projects and performances worthy of reporting.

In Joan Simmon's classroom in Craftsbury Common, Vermont, 7th and 8th grade students conduct professional discussions about the quality of their writing, applying the Vermont scoring rubrics to one another's work. It is not uncommon to hear one student say to another, "This is an interesting piece, but I don't hear your voice in it," or "I think you use too much detail in this piece; it confuses the reader." Students often rate other students' pieces by voting in their peer conferencing groups or as a whole class. In Ann Rainey's 8th grade mathematics classroom in Shelburne, Vermont, a boy standing in the back of the room was heard to say "Jeez, that's sweet!" after a girl had presented a particularly elegant solution to an algebra problem.

Technology is wasted on reporting shoddy work. Students must understand what quality work is before they can be expected to produce it. This means that they must learn to self-assess, to listen to the critiques of others, and to use that information to improve what they have started. In many classrooms in Vermont, students use self-assessment sheets in mathematics and writing to evaluate their work before they ever hand it in. They listen closely to the comments of their peers as well. Often, students and teachers will compare their assessments. Over the last several years, agreement between student and teacher on levels of performance have become closer as each has become more familiar with the standards.

Support for Staff Members

Using technology to report and facilitate discussion about student achievement requires a management system that will support technology in and out of the classroom. In this vision, teachers are coaches, assessors, and communicators. They are not VCR operators, photographers, data-entry clerks, or computer programmers. A system is needed to allow for audiotaping and videotaping, photographing, scanning, and entering information into the computer. The most obvious sort of talent for this work is students themselves, who are generally more sophisticated than their teachers in this realm.

For example, student volunteers helped to prepare the VCR report card at the Burris Laboratory School. In addition to the full-time technology coordinator in Williston, another teacher is released half-time to work with teachers in adapting and adopting technology to their teaching, assessing, and reporting needs. Williston plans to rely heavily on students to record the work for their portfolios on CD-ROM.

In a summer institute sponsored by Teaching and Technology Consortium, parents, teachers, administrators, and board members became members of a learning community, modeling the uses of technologies as significant tools for learning and reporting. Instructors in the Institute included high school students. Once again, participants were amazed by the comfort and capability the students demonstrated with the technologies. As one teacher exclaimed, "I now realize how underutilized the students are in our high school!" As we move toward school-to-career considerations, technologies will serve as a catalyst for bringing students to the workplace for learning. The lines between school and community will disappear; and teaching, learning, and reporting will increase in credibility as intergenerational groups work more closely together.

In our vision, school is organized around assessing the authentic achievement of its students, reporting the results widely to many audiences, and acting on the results using technology to make these conversations more powerful for everyone. In Victoria Bernhardt's book *The School Portfolio* (1994), a case is made for using technology to inform schools about their progress around dimensions such as leadership, information and analysis, quality planning, and student achievement. Bernhardt's work provides a clear example of how the use of computers as tools makes data-based decision making possible. The concept of a feedback spiral (Figure 12.1) demonstrates a frame of mind that we must have if we are to use assessment data to report on continuous improvement. The reporting system will help us move from our present summative frame of mind in which we make judgments and interventions on a yearly basis to a continuous relationship with assessment data that help us monitor and adjust on a formative basis.

Tips for Success

Of course, there is no single way to achieve this vision. Each school will do it in its own way. However, if some elemental ideas are followed, success is much more likely.

1. **Plan well.** Careful planning is the key to success. Take into consideration both the technological and nontechnological pieces of the puzzle. Think expansively as you plan. This is about system change, not just technology or reporting results.

FIGURE 12.1

CONTINUOUS GROWTH THROUGH FEEDBACK SPIRALS

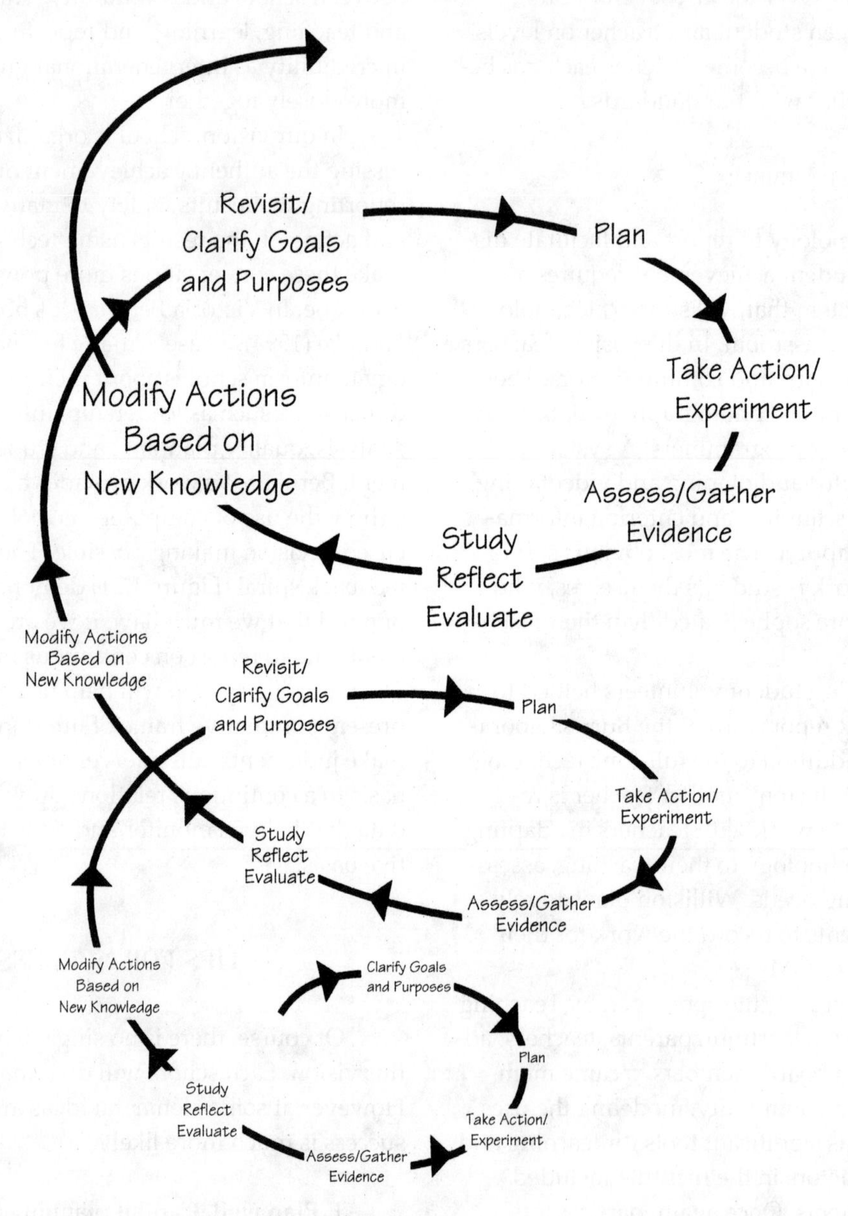

Source: Costa, A., and B. Kallick. (1995). Assessment in the Learning Organization. Alexandria, VA: ASCD. Reprinted by permission.

2. **Make planning a community effort.** Assessment and reporting systems fail if they do not have the backing of community members who will receive reports. Be sure they are part of the planning process.

3. **Start slowly and build carefully.** Don't overwhelm people at the beginning. Williston started with a simple piece of online software that described goals and objectives for each student. Gradually, other pieces like the rubrics and comments section were added as needs became apparent and familiarity with the system grew. Williston is now ready to add a CD-ROM portfolio.

4. **Be forward looking in the equipment you buy.** Don't purchase equipment that will be obsolete in a few years. You may need to create a partnership with companies that keep their equipment updated and are willing to donate their used models. Leasing equipment is another possibility.

5. **Support teachers as they go through the process.** Professional development is vital. Support for the technology is important as well. The concept of "just in time" learning suggests that adults are most eager to learn something like uses of technology when they need to apply it. Find reasons to use the tools. Rather than offer staff development on word processing skills, give laptop computers to a group of teacher researchers so they can write up their work for a conference.

6. **Connect with community resources.** Many community members are making good use of technology. Join them in learning!

References

Bauch, P.A., and E.B. Goldring. (1995). "Parent Involvement and School Responsiveness: Facilitating the Home-School Connection in Schools of Choice." *Educational Evaluation and Policy Analysis* 17, 1: 1–21.

Bernhardt, V.L. (1994). *The School Portfolio.* Princeton Junction, N.J.: Eye on Education.

Connors, L.J., and J.L. Epstein. (1994). *Taking Stock: Views of Teachers, Parents, and Students on School, Family, and Community Partnerships in High Schools.* (Report No. 25). Baltimore: Center on Families, Communities, Schools and Children's Learning.

Elam, S.M., L.C. Rose, and A.M. Gallup. (1991). "The 23rd Annual Gallup Poll of the Public's Attitudes Toward the Public Schools." *Phi Delta Kappan* 73, 1: 41–56.

Elam, S.M., L.C. Rose, and A.M. Gallup. (1992). "The 24th Annual Gallup/Phi Delta Kappa Poll of the Public's Attitudes Toward the Public Schools." *Phi Delta Kappan* 74, 1: 41–53.

Elam, S.M., L.C. Rose, and A.M. Gallup. (1994). "The 26th Annual Phi Delta Kappa/Gallup Poll of the Public's Attitudes Toward the Public Schools." *Phi Delta Kappan* 76, 1: 41–56.

Greenwood, T.W. (1995). "Let's Turn on the VCR and Watch Your Report Card." *Principal* 74, 4: 48–49.

About the Authors

Thomas R. Guskey, the Editor of the 1996 ASCD Yearbook, is Professor of Educational Policy Studies and Evaluation at the College of Education, University of Kentucky, Lexington, KY 40506. Phone: 606-257-8666. e-mail: guskey@ukcc.edu

Jane Bailey, Professional Development Coordinator, CHAR EM, 08568 Mercer Boulevard, P.O. Box 318, Charlevoix, MI 49720-0318. Phone: 616-547-9947; fax: 616-547-5621

Susan Unok Brengelman, Research Associate, Eugene Research Institute, University of Oregon, 1400 High Street, Suite C, Eugene, OR 97401. Phone: 503-342-1553.

W. Ross Brewer, R.R.1, Box 7390, Underhill, VT 05489. Phone: 802-899-4825.

Kenneth Eastwood, Director of Planning and Evaluation, City School District of Oswego, 120 East First St., Oswego, NY 13126. Phone: 315-341-5838; fax: 315-341-5877.

Russell Gersten, Professor of Special Education, University of Oregon, and President of Eugene Research Institute, 1400 High Street, Suite C, Eugene, OR 97401. Phone: 503-342-1553; e-mail: rgersten@oregon.uoregon.edu.

David W. Johnson, Professor of Educational Psychology, Department of Educational Psychology, University of Minnesota, 202 Pattee Hall, Minneapolis, MN 55455. Phone: 612-624-7031; fax: 612-626-1395.

Roger T. Johnson, Professor of Education, Department of Curriculum and Instruction, University of Minnesota, 202 Pattee Hall, Minneapolis, MN 55455. Phone: 612-624-7031; fax: 612-626-1395.

Kery Kafka, Assistant Superintendent for East Area Schools, Madison Metropolitan Public Schools, 545 West Dayton St., Madison, WI 53703. e-mail: rjkafka@aol.com

Bena Kallick, Education Consultant, 12 Crooked Mile Road, Westport, CT 06880. Phone: 203-227-7261; e-mail: bkallick@aol.com

Kathy Lake, Associate Professor, Alverno College, P.O. Box 343922, Milwaukee, WI 53234-3922. e-mail: klake64@aol.com

Jay McTighe, Director, Maryland Assessment Consortium, c/o Frederick County Public Schools, 115 East Church Street, Frederick, MD 21701. Phone: 301-694-1337; fax: 301-694-1800.

Kathy Bearden Peckron, Coordinator of Gifted Education Programs, Center for Creative Learning, Rockwood School District, 265 Old State Road, Ellisville, MO 63021-5912. Phone: 314-394-2597; fax: 314-230-0721; e-mail: ibi008@mail.connect.more.net.

Bernard Schwartz, Professor, Department of Elementary Education, Faculty of Education, 551 Education Building South, University of Alberta, Edmonton, Canada T6G 2G5. Phone: 403-492-4273; e-mail: bernard.schwartz@elem.ed.ualberta.ca.

Sharon Vaughn, Professor, Departments of Teaching and Learning, and Psychology, University of Miami, Florida.

K. Heidi Watts, Director, Experienced Educators Program, Antioch New England Graduate School, 40 Avon Street, Keene NH 03431-3516. Phone: 603-357-3122; e-mail: hwatts@antiochne.edu.

Grant Wiggins, President and Director of Programs, Center on Learning, Assessment, and School Structure (CLASS), 648 The Great Road, Princeton, NJ 08540. e-mail: classnj@aol.com

ASCD 1995–96
Board of Directors

Elected Members as of November 1, 1995

Denrick Richardson, Deninoo School, Ft. Resolution, Northwest Territories, Canada

Douglas Schermer, Waco Community Schools, Wayland, Iowa

Joseph Taylor, New Orleans Public Schools, Louisiana

Robert Watson, Wright Junior-Senior High School, Gillette, Wyoming

Jill Wilson, Pembroke Pines, Florida

Fran Winfrey, Dade County Public Schools, Miami, Florida

Ellen Wolf, Walla Walla SD, Washington

Donald Young, University of Hawaii, Honolulu

Thomas Zandoli, Yaquina View School, Newport, Oregon

Affiliate Presidents

Alabama: Betty H. LeGrone, Tuscaloosa City Schools

Alaska: Patricia R. Chesbro, Mat-Su Borough School District, Palmer

Alberta, Canada: Nancy Lukey, David Thompson Junior High School, Calgary

Arizona: Sarah Hartley, Camp Verde Middle School

Arkansas: James Dalton, Cabot Public Schools

British Columbia, Canada: Frank Dunham, Fraserview Elementary, Mission

California: Patrick Perry, San Luis Coastal Unified School District, San Luis Obispo

Colorado: Beverly Bjork, Colorado Springs School District #8

Connecticut: Richard Nabel, Hamden High School

Curaçao, Netherlands Antilles: Suze M.L. Giskus, Fundashon Material Pa Skol

Delaware: Carole White, Department of Public Instruction, Dover

District of Columbia: Barbette Thorne, M.C. Terrell Elementary School

Florida: Nancy G. Terrel, Broward County Schools, Plantation

Georgia: Annette B. Rougeou, Gwinnett County Schools, Lawrenceville

Germany: Wilhelmina Szopiak Pearson, Ansbach Elementary School

Hawaii: Linda K. Kamiyama, Kapunahala Elementary School, Kaneohe

Idaho: Doris Matthews, Kuna

Illinois: Sarah J. Booth, Metcalf Laboratory School, Normal

Indiana: Robert A. Fallon, Indiana Department of Education, Indianapolis

Iowa: Lou Howell, Urbandale Schools

Japan: Maynard Yutzy, Sendai American School

Kansas: Joy L. Kromer, Unified School District #401, Atchinson

Kentucky: Patricia Marshall, Gheens Academy, Louisville

Louisiana: Sandra Wilson, Langston Hughes Elementary School, New Orleans

Maine: D'Lila Terracin, Sanford Junior High School

Manitoba, Canada: Charles Tinman, St. Boniface Teachers Centre, Winnipeg

Maryland: Brian Lockard, Carroll County Public Schools, Westminster

Massachusetts: Janice C. DeSantis, Buker Middle School, Wenham

Michigan: Henry L. Cade, Wayne County Regional Educational Service Agency, Wayne

Minnesota: Robert M. Jernberg, Moorhead Public Schools

Mississippi: Doris Smith, Winona School District

Missouri: Lewis Gowin, University of Missouri at Kansas City

Montana: Todd Taylor, School District #19, Colstrip

Nebraska: Jim Walter, University of Nebraska-Lincoln

The Netherlands/Flanders: Atse R. Spoor, Violenschool, Hilversum

Nevada: Sandra Ingram, Whitney Elementary School, Las Vegas

New Hampshire: Paul F. Ezen, Kearsarge Regional High School, North Sutton

New Jersey: Patricia E. Abernethy, Teacher Education Institute, Cherry Hill

New Mexico: Carolyn Brownrigg, Pinon Elementary, Los Alamos

New York: Bette Cornell, Fayetteville

North Carolina: Barbara M. Parramore, North Carolina State University, Raleigh

North Dakota: Gerald Roth, University of Mary, Bismarck

Northwest Territories: Peter Grimm, Princess Alexandra School, Hay River

Ohio: Ronald Anderson, Greene County Office of Education, Yellow Spring

Oklahoma: Stacy Lee Nix, Tulsa Technology Center

Ontario, Canada: Wendy Lawton,V.K. Greer Public School, Utterson

Oregon: Patricia A. Thompson, St. Mary's Academy, Portland

Pennsylvania: John Linden, School District City of Erie

Puerto Rico: Noemi Alvarado, Pontifical Catholic University, Ponce

Rhode Island: Marylou Mancini-Galipeau, Chariho Regional School District, Wood River Junction

Singapore: Kan Sou Tin, Ministry of Education, Singapore

South Carolina: Sandra R. Lindsay, Dorchester District Two, Summerville

South Dakota: Josephine Hartmann, Meade School District 46-1, Sturgis

Spain: Manuel Wood, Universidad/Las Palmas de Gren, Canary Islands

St. Maarten, Netherlands Antilles: Juliana Hodge-Shipley, Methodist Agogic Centre, Philipsburg

Tennessee: Larry Peach, Tennessee Tech University, Cookeville

Texas: Elizabeth A. Clark, Hallsville Independent School District

Trinidad & Tobago: Paula Daniel, Diego Martin Government

United Kingdom: Gwyn Edwards, Goldsmith's College, London

Utah: Carolyn Schubach, Parkside Elementary School, Murray

Vermont: Stephen Sanborn, Chittenden Central Supervisory Union, Essex Junction

Virgin Islands: Dolores T. Clendinen, Department of Education, St.Thomas

Virginia: Margaret VanDeman Blackmon; Fredericksburg City Schools

Washington: Joan Hue, Richland High School

West Virginia: Helen Hazi, West Virginia University, Morgantown

Wisconsin: DuWayne Kleinschmidt, Wausau School District

Wyoming: Susan Staldine, Campbell County High School, Gillette

ASCD Headquarters Staff

Gene R. Carter, *Executive Director*
Diane Berreth, *Deputy Executive Director*
Frank Betts, *Associate Executive Director, Operations*
John Bralove, *Assistant Executive Director, Financial and Admistrative Services*
Ronald S. Brandt, *Assistant Executive Director*
Susan Nicklas, *Assistant Executive Director, Constituent Relations*
Michelle Terry, *Assistant Executive Director, Program Development*

Jocelyn Abner
Kevin Adler
Diana Allen
Barry Amis
Pam Bailey
Carla Baker
Charlie Barbour
Vickie Bell
Karen Berry
Jennifer Beun
Steve Blaufeld
Gary Bloom
Maritza Bourque
Joan Brandt
Arni Brown
Dorothy Brown
George Bryant
Colette Burgess
Liz Byrne
Angela Caesar
Kathryn Carswell
Sally Chapman
John Checkley
Kathy Checkley
Raiza Chernault
Sandra Claxton
Lisa Manion Cline
Andrea Corsillo
Agnes Crawford
Sandi Cumberland
Marcia D'Arcangelo
Jay DeFranco
Keith Demmons
Becky DeRigge
Michael DeVries
George Ellis
Sheila Ellison
Don Ernst
Kathie Felix
Gillian Fitzpatrick
Frederick Fleming
Chris Fuscellaro
Troy Gooden
Loyd Gore
Nora Gyuk
Dorothy Haines
Joan M. Halford
Susan Hlesciak Hall
Vicki Hancock
Nancy Harrell
Dwayne Hayes
Helené Hodges
Davene Holland
Julie Houtz
Angela Howard
Debbie Howerton
Peter Inchauteguiz
Bethany Jackson
Todd Johnson
Jo Ann Jones
Mary Jones
Teola Jones
Stephanie Justen
Beth Kabele
Sandra Kashdan
Leslie Kiernan
Crystal Knight-Lee
Shelly Kosloski
Jennifer Lane
John Mackie
Indu Madan
Gina Major
Larry Mann
Helen Marquez
W. Frank Masters
Jan McCool
Clara Meredith
Ron Miletta
Frances Mindel
Nancy Modrak
Cerylle Moffett
Kenny Moir
Karen Monaco
Donna Motley
Jennifer Mulligan
Margaret Murphy
Dina Murray
Mary Beth Nielsen
Aubin Odah
John O'Neil
Margaret Oosterman
Jayne Osgood
Millie Outten
Diane Parker
Kelvin Parnell
Margini Patel
Terrence Petty
Carolyn Pool
Ruby Powell
Tina Prack
Pam Price
Lorraine Primeau
Gena Randall
Karen Rasmussen
Hope Redwine
Melody Ridgeway
Mary Riendeau
Judy Rixey
Amy Roberts
Rita Roberts
Gayle Rockwell
Cordelia Roseboro
Carly Rothman
Jeff Rupp
Lois Saboe
Jamie Sawatzky
Marge Scherer
Beth Schweinefuss
Timothy Scott
Judy Seltz
Bob Shannon
Darcie Simpson
Tracey Smith
John Somers
Valerie Sprague
Karen Steirer
Lisa Street
Judy Walter
Donald Washington
Vivian West
Kay Whittington
Linda Wilkey
Helena Williams
Scott Willis
Carolyn Wojcik
David Zamora